The Guided Acquisition of First Language Skills

Advances in Applied Developmental Psychology

Irving E. Sigel, Series Editor

The Guided Acquisition of First Language Skills

by Ernst L. Moerk
California State University, Fresno

Ablex Publishing Corporation
Stamford, Connecticut

Copyright © 2000 by Ablex Publishing Corporation

Printed in the United States of America

Library of Congress Cataloguing-in-Publication Data

Moerk, Ernst L.
 The guided acquisition of first language skills / by Ernst L. Moerk.
  p. cm. — (Advances in applied developmental psychology; v. 20)
 Includes bibliographical references and index.
 ISBN 1-56750-468-X (cloth) — ISBN 1-56750-469-8 (pbk.)
 1. Language acquisition—Research—Methodology. I. Title. II. Series:
Advances in applied developmental psychology (1993) ; v. 20.
P118.15.M64   2000
401'.93—dc21   99–39681
                                 CIP

Ablex Publishing Corporation
100 Prospect Street
P.O. Box 811
Stamford, Connecticut 06904-0811

Contents

Preface

Irving E. Sigel
Educational Testing Service

Ernst L. Moerk writes, "the exploration of language acquisition requires conceptual tools for informational, motivational, and straight behavioral-learning analyses" (Moerk, in this volume, p. 2) as necessary to comprehend so complex a phenomenon such as acquisition of language by very young children.

In this volume, the product of many years of productive research, Professor Moerk continues to fulfill a major career objective by providing an integrative view of his work on early language acquisition. He has set a major task for himself because he describes a tremendous body of research, along with scoring some critical points regarding language acquisition, as he describes the body of knowledge that has emerged in the field over the last three decades. There has been, and still is, little agreement on how children acquire language. We have the early postulation of Stern (1969) that there is "an innate component in the brain function without which a human infant could not respond to the complexities of language. Undoubtedly, the actual acquisition of language involves some form of learning although the learning processes involved, if we reject a stimulus-response model as I think we must, are not at all clear." (p. 25)

In spite of Stern's rejection of a stimulus-response model, Moerk (1983), in his reanalysis of the classic material presented by Roger Brown (1973) on language samples of three children in their second year, did identify teaching techniques that fit within a stimulus-response paradigm. This finding was not included in Brown's analysis either.

For Moerk, however, a behavioral paradigm is but one aspect of the complex posture that must be taken in order to get a meaningful understanding of so complex a process, one that he develops in this book. An earlier publication was prescient to what we have before us now. In this publication, Moerk (1976) described complex processes used by mothers as they were engaged verbally with their children. He studied these verbal transactions among a group of 20 mother–child dyads (1.9–5.0 yrs.) He found that the "mothers actively taught all aspects of language, including syntax and morphology. The interactional structures employed in the course of this teaching included feedback cycles and calibration processes" (p. 1064). His interpretation of these findings was that the acquisition of language occurs in a self-regulating, closed system and that the teaching process as a whole plays a significant role in first language acquisition.

The prelude to this book came in 1990 when Moerk reported using a large longitudinal data set in which "behavioral conceptualizations of the learning process are supported by the analyses" (Moerk, 1990, p. 293). The analyses he refers to are based on Markov-chain logic. From these he comes to the final conclusion explicated in this book in context and greater detail: "Maternal rewards and corrections should be integrated with perceptual, cognitive, and social learning conceptualizations in a skill-learning approach to explain the complexity of language transmission and acquisition process" (p. 293).

Now, 10 years later, Moerk presents us with his perspective on language acquisition which moves away from singular, thematic thinking, such as those who focus on neural organization or maturational processes, to a conceptual framework recognizing the complexity of the acquisition process. In providing this broader perspective he presents a rationale for the psychological science to seek rational integration among the diverse theories, methods, and data in the field. This book is a systematic documentation regarding the arguments for the *learnability* and *teachability* of language. In this way, in addition to scientific material, he also offers a practical basis for remedial application. His conclusions and recommendations are not speculative, but rather grounded in careful observations and data. He eschews speculations such as those presented by Chomsky and many of his supporters who have extensive theoretical exegesis, but not much of a sound database for their claims. Moerk carries out his observations in ecologically appropriate settings.

From a personal perspective, I found the book to be particularly appealing because attention is paid to epistemological contexts in which the research is carried out. Such an approach speaks to the need to clarify a common misunderstanding among many publics, including scientists, that the scientist is value-free and objective. The question is, what philosophy (usually unspoken) does the particular investigator hold and which epistemology is expressed in the research program presented in every category from the theory of the methodology and the interpretation of findings?

When the research is read, not only in this book, but in any psychological treatise, the reader should note the perspective of the investigator, or, colloquially, where the particular scientist is coming from. Understanding this aspect of the work provides a deeper understanding of the vagaries of empirical research. Ernst Moerk has provided the readership interested in first language acquisition an opportunity to have such an intellectual experience.

References

Brown, R. (1973). *The first language: The early stages.* Cambridge: Harvard University Press.

Moerk, E. L. (1976). Processes of language teaching and training in interactions of mother-child dyads. *Child Development, 47,* 1064–1078.

Moerk, E. L. (1983). A behavioral analysis of controversial topics in first language acquisition: Reinforcements, corrections, modeling, input frequencies and the three-term contingency pattern. *Journal of Psycholinguistic Research, 12,* 129–155.

Moerk, E. L. (1990). Three-term contingency patterns in mother-child verbal interactions during first-language acquisition. *Journal of the Experimental Analysis of Behavior, 54,* 293–305.

Stern, H. J. (1969). Foreign language learning and the new view of first language acquisition. *Child Study Journal, 30,* 25–36.

1

Broader Perspectives on Language Acquisition Research and its Epistemological Contexts

> This is the foundation of all, for we are not to imagine or suppose, but to discover, what nature does or may be made to do.
> —Francis Bacon, *The Advancement of Learning*

The overall goals of the present book are integrative in four senses: (a) an integration of broader developments in overall world views or the zeitgeist of the last centuries with the epistemological positions in first language research, (b) an integration of past and present empirical language acquisition research with reference to the analyses presented under the preceding section, (c) an integration of contributions from diverse schools of psychology to encompass both the behaviors and the underlying rather stable cognitive schemas of language and its acquisition, and finally (d) an integration of domains of language acquisition research is tentatively envisaged wherein differential acquisition across social classes and diverse cultures are related to findings from typical first and second language transmission/acquisition.

Whereas topics (a) and (b) are discussed in sections of Chapters 1 and 8, Chapters 6 and 7 focus on topic (d), class and cultural differences. The central chapters of the book are devoted to topic (b), the review of empirical research on the principal training/learning phenomena and their relations to theoretical postulates. This review extends over Chapters 3, 4, and 5 where the facts are contrasted with the common negation of "learnability" and "teachability" of language. With the strong emphasis on empirical evidence for effective language teaching and learning, the book is also intended to provide firm bases for remedial applications, whose beneficiaries will be language-delayed children and their parents.

The empirical evidence, in turn, has to be gauged as a function of the methodology employed in gathering it. Whether the methods accord with the structure of the object investigated or do not accord with it determines the soundness of the evidence. The methodological bases are, therefore, explored in Chapter 2. Less frequently employed methods are suggested which seem to have great potential in capturing the longitudinal and multivariate nature of the data.

Topic (c), the integration of psychological schools, is not explicitly spelled out, but it informs the entire book and is reflected in an eclectic or "integrative" use of terms and concepts from diverse schools, as they are fit for describing the processes at hand. Such an integrative "behavioral-cognitive" approach has proven useful in explorations of language acquisition (e.g., Moerk, 1977, 1992) and has also manifested its utility in the field of cognitive behavior modification (Meichenbaum, 1977). Catania (1972) and Richelle (1973) have explicated this principle with respect to the Skinner–Chomsky controversy.

Generally, it is presupposed that perspectivism, whether in the form of psychological schools or as postmodern social-functional perspectives, and objectivism are not mutually exclusive. The parable of the blind men describing an elephant exemplifies the complementarity envisaged. Perspectivism is even seen as necessary for comprehending any complex object of study. Such perspectivism should not be confused with a mixing of paradigms but as an analytical tool doing justice to the task at hand. Similarly, as electric and electronic tools are used together with screw drivers and ratchets in car repairs, depending on the problem to be fixed, so the exploration of language acquisition requires conceptual tools for informational, motivational, and straight behavioral-learning analyses.

THE ZEITGEIST AND EPISTEMOLOGY

Before the focus is more narrowly directed to the main topic of the present chapter and the entire book, first language (henceforth L1) transmission and acquisition, the changing zeitgeist into which this research has been embedded needs to be briefly considered. It is presently fully acknowledged that scientific conceptualizations are not only influenced by changing technical "paradigms," as emphasized by Kuhn (1962), but also by much broader shifts in the zeitgeist or in world views, as explored by Pepper (1942). Two dimensions seem most pertinent to the present concerns: (a) scientific empiricism versus speculative romanticism and (b) ontogenetic/learning-based versus evolutionary/genetic views. On both dimensions, cyclical changes have occurred that had and still have broad implications for scientific problem formulations, methodological choices, the resulting data, and the conclusions drawn from them.

Scientific Empiricism Versus Speculative Romanticism

Whereas the concept of empiricism is clear enough, the meaning of the present, somewhat restricted use of the label romanticism needs a brief clarification. "Romantics" (in the epochal sense), are prone to ask broad questions when they focus on science. Consequently, their reach generally exceeds their grasp. They also lack the patience to engage in the often laborious empirical studies needed to explore the domains they are interested in. As a result, they are tempted to answer their grandiose questions by means of impressively sounding labels (phlogiston, élan vital, language acquisition device) without bothering with the careful delimitation and even less the empirical justification of the labeled concepts. This is exemplified later for several well-known authors. In brief, romantic theories tend to be speculative, often in advance of available methodologies, and little concerned with detailed empirical evidence.

Three major shifts from scientific empiricism to speculative romanticism can be discerned over the last centuries: first, that from the Enlightenment to the original romantic period of the turn of the 19th century. The romantic reliance on labels led to the Scottish "faculty psychology" between about 1770 and 1820, positing about 30 "powers of the mind," of which Boring (1957, p. 207) concluded so succinctly that "such naming is word magic." (The analogy to Chomsky's [1965] language acquisition device [LAD] and Fodor's [1983] "modularity of the mind" is evident).

The second shift happened around the turn of the 20th century as reaction to the scientific-industrial revolution of the 19th century and is mostly referred to as neoromanticism. It culminated in the Nietzschean neoromantic nihilism, perspectivism, and in widespread philosophical antiempiricism. This was the time when Bergson lectured to large and enthusiastic audiences at the Sorbonne about the élan vital, an animistic romantic label without substance, *un terme au defaut du concept*, as the French express it in their more critical moments. At the same time, Dilthey (d. 1911) argued against explanatory psychology and for a vague *Verstehende Psychology* (understanding psychology), including hermeneutics; both equally based on intuitive approaches.

The third shift developed as a reaction to the logical positivism or the logical empiricism of the Vienna circle and to American behaviorism. It has been gaining force since the 1960s and has involved the enthusiastic revival of Nietzsche, mainly by French writers, such as Foucault, Derrida, and Lyotard, and has produced an increasingly hostile attitude toward empiricism and objectivity (cf. the discussions in Gross, Levitt, & Lewis, 1996). It has also resulted in the resuscitation of Dilthey's hermeneutics as a substitute for traditional epistemology (Rorty, 1979). Especially

Feyerabend, with his slogan that "anything goes," argued forcefully "against method" (Feyerabend, 1975) and for an anarchistic relativism. In psychology, this turn against objective method was first reflected in the school of humanistic psychology and it has been put on epistemologically somewhat sounder footing in Gergen's constructivism (e.g., 1985). In developmental psycholinguistics, Chomsky exemplifies the romantic trends of antiempiricism combined with the speculative invention of entities. These antiempirical and antifoundational tendencies are propounded by many present-day intellectuals as "postmodernism," "deconstruction," "postempiricism," and "poststructuralism." This most recent vogue is referred to here as postromanticism.

Three major features derive from speculative romanticism that are relevant to the present topic: (a) a basic hostility to objective methods and to a representational conception of knowledge combined with a quite extreme relativism, and even subjectivism. The latter is often expressed in the argument that scientists tell "a story" (or "narrative"), with the implication that any "story" is equally valid. (Feyerabend equated shamanism with modern medicine!—before he himself became seriously ill.) (b) From the urge for explanation and the neglect of empirical research follows the uncritical introduction of undefined and unsubstantiated terms, whether the numerous *faculties* of the Scottish philosophers, Hegel's *Weltgeist*, Nietzsche's *will to power*, Bergson's élan vital, or Chomsky's *language acquisition device* (LAD). Concerns for ontological justification and empirical foundation are minimal or are even rejected, though the terms are employed as explanatory variables. As these diverse concepts with their dynamic causal implications reflect the zeitgeist, they are eagerly and uncritically accepted in wide circles. (c) Yet, because these terms and their presumed dynamics are merely invented, they can take on any implausible features. The *Volksseele* of extreme nationalism is perhaps most notorious in its impact, but Hegel's *cunning of reason* or Adam Smith's *invisible hand* have perhaps proven not less dangerous and destructive.

Evolutionary/Genetic Versus Ontogenetic/Learning Approaches

The present evolutionary/genetic conceptions have their roots in the theories of Darwin/Wallace and Mendel/de Vries. Yet it is thought provoking to contrast Darwin's extensively empirically based evolutionary theory (e.g., the voyage of the Beagle), or Mendel's life-long experiments, with the dearth or absence of empirical, species-relevant data in the theorizing of sociobiologists such as E. O. Wilson, an entomologist who wrote so much about human societies, and of Chomsky who postulated a "language organ." As Darwin and Wallace wrote close to the peak of the Industrial Revolution, an empirical and scientific period *par excellence*, they relied on empirical bases and on induction in constructing their theories. Wilson and Chomsky are products of postromanticism and chose the speculative-romantic approach in the genetic versus learning controversy.

Speculative genetic explanations were somewhat constrained during the pre-dominance of the empirically minded logical positivists and later the behaviorists (although the social Darwinists in the political domain followed a different course). The evolutionary concepts of "instinct" and "innate" came to be seen as empty labels rather than as explanatory variables through critical analyses of the work of Tinbergen and Lorenz. These labels were therefore rejected as substitutes for causal analyses (cf. Lorenz, 1965). When evolutionary speculations came to the forefront again with the latest romantic turn (Chomsky, 1965; Wilson, 1975), it happened in the conducive scientific context of the "human-genome" project in biology. At present, speculative nativism can borrow its truth-claims from this empirical work without providing comparable empirical evidence. It then overgeneralizes these claims to domains wherein empirical evidence does not justify them. Just as newspapers quite frequently report on the discovery of the genetic basis of yet another illness (or even of homosexuality), a "language instinct," "a language organ," possibly even a "language gene" may be seriously propounded in the absence of any positive evidence and even despite strong counter-evidence from clinical brain resections. Yet both dimensions of the zeitgeist, the romantic and the genetic emphases, make these empty labels readily acceptable to large, and not only lay, audiences.

Chomsky who spoke so often so "authoritatively" about L1 acquisition is an exceptional example of this romantic antiempiricism. Not only has he never published even a single empirical study on verbal input and adult–child verbal interaction, his book *Rules and Representations* (Chomsky, 1980a) that extensively discusses the development of a first language, does not contain any references to recent empirical studies on adult–child interaction. Instead, Chomsky relies exclu-sively on "imagination." Two quotes exemplify his style of argument: "It is hard to *imagine* that children receive specific training to establish this shared knowledge [of a specific linguistic structure] or even that this knowledge is derived inductively from experiences. These observations suggest at once that there is a language related faculty of mind" (Caplan & Chomsky, 1980, p. 98, emphasis added). Note the shift in the wording from "imagine" to "observations"—the latter sounds much more scientifically acceptable although no "observations" were ever made. And: "It is difficult to *imagine* that people capable of these judgments have all had the relevant training or experience...Rather, it seems that some specific property of the human language faculty" (Chomsky, 1980a, p. 42, emphasis added). This was the same Chomsky who argued in the same year: "from ignorance it is impossible to draw any conclusions" (Chomsky, 1980b, p. 36). It is a well-known feature of ideologies that they "have a contempt for facts and reality" (Boesche, 1996, p. 445). They differ in this respect most drastically from science, as do Chomsky's "imagina-tions."

In contrast to Chomsky's reliance on mere imagination, considerable evidence on parent–child interactions and on the training provided through these interactions already existed in 1980. Brown and associates had begun publishing their impressive findings in the early 1960s (Brown & Bellugi, 1964; Brown & Fraser, 1963). Moerk (1972) as well as Snow (1972), beginning their research programs in the early 1970s, had reported instructional interactions. Many further investigations followed. Nevertheless, the zeitgeist condoned persistence in ignorance and imagination, making an unsubstantiated "language organ" carry the major explanatory burden of language acquisition and linguistic competence. During the last few decades, extensive research on partly prenatal and early postnatal learning of phonetic and phonemic aspects has shown beyond any doubt how early infants are capable of learning perceptual features and of establishing concepts. Subsequent vocabulary learning equally has been demonstrated as rather efficient. A great deal of evidence for the teaching of morphology and syntax during the ensuing years exists but is ignored.

The above brief epistemological sketch would need to be supplemented by finer differentiations to reflect the complexity of the history of ideas. For example, the trend towards romantic speculations appears to have been strongest in the spokespersons of the eras: Rousseau, Bergson, and Chomsky. Probably a more accurate formulation would be: Romantic simplifications caught the fancy of the layman and created famous spokespersons whose influence became predominant. Practitioners, in contrast, remained more in touch with the requirements of empirical substantiation. Even during the height of the romantic revolutions the Industrial Revolution did not suddenly end, nor did empirical and remedial work in child language acquisition end when Chomsky propounded his speculations about innate linguistic knowledge. In the domains of phonemic and vocabulary acquisition, where innateness is almost necessarily precluded due to wide differences in languages and where learning cannot be doubted, empirical research made impressive strides. Also, educators soon realized that a reliance on a language acquisition device was counterproductive for their tasks, and second language (L2) research returned to teaching and learning conceptions (Gass, 1997; Larsen-Freeman & Long, 1991). This persistence of empiricism does not prove, however, that progress was not delayed by the invented, easy, pseudo-answers. The delay is indicated by the fact that many L1 intervention programs are often built upon simplistic behavioral conceptualizations that go back to the pre-Chomsky period of the 1950s. It is also sadly demonstrated by the millions of children who experience unremedied delays in their language acquisition and suffer under lifelong deficits.

PAST AND PRESENT RESEARCH IN THE FIELD OF L1 ACQUISITION

The broader intellectual and epistemological background sketched out earlier can explain some of the dynamics encountered in the field of first language acquisition over the last century. Certainly, the specific nature of the data and of the contexts of language transmission introduce additional aspects that interact with the more global factors. Both are briefly considered in the following sections.

The field of L1 acquisition is exceptionally fortunate in never lacking participants or evidence. Observant parents are intimately and almost automatically familiar with the increasing verbal skills of their children (Rondal, 1979). If these parents are also scientists, they have their database basically home-delivered. Accordingly, most of the early, and many of the present, investigators took advantage of these propitious circumstances and reported on the gradual phonetic, phonological, semantic, and morphosyntactic development of their own infants and young children. Data-centered research should therefore predominate in the field.

The verbal productions of children are, however, only one aspect of the database, pertaining to the effect-side. In contrast to the ready recordability of early output data, an approximate exhaustive coverage of the input is much more difficult. Even more demanding is the full documentation of the child's intake and learning processes. The latter is at present still beyond the capacities of the field. These three aspects, output, input, and intake/learning, are considered briefly in historical perspective.

Children's Output of Verbal Messages

First-language acquisition research, focusing on filial productions, has a quite venerable history. Whether beginning with Tiedemann's (1787) publication or with Taine's (1870) and Preyer's (1882) major studies, it is between one and two centuries old. The three mentioned authors preceded the first and second romantic eras, respectively, and are extensively empirically based. Whereas Ament (1899) and Clara and Wilhelm Stern (1928/1987) continued these scientific and empirical approaches, Meumann (1902) seemed to respond in part to the neoromantic zeitgeist by emphasizing emotional and voluntaristic aspects of language development. Speculative accounts became so common around the turn of the 20th century that Cohen (1930) complained about speculative interpretations and broad generalizations replacing empirical investigations in many publications. With Guillaume's (1926/1971) book on imitation and the four-volume project of Leopold (1939-1949) the field returned to empirical emphases during the behaviorist era. McCarthy (McCarthy, 1946, 1954) and associates extended this research to larger samples of children. And soon afterwards, Brown and associates initiated the path-breaking Harvard project, as discussed below. This period after the 1920s could be labeled the period of "normal science" in Kuhn's (1962) terminology. The research was cumulative, amassing rich details about the course of language mastery.

From an explanatory perspective, it appears there was quite broad agreement that language acquisition was a learning process. Preyer (1882) already devoted a whole volume to *Learning to Speak*. Guillaume (1926/1971) emphasized imitation—a presumably sufficient learning process. Leopold (1971) considers his work as "a systematic examination of the *language learning* of the first two years..." (p. 10, emphasis added). Yet, a certain ambiguity existed in many reports. Several of the investigators of the 19th century were physiologists (psychology did not yet exist as a field during the earlier period) and they often did not make a clear-cut distinction between a learning process and "language growth," which seemed to resemble organ growth in its gradualness. The still-common term "language development" shares in this confounding of physiological maturation and the products of learning processes.

The advantages of the ready availability of rich data turn into a problem when the language skills of children expand and their verbal behavior becomes so copious that it cannot be exhaustively recorded—and even less analyzed—without sophisticated technology. Consequently, the informativeness of almost all the early studies decreases steeply after the second year of life. Like many other authors, Leopold, in his fourth volume (1949), discontinued his detailed records of language acquisition long before his children reached full competence. A large gap remains up to the present between the levels explored in early childhood and the level of adult competence: Many intervening steps remain undocumented.

The lack of documentation resulted in two logical traps into which some researchers predictably fell: The first is the frequent assertion that language development is essentially complete around the age of 4—the emphasis on early perfection providing gist for nativistic causal explanations. The second is implicit in the first and is often encountered in Chomsky's arguments. It is the postulate of insufficient input ("the poverty of the stimulus") and was most explicitly expressed by Baker (1979) as "the projection problem." It was defined as "the problem" that child-input data could not explain adult performance. As fifteen or more years of learning (from 4 to about 20 years of age) and much systematic schooling were neglected in this conception, a recourse to "innate linguistic creativity" seemed again required to explain sophisticated adult performance when only input provided to the very young child was considered.

Descriptions of readily observable phenomena, as briefly surveyed, commonly reflect the first steps in scientific endeavors. They serve to establish the basic factual evidence for subsequent explanatory advances. In the present field, however, this necessary descriptive approach was completely one-sided: considerations of causes of the development in the input and in the child's learning strategies (excluding a generally presumed imitation) were at best implicit. Only the evidence of extreme language delay or deficit as a consequence of deprivation (Dennis, 1960; Spitz & Wolff, 1946), made the overwhelming dependence of normal development on sufficient input obvious. However, types of input that are conducive to learning, or those that delay it, were not differentiated until recently.

Parental Input and the Question of Causality

Even compared to the wealth of data of children's output after the age of two or three, the *embarassement de richesse* regarding the causal factors in the input is exponentially greater. The total speech addressed to and heard by children while they acquire their first language is almost unrecordable even with present-day technology. The situation becomes even more unmanageable once children begin reading independently. Probably due to these difficulties, early researchers almost systematically neglected the recording of any of the causal factors that result in the learning of language. In the reports of Leopold (1939-1949) there is some global evidence for cause-effect relationships, when the family moved from German to English speaking environments and the child acquired skills in the new language. The same applies to some further studies on bi- and multi-linguality. Yet, for most of the observed children, only very few examples of model utterances that were imitated are encountered in the literature. Rote reproductions of traditional texts, such as nursery and play rhymes (Chukovsky, 1963; Opie & Opie, 1959), where the source is obvious, implicate the input in a general manner. However, these texts are neither necessary nor sufficient causes for general language acquisition. Broader causal explanations of the relations between input and output, over shorter and longer time-spans, required data—and methodologies for recording them—that did not exist before the 1950s and 1960s.

As science is humankind's attempt to *rerum cognoscere causas* (Lucretius: "to understand the causes of things/events"), the logical step after descriptions of effects was to add causal explanations. Three approaches were embraced, two speculative ones and one an empirical endeavor. One was the vaunted "Chomskyan revolution," which relied on Darwinian genetic analogies to postulate a cause, a *language organ* or even a *language instinct* (Pinker, 1994). The second approach to causal explanation was the behaviorist one, presuming homologies between animal classical and operant conditioning and human language acquisition. Skinner (1957) and Mowrer (1960) are the most prominent exponents of this approach. Yet, the gap between species, rats versus humans, and between domains of behavior is certainly wide. The association of "emitted" responses (which appear to be seen as innate, judging from Skinner's writings) to stimuli is categorically different from the actual construction of patterned responses in language. Additionally, meaning and reference, the representational functions of language, are almost totally absent in lower vertebrates. Neither Skinner's nor Mowrer's speculative extrapolations could therefore suffice for explaining language acquisition, even if behaviorist principles are useful in describing some aspects of learning, as was shown by Moerk (1983a, 1992).

Both the nativist and behaviorist speculations were presented at a time (Skinner 1957; Chomsky 1959 and later) when the zeitgeist changed from positivist empiricism to relativist romanticism, the latter accepting well-told stories and catchy labels as causal explanations. Chomsky's nativism prevailed therefore for a time and caught the imagination of many scientists and lay persons alike, although Skinnerian-based remedial interventions, providing evidence of cause-effect dynamics, were not negligible by far(e.g., Warren & Kaiser, 1986; Warren & Rogers-Warren, 1985). The recent connectionist proposals, discussed, for example, by Bates and Carnevale (1993), reflect a renewed turn of the ideological wheel toward a learning approach.

The one empirical approach to causal explanations that overcame some of the obstacles to the recording of the input and the exploration of processes, was that of Roger Brown (e.g., 1973) and his team at Harvard. They utilized the technical innovation of the tape-recorder and recorded the *interactions* of children with their parents. Now, input, the causal factor, became known together with immediately contingent and somewhat delayed responses of the children. Equally, parental feedback to children's utterances could be specified from the data. From the relation between input and acquisition, the second causal factor, learning strategies of the children, could be abstracted. Consequently, Brown and associates emphasized process analyses even in their earliest publications (e.g., Brown & Bellugi, 1964). Brown's example was followed widely, resulting in the CHILDES data collections, nurtured by MacWhinney and Snow (e.g., Sokolov & Snow, 1994). This was and is accompanied by other impressive empirical projects in a rapidly expanding literature that is the focus of the subsequent chapters. As Brown's project and many of those collected in the CHILDES database were, in principle, longitudinal, both short-term and longer-term cause-effect relationships became accessible to exploration.

However, enormous gaps remain in the data, because Brown and most of his followers recorded a few hours per month at most for individual children and only over a span of one to two years. The cause-effect relationships that occur *between* the recorded hours are necessarily missed with this design. If the input preceding specific productions was not recorded, misleading inferences about miraculously creative productions could be and have been drawn, as shown by Moerk (1980, 1981). Despite this gap, the most important type of dependencies, immediate and short-term cause-effect relationships and multiple feedback cycles can be explored—if fitting analytical methodologies are employed. Such sequential methodologies, relying on contingencies, are discussed in Chapter 2.

The second gap, that between early childhood learning and adult competence, still needs to be filled, although valuable beginnings exist (e.g., Nippold, 1988). An exhaustive recording of the causal factors for more advanced skills, including the effects of schooling and private reading, has not even been attempted and would be beyond the facilities of most individual investigators. Consequently, the presently available data and analyses, both for early, and even more for later acquisitions, are so fragmentary, despite much progress, that for the causes of most advanced performances the only honest answer can be: "Not yet known/not yet explored." The urge for immediate causal answers needs therefore to be restrained and directed toward systematic empirical studies instead of fulfilling it through mere labeling.

Intake and the Problem of Processing

The most difficult challenges are encountered when trying to ascertain the processing of the input. Whereas input and output are fully observable, processing can only be inferred through complex indirect approaches. It has to be abstracted from the multiform and multi-interval relationships between input and output. Presuming a memory span that retains input longer than a few seconds or minutes, a presumption that is necessary to account for lasting learning, evidence of processing could be exhibited considerably after the input was provided. Also, every input has phonetic, semantic, morphosyntactic, and pragmatic aspects, and multiple perspectives are needed to capture its processing. Processing of input can be partial or full, exact or approximate, producing mistakes that require corrections, and exhibit many other variations. The following chapters focus on this processing.

Additional problems arise: Before infants even approximate their first word, they have been subjected for about a year or more to rich input to which they respond only minimally and very imperfectly. While research has shown that this input already has effects during the first half year of life, and even during the last months of pregnancy (Mehler et al., 1988), no immediate behavioral evidence of its processing is readily available during this early period. Later, when evidence becomes available, it cannot be traced to specific input items, requiring different, that is, wholistic (as contrasted to one-to-one) cause-effect conceptualizations. (A shot in the head resulting in death is labeled one-to-one causation; the deposit of sedimentary layers over geologic time is a wholistic one).

Processing could consist of rote memory storage, of pattern abstraction, of rule learning (MacWhinney, 1978) and possibly of other procedures. As an exhaustive specification of forms of processing cannot be provided at present, multiple approaches are needed for exploring diverse strategies infants and young children might employ during language acquisition. Three seem most promising: (a) Most of all, the "object" (note the reification) to be learned needs to be conceived from a (child)-psychological, as against an adultomorphic philological or linguistic, perspective. As is well known from L2 teaching, traditional philological presentations of the "object" of instruction generally did not result in very effective acquisition, and "language" input certainly must appear very different to the toddler, or the average schoolchild, as contrasted to linguists of diverse persuasions. (b) Furthermore, children's processing tendencies in similar, more widely explored areas of skill learning can be employed as general guidelines, if empirical evidence suggests that the compared domains are similar. Such an analogical procedure can preclude the postulation of overly advanced processing in the domain of language. For example, children learn from feedback how to hit a target with a stone while nobody would assert that they have understood the laws of physics underlying this achievement. Seemingly rule-following behavior in other domains can therefore be—and often is—contingency based. (c) Finally, multiple methodological improvements are needed to capture processes by studying the relationships between input and output over varying intervals. The first two tasks, describing the "object" of learning and suggesting some acquisition processes, are focused on in the last section of Chapter 1. Chapter 2 focuses on methodological concerns.

In summary, causal analyses of L1 acquisition encounter extensive technical difficulties, not to speak of the conceptual problems of causal explanations that

Hume emphasized. Considering these technical and conceptual difficulties, Levy and Schlesinger's (1988, p. 273) pessimistic conclusion that "there is hardly any study in the field that purports to show us the learning process in action" seems not only to reflect the research endeavor but is an almost predictable result of the difficulty of the task and the tendency of "the best and the brightest" (Halberstam, 1969) to replace laborious empirical research through easy imagination.

"LANGUAGE" OR THE TASK CHILDREN FACE

Whenever the term "language" is employed, a serious mistake of reification threatens. "A language" does not exist, and nobody ever learned "a language." What does exist and is learned are utterances, spoken and heard, and in literate societies also written and read. After rhetorical or philological analyses, going back to the ancient Greeks, utterances *about* "languages," reflecting suggestions for use, abstractions of patterns or of rules (grammar and pragmatics), are mostly included in what is labeled "language." (The latter aspects certainly were central in most L2 teaching.)

The point to be made might profit from clarification through several analogies: The referent of "language" is similar to that of "music," "dance," "etiquette," or "law." All these abstract terms refer to a wide range of socially trained and learned behaviors, including codifications of rules and prescriptions for these behaviors, such as in books of etiquette or of choreography. If either of these terms would be taken as referring to a unitary entity, one would commit an ontological mistake, confounding an abstract reference with a myriad of behaviors and codified analyses of behaviors. Singing/playing a piece of music, performing complex dance configurations, and acting according to etiquette, are learned social skills, and the codifying of underlying rules is another learned skill. These rules are often taught, facilitating the planning of skilled actions. All these sets of skills can be recorded in a variety of media. Once recorded, they appear much more "thing"-like, giving easily rise to reification.

Because "music" performance relies largely on instruments, "dance" presents an even closer analogy to "language." It employs only body organs, is based on the (probably innate) stepping pattern, and is encountered in all human groups. Yet, dance forms are very different across human groups. Dance entails multiple levels, from a simple two-step country dance to a sophisticated ballet or minuet with complex choreography. It is largely learned through modeling and imitation, but is also taught didactically and has been recorded in graphic form. Yet, nobody would (as yet?) argue that "dance" is innate.

On the basis of this ontological confusion of an abstract label with an enormous set of skills, Chomsky and his followers inquired about the biological substrates of "language" or of "rules of language." As a result they committed two logical mistakes simultaneously: First, they committed a category mistake by confounding multiple social products, established over time and integrated from many geographic locations, with a genetic, and therefore individually-based, knowledge structure. As "language" is a subset of "culture," the underlying logic is fully homologous to exploring the biological roots of "culture" in a "culture organ," or to searching for a "law organ." (Whereas the last conclusion might sound bizarre, speculations about an innate, God-given conscience or "moral sense" were quite common until the 18th century and they still occur in religious sermons. In contrast, psychological research has clearly demonstrated the social roots of moral decisions and moral behavior.)

Second, this argument of Chomsky and associates also confounds material causes and formal causes (in Aristotelian terminology), or necessary causes with sufficient ones, in modern terms. To clarify this confusion: Does a piano-player have "piano-playing organs?" Of course, he does: two arms and hands with ten fingers. Does this mean a Beethoven piano sonata or even the Western eight-tone scale are part of innate knowledge? This somewhat oversimplified analogy exhibits the logical mistake of presuming that cerebral structures, while necessary, are sufficient to explain the existence of a skill. No recourse to "triggering" environmental input will justify inferring an information-carrying "piano-playing organ" on the basis of anybody's piano-playing skills.

By overcoming the simplistic entification (reification) lurking behind the label "language," the researcher avoids, however, only the grossest pitfall. Many finer clarifications are needed: As philologists and linguists have discussed for millennia, each utterance entails many features, which could be attended to singly, in various combinations, or as a wholistic unit. As is known from both L1 and L2 acquisition, the perception of the input changes sequentially in the course of the learning process. In the early stages, perception is generally wholistic. Utterances in a foreign language are perceived as unanalyzed wholes. Later, differentiation and articulation become possible, and single words or brief phrases stand out. Finally all elements are integrated into a complete understanding of an utterance. (This is obviously Heinz Werner's [1940] "orthogenetic law" in a process of relative macrogenesis.)

These brief remarks indicate that even one specific utterance presents profoundly different tasks—and learning opportunities—depending on the level of the learner. From an informational angle, the same maternal utterance entails completely different informational aspects for the six-month-old baby versus the six-year-old sibling. The "object" of learning changes therefore with the development of a child, from wholistic intonation contours to the discrimination of words, to word combinations, and the analysis of some words into stems and bound morphemes. Only gradually do integrative tasks come to predominate after the elements have been rather well mastered. With multiple and densely spaced experiences of the same underlying structures, such as the subject–verb–object (S–V–O) structure, (invariants over transformations in L1, substitution drills in L2 training), pattern abstraction occurs. Only much later do questions of complex sentences, of paragraph structure, and of essay writing become the tasks of "language" learning.

It follows that neither input effects nor learning processes can be clearly conceived and explored without the investigator being as specific as possible about the "object" of learning at each developmental level, or without at least being openminded about inferring the "object" from the child's responses to the input. To exemplify this point from a notorious mistake in the literature (which is discussed in detail in Chapter 5): It has often been argued that "children do not learn from corrections," because two researchers presented one example each of lack of learning from repeated corrections. However each example was reported without considering the child's language level in relation to the complexity of the correction provided. This would be analogous to watching a beginning skier not immediately acquiring the skills of an Olympic competitor and arguing that skiers generally cannot learn advanced skills from models.

Having argued that the tasks the child encounters have to be considered in a "differential" manner ("differential" as in calculus, meaning differing at each specific moment) it follows that the children's tasks are relatively simple at each step in the long learning process: Children perceive one input utterance at a time and can—but do not need to—compare it with a preceding one. They can also produce an utterance and observe the adult's reactions to it—and those are not reactions to any of the potentially infinite varieties of the utterance. Extensive evidence on mother–child interaction has shown that input is generally provided as "intelligent text presentation," in Levelt's (1974) terminology. This means that utterances are closely tuned (see Chapter 4) to the child's previously demonstrated competence. If not tuned well enough, the child provides feedack of lack of mastery, and the mother makes simplifying adjustments (Bohannon & Marquis, 1977) or provides corrections (see Chapter 5) in order to reestablish effective interactions. The adult's feedback to filial utterances is almost necessarily tuned to them and therefore easy to process. In all these cases, the general task could be defined for the child: recognize familiar patterns and notice the (few) new element(s) that is/are presented in an optimum-level-of-discrepancy format.

This reference to adult fine tuning introduces one of the main topics in this book—that of expert–apprentice relationships. The extensive scaffolding, or the lack of it that results in delayed or defective acquisition, is discussed in subsequent chapters. The principle is analogous to the acquisition of the knowledge of physics: It took mankind two to three thousand years to establish this knowledge, but good teachers can convey the important principles within a few years of high school and college education. Therefore the task of the child has to be largely judged in relationship to the scaffolding provided: the better the scaffolding, the easier the task, the quicker the acquisition, and vice versa. It goes without saying that the level of the end product is another factor that needs to be differentiated: from the taciturn peasant, to the loquacious bourgeois, to the college professor, and the Pulitzer Prize winner, levels of accomplishment and requisite learning tasks greatly increase in complexity, as do demands on the input.

THE NATURE OF THE INFORMATION PROCESSOR

It is a logical truism that the varying social interactions that contribute to language acquisition presuppose a range of learning competencies and learning constraints in children. Therefore processing capacities and input need to be conceptually related. Slama-Cazacu (1983) expressed this concisely: "Theories that do not locate language in the sense of the French term *language*, that is, the ensemble of psychological processes involved in language functioning in the social context are useless to applied linguistics." Fodor, Bever, and Garrett (1974) argue similarly that "any model of the ideal speaker–hearer which is incompatible with whatever is known about the rest of human psychology is ipso facto disconfirmed" (p. 279). For the present purposes, the words "human psychology" should be replaced by "child psychology at various levels of development." In case of incompatibility between acquisition theories and confirmed processing tendencies, better models about the language learning processes have to be formulated on the basis of the *observed verbal interactions*.

As to human psychology generally, a reminder might be useful that even rather sophisticated adults function as "cognitive misers" with "bounded rationality" (e.g., Simon, 1985). That is, adults minimize complex analyses and for the most part cannot perform them even if they try. Even experts rely extensively on recognition processes and on stored patterns, that is, simple cognitive strategies, in handling everyday tasks (Simon, 1990). Analogies employed and rules abstracted even by "the best and the brightest" (Halberstam, 1969) are frequently oversimplified and incorrect (Howard, 1991), and even simple principles may not be abstracted from experience (Kahneman & Tversky, 1972). If this is the case with "sophisticated" adults, great caution might be advisable when postulating complex cognitive performances of the infant and young child.

On the other hand, the long-term memory of human beings is impressive. It has been found that chess masters store from 10,000 to 100,000 different chess patterns and recognize 50,000 different patterns on the average. It is almost certain that the preschooler needs to employ a far smaller number of linguistic patterns, mainly the S–V–(O) and the S–Copula–Complement pattern, complemented by a few rather formulaic prepositional phrases and modal verb constructions (e.g., *I want to...*). Therefore much of the acquisition of verbal skills could be based mainly on rote learning with versatility derived from pattern abstraction, combined with slot-and-filler principles.

When deciding between the predominant tendency of assuming early rule learning and the alternate possibility of simple rote learning and flexible combinations of subroutines (as widely shown in skill learning), the infant's and preschooler's processing tendencies need to be scrutinized. It would obviously require several volumes to fully describe the processing capacities and changing tendencies of children between birth and four years. A different approach has therefore been chosen, relying on two principles: First, a conceptualization of language acquisition as analogous to skill acquisition provides guidance as to which processing tendencies might be important. Second, a focus on the actual verbal interactions, that is, the input as it is related to children's uptake and production, can demonstrate predominant inclinations. In this way, children's verbal performance in context can be related to evidence from cognitive development and skill learning to allow further refinements.

Input Frequency and Rehearsal

Chapter 3 documents, in considerable detail, that frequency of input, implying much rehearsal, is an important factor in language acquisition. Chapters 6 and 7 then demonstrate the language delay that is common in the absence of such intense input and high rehearsal frequency. Both these facts indicate a heavy reliance on memory—as every L2 learner knows. This evidence from early verbal interactions fits closely with research from early memory development.

Infants are already relatively competent in information intake, and their memories are quite robust (Cohen, 1979). With frequently repeated patterns in the input, they are also successful in pattern recognition, at least on the acoustic level, where recognition of the mother's voice can be shown for the first month of life. Visual patterns (Bower, 1972) seem to be stored somewhat latter, but clearly before the appearance of the first word, as the "seven-months-anxiety" indicates. Generally, recognition memory, which typically does not involve strategic aspects, arises early and changes little during the life span (Brown, 1975; Perlmutter, 1980).

Reliance on short- and long-term memory in language performance is supported by the fact that young children build extensively on previous utterances (cf. Clark, 1974). These prior utterances could have been produced either by the adult partners or by the children themselves (in build-up sequences). Children replace one or two elements to adapt the borrowed forms to new or changed pragmatic purposes. For example, the mother's question: *Do you want milk?* might receive the reply: *I want juice*. Not only is the model's frame retained but the construction has been extensively overlearned due to pragmatic exigencies.

The same principles apply both to early and later L2 acquisition. Powerful evidence for formulaic speech during the early stages of acquisition was provided by Wong-Fillmore (1976). Becker (1984), a specialist in L2 training for later ages, emphasizes "an accumulation of remembered prior texts" and that "our real language competence is accessed via memory to this accumulation of prior texts" (p. 218).

It could be argued that receptive memory is not sufficient, because children below the age of four or five years have not yet caught on to the need for active rehearsal (Flavell, 1985). Yet, the extensive repetitions provided in everyday conversations (see Chapters 2 and 3) establish the rehearsals that are needed for longer term storage. After immediate, relatively massed repetitions, conversational exigencies (and probably some intentional planning by the adult) result in spaced rehearsals and long-interval reinstatements, as was shown by Moerk (1992). The children only need to attend to the input and repeat some of the models—which they demonstrably do.

In the realm of verbal productions, abundant research has shown that children begin with highly overlearned formulas. In only four hours of input Moerk (1992) counted 327 models of *one-syllable-verb* + *"it"* constructions, such as "have it," "get it," "did it," "see it," "find it," and "taste it,"—only six slightly differing surface forms of the same pattern. These constructions were then gradually employed by the child. Then, some additions modeled frequently by adults, such as the insertion of new fillers in the slots of the established frame or inclusions of adverbs or prepositional phrases, were imitated, resulting in what looked like pattern abstraction and flexible use by the child, but which could be fully based on rote learning. As obvious from the earlier six instances of the *"verb it"* constructions, the early patterns are pragmatically important for the child, their semantic structure is clarified by their situational contexts (wherein the *it* is specified nonverbally), and they are also based on a simple prosodic pattern of a stressed syllable followed by an unstressed one, the trochaic pattern. That such simple prosodic patterns support retention is well known from the rote learning of poems.

Pattern Abstraction

When emphasizing the importance of rote memory and the learning of formulas, it is not asserted that every sentence the child utters has been heard before (although for the early stages this possibility should not be discounted). With a considerable variety of heard and produced utterances that are based on the same few patterns, pattern abstraction is an automatic product of memory restrictions, that is, of forgetting. Similarly in motor development, children employ a few overlearned schemas, such as reaching and grasping, or stepping, in a wide variety of circumstances, but do not remember every item reached for and grasped, or every step made. So in verbal performance, a few syntactic patterns fulfill many objectives, as indicated earlier with the *"verb it"* pattern. This is the common "novelty problem" (Schmidt, 1975), which applies to all skilled behavior and not only to language. No miraculous generativity is needed to explain it. As adults necessarily employ a narrow range of vocabulary and of syntactic constructions while interacting with young children, they facilitate the necessary pattern abstraction.

Being aware of children's processing restrictions and following Morgan's canon, a parsimonious interpretation of early language learning should mainly be based on rote learning, the abstraction of a few patterns, and consequent element substitutions. This is largely perceptual learning, already well developed in many animals below the human species.

Rules and Production Systems

As is well known, "rule following" is a highly emphasized topic in L1 research (and especially in nativistic explanations). Although extensive analyses exist (Baker & Hacker, 1984; Herrmann, 1995; Herrmann & Graf, 1996; Root, 1973) exploring the concept of "rule" and how it has been misapplied in developmental psycholinguistics, a few brief remarks might still be useful to place these questions into a broader perspective.

These considerations start with Anderson's (1981) "production system" as it is employed extensively in computer science. This is basically an "IF–THEN" principle: If conditions x and y are given, then produce step z. These productions systems are not only central to computers (which, after all, have been programmed by human beings), they are also the core of classical conditioning, of all operant conditioning, and of adapted goal-directed behavior. They are equally the basis of labeling: If a dog is within sight and a question is asked "*What is this?*", label it "dog."

Such production systems could also explain bound-morpheme use at somewhat higher developmental levels: "If two or more items are referred to, use -*s* at the end of [most] nouns;" equivalently in case of the past tense -*ed*, and so forth. Although the condition definitions become somewhat more abstract, it might be difficult to argue for substantive differences between these diverse condition–action sequences. Harlow (1959), in the case of oddity learning, and Kendler and Kendler (1959, 1962), in the case of the reversal shift, have shown that even subhuman species can master relatively abstract condition definitions. Therefore the latter cannot be considered as highly complex.

The recommended caution against premature imputation of complex cognitive performances seemed, however, to be counter-indicated by an often quoted study. After the famous experiments of Berko (1958), summarized admiringly by Brown (1973), an overwhelming tendency arose to employ rule interpretations of early language performance—very much in accordance with the predominant cognitive zeitgeist and the tendency to draw rather biased inferences from incompletely analyzed evidence. A closer study of Berko's procedures shows, however, that all the children's more successful performances could have been based on intertextual cues and not on anything resembling a rule. For example, in the case of the plural, the leading question of the experimenters was: "*Those are two ...*" Here three textual cues are given: the plural form of the pronoun, the plural verb "*are*", and the numeral "*two*". Any of these cues should be associated in the child's memory with the plural morpheme. Similarly for the past tense, the experimenters asked "*What did he do yesterday?*" or "*What happened to it?*" providing in both instances a model of a past tense, and in one construction the word "*yesterday*" also. For example, Moerk and Vilaseca (1987) have shown that young children often utilized the past tense "*did*" of the input as an indicator that an "*-ed*" was required in their own verb construction, and without the preceding "*did*" in the input, they often did not provide the past tense morpheme in required contexts, even with verbs for which they had provided them at other times. Also consider what *sounds* more familiar: "*Yesterday I go to school*" or "*Yesterday I went to school*." Both considerations suggest that Berko's participants could easily have relied only on textual cues and rote memory in their answers.

Similar arguments apply to other constructions in Berko's study, especially in the case of the present progressive "*-ing*," which was always tested by Berko by means of "*What are they doing?*" Again, Moerk's (1992) finding that "*doing ,*" employed in a question, is an effective cue for eliciting the morpheme "*-ing*" in the child's verb construction suggests mere intertextual cue use. But most interesting are Berko's tasks, such as "derived adjective," and the "comparative and superlative," where no intertextual cues were provided by the experimenters. The children failed quite abysmally in these categories. Berkos' study, fully analyzed instead of selecting only data interpretable as rule use, would therefore suggest *lack* of morphological rule awareness in her participants and reliance on briefly preceding textual cues.

The preceding argument does not deny that—sometimes—children will catch on to grammatical principles. It is, however, a reminder to at least consider more parsimonious interpretations that might be more appropriate for the early stages of acquisition. As is well known, and as was already shown by Brown (1973), during the acquisition period children do not consistently supply morphemes when they would be required. Rule interpretations would require auxiliary hypotheses to explain this inconsistency; a fact that suggests that these rule interpretations might be misleading and that proximate input variations might account for performance variations.

If, however, some still prefer to label these performances "rule-governed," Miller's (1970) cautionary remark should be kept in mind: "In spite of increasing reliance on rules as explanations of thought and behavior, I do not know of any clear account of what rules are or how they function" (p. 191). Baker and Hacker (1984) have shown the many nonsensical uses of the concept of "rule." It seems therefore that a romantic explanatory principle, *un terme a defaut du concept*, again supplanted careful empirical analyses. If this is the case, it will not contribute to the clarification of the acquisition problem.

In contrast to the high-level cognitive implications of the term "rule," classical and operant conditioning in animals suggest that the establishment of production systems is a very basic process, found far back in evolutionary history and therefore also in low level animals. It is a basic biological principle that is needed for survival. In its simplest form it is found in reflexes and even in taxes, such as phototaxis.

While reflexes are innate, and species-specific propensities to respond differentially to diverse forms of conditioning seem to exist, this is almost certainly not what a linguistic nativist would want to fall back on exclusively in explaining language acquisition.

Prescriptive Rules

Rules for how to do things, are, of course, taught mainly in L2 courses and also during elementary and later schooling. Inductive rules of this kind have been developed by linguists over centuries and millennia. Whereas they can be taught quickly, they require advanced abstract thinking for their formulation and some abstraction for their comprehension. Some of these rules might be used by older children and adults in *planning* an utterance *before it is spoken*. Yet, as Becker (1991) has argued persuasively (persuasive because it is well known to everybody who ever learned a second language) it is impossible to simultaneously plan a sentence in accordance with consciously formulated rules and to speak it.

It seems therefore that Chomsky committed another category mistake, misled by his familiarity with linguistic rules, by implying that the infant's, child's and normal adult speaker's performance is based on such prescriptive rules. He confounded high-level academic competence with preschool performance. Presuming the child has established major semantic categories, as is obvious from much of his nonverbal behavior, and acknowledging the wealth of the well tuned input, Maratsos' (1983, p. 772) conclusion can be fully seconded: "The acquisition of grammar is essentially fairly straightforward, requiring little information processing capacity, which is a good thing because the child has very little."

The earlier arguments suggest that empirical, more empirical, and better-structured empirical studies are needed in the field of L1 acquisition, which is still quite immature as far as process analyses are concerned. Premature speculations without any evidence or biased interpretations of evidence retard the field, as Leopold's (1971) survey has emphasized. Empty labels prove even more useless. Who would want to explain a biological process today through Bergson's élan vital or a psychological one by means of McDougall's (1908) instincts—products of the neoromantic era.

Additionally, Morgan's canon and also Occam's razor have to be kept in mind, especially with infants and young children, who have shown themselves as relying on relatively simple perceptual-memory (sensorimotor) processes, processes that provide the explanation for early performance in other domains. High-level abstractions of rules appear to be difficult even for adults, while everybody remembers having checked, when unsure, "what an utterance sounds like" or "what it looks like." Perceptual-memory procedures and not rule analyses are therefore employed by most adults in everyday performance when deciding about linguistic correctness.

INTEGRATIONS, EVALUATIONS, AND A PROSPECTUS

The Paradoxical State of the Field

The extreme logical weakness of Chomsky's original argument, based on a lack of easy imagination, has been summarized earlier. Absolutely nothing follows as to causal factors whether learning processes are "easy or hard to imagine." Counterevidence against the claim of the "poverty of the input" is abundant. Consequently, Givon argued more than a decade ago, that extensive research results not only in "a realization that the input in the acquisition of one's first language matters ENORMOUSLY. We have, so it seems, put behind us Chomsky's cavalier trivialization of input" (Givon, 1985, p. 1007). However, Chomsky perhaps remains the most cited living scholar.

Even the basic sequence of the development of diverse skills argues against a nativistic thesis, as the following considerations show: The evidence that the acquisition of a first language proceeds quite slowly, extending over two decades in the case of advanced language skills, is too strong to be denied. (When the mastery of *two* simple patterns, the S–V–O and the Copula-sentence pattern, after three to four years of extensive input, is described as fast progress, one wonders by which measurement criteria.) Only the perceptual learning of phonetic and phonemic characteristics has been shown to occur relatively quickly, as in the cases of visual and olfactory perceptions. A serious contradiction arises therefore when linguistic knowledge in any form is considered innate: Children recognize smells, sounds, and faces within the first months of life; they reach by six months and walk by 12 months, both partly innate and partly learned patterns, and they babble by the age of six months—a seemingly innate tendency that is, however, transformed by perceptual-motor learning, as revealed by sound patterns of the mother tongue that occur in babbling.

As learning can be demonstrated so early, and considering the amount and appropriateness of verbal input in middle-class homes, infants should speak quite fluently and grammatically at the age of one year if this behavior were supported by strong innate predispositions. Only in postulating an extremely impoverished input—a postulate that had already been disproved when it was made—could the contrast between the slow acquisition and innateness assumptions be resolved. Impoverished input, is of course, the argument that Chomsky and his disciples relied on—and still rely on in part, when they deny corrections and other instructional strategies, such as fine tuning and frequency effects. The evidence pertaining to these most central aspects of training and learning are surveyed in Chapters 3, 4, 5, and partly in Chapters 6 and 7. The latter chapters focus, however, more on the reciprocal of enrichment—input deprivation and its effects. Combined, these chapters provide considerable indications of which specific features of the input lead to successful language acquisition and which delay or impede it, that is, they suggest causal explanations. Each issue of L1-acquisition journals provides more evidence for learning. Yet, Pinker's *The Language Instinct* (1994) became a best-seller.

Avoiding an Extreme Antithesis

As necessary as the accumulating evidence of rich input is, a real danger exists of overemphasizing the counterargument to Chomsky's postulate of deficient input. Not all parents display uniformly rich input—the range of variation in input provision is large, both as far as quantity and quality are concerned. Hart and Risley (1955) provided impressive quantitative evidence. The relation of qualitative input deficits to deficits in advanced language skills, suffered by some social groups and possibly by entire cultures, is the main focus of Chapters 6 and 7. These common deficits in language skills indicates not only the weakness of the nativistic argument (as almost all children become skillful walkers, a skill strongly based on an innate pattern), but they also emphasize the vulnerability of dyadic interactions and of training/learning procedures to interference, at least as far as modern high-level language requirements are concerned. Insufficiency of the home for high-level language training has been implicitly admitted in all advanced societies where eight, twelve, or more years of educational endeavors include extensive instruction in the mother tongue. For even higher performance on the level of Nobel or Pulitzer Prize winners, much more extensive literary training is required, as all biographical evidence about such outstanding achievers confirms. On the opposite end of the continuum, large numbers of children are found whose home-based language is insufficient to succeed even in elementary school.

Chapter 6 focuses on the established concomitant variations across social classes. In contrast to some reports, Chapter 7 shows that the same covariation seems to exist across entire cultures: with vastly suboptimal input, the acquisition of language skills is delayed for years, and advanced skills are never attained. A well-established covariation of children's behavioral and psychiatric problems, indicating family problems, with language deficits and difficulties (Baker & Cantwell, 1982), also points to a common environmental deficit that has negative impacts in both domains. However, psychiatric family-dysfunction and its effects on language acquisition are not included in the present survey. A differential focus on the poverty of the stimulus in diverse ecological settings, and how it differs from the optimal input that leads to high levels of competence, is therefore certainly required. Neither the notorious wholistic declaration of a universal poverty of the stimulus, nor its opposite, a relativistic assertion that all input is equivalent, has any practical utility.

Facets of Training and Outcomes

Before proceeding to the empirical analyses, one further conceptual clarification is desirable. This differentiation can utilize the emphases of postmodernists and poststructuralists who insist on the multifaceted nature of all phenomena. For verbal interactions, logical positivism's emphasis on "observation statements" is certainly oversimplistic: One hears directly only the surface forms of sentences and of extended discourse. Both the grammatical pattern of the sentence, and even less the teaching techniques and learning strategies entailed in the discourse, are not immediately obvious from the stimulus pattern. They can, however, be conceptualized on the basis of diverse theoretical perspectives, involving behavioral, perceptual, and cognitive principles. This is the notorious fact that all data are theory laden. All these conceptualizations can, however, be empirically evaluated. Repetitions involve rehearsals, which can be counted, and their intervals can be measured. Juxtapositions of incorrect and correct forms have corrective potential; repetitions of identical structures with variations of elements can serve as pattern drills, and so forth. Yet, while rehearsals, corrections, and pattern drills are theory-based inferences, they are based on observables and can be refuted if pertinent evidence is not forthcoming. This is the basic principle of any science— to formulate refutable hypotheses and evaluate them empirically.

Different theoretical approaches can therefore produce complementary, instead of conflicting, insights: A Gothic cathedral can be approached with an interest in the type of stone employed, in architectural forms, or in religious expression. Only all three, and probably more, perspectives combined will do justice to the Gothic cathedral. Similarly for language transmission and acquisition, philological-linguistic approaches need to be supplemented by semiotic, paralinguistic, and especially skill training/learning perspectives. Multiple aspects of language, its form, meaning, function, and (during the acquisition phase) training as well as learning perspectives (relevant for transmission and acquisition), need to be selected for study for a comprehensive understanding. Whether children are predominantly trained to be skillful in social interactions or in academic discourse should affect which subskills of language are taught and how they are taught. Also from this perspective of the end product, multiplicity is to be expected: Most of the research on these topics still needs to be performed.

An Overview of the Following Chapters, Present Aspirations, and Imminent Dangers

A great deal of epistemological guidance can be derived from the homologous domain of skill learning, including sports and industrial skills. This paradigm is emphasized: From a skill learning perspective, some of the points most needing evaluation are: contingencies, especially fine tuning and corrections; frequency effects; pattern abstraction; covariations between differential input and acquisition; and the continuity of development from the earliest to higher levels of language skills. The following chapters survey most of these topics with the exception of the long-term continuity aspect, for which the available empirical evidence is still too fragmentary. Two topics are conspicuous through their absence: the neurological bases of language and connectionist learning theories of language development.

While their promise is not doubted, the modeling of neural processes lies outside the scope of analyses of naturalistic adult–child interactions.

The perhaps too optimistic aspiration guiding all chapters is that the massed presentation of empirical perspectives and the forceful analysis of logical flaws in some conclusions drawn from empirical findings might nudge some of the spokespersons of the field away from their romantic escapades and induce them to return to critical, empirically-based research and theorizing. Otherwise, both theoretical conceptions and practical applications will remain stymied. The contemporary nativistic tendencies certainly hindered research on the functional and instructional analyses of language transmission, that is, of the teachability of language. They thereby delayed the development of optimal methods to intervene in the frequent instances of delay and deficit.

As romantic ideologies of the previous two turns of the centuries, when the *Volksgeist*, the élan vital, and *Blut und Boden* (blood and soil), were argued as major factors shaping languages, contributed to invidious comparisons of nations and nationalistic conflicts, so nativistic explanations of differences in language skills can support invidious comparisons of social classes and races whenever some social groups quite consistently perform below the average of the population. Herrnstein and Murray (1994) argued genetic causes for IQ differences, although nobody would deny that intelligence is strongly influenced by the environment. Yet, if scientists declare the environment quite unimportant for the acquisition of language, politicians will quickly withdraw the resources for improving it, and the futures of millions of children will be destroyed.

2

Sequential Analyses in the Exploration of L1 Acquisition

> The skills required for the study of long-term processes may still need some time to mature. Specific hurdles have to be overcome before social processes of long duration can become a regular study object.
> —N. Elias, *The Symbol Theory* (1991, p. 16)

The arguments of Chapter 2 and the evidence of the following chapters demonstrate how closely Elias's conclusion applies to the field of first language transmission and acquisition. Yet it is also generally agreed that the structure of inquiry must be compatible with the structure of its object. If it is not compatible, the real nature of the object will be distorted or its existence will be overlooked entirely. The contrast between this generally acknowledged methodological requirement and Elias's conclusion, drawn after a long life of research, expresses the dilemma in the field of first language acquisition. The object of study, language acquisition, is a process extending over about twenty years (or the entire life for advanced levels of skill), relying upon cumulative learning, but also on iterative cycles of input–progress–renewed-input that extend over seconds only. Yet nobody in language acquisition research has tried to employ the full range of methodologies that would be commensurate with the structure of this object of investigation, which entails microlongitudinal contingencies, multi-year processes, as well as all the time spans between these extremes.

Nevertheless, Elias might have been a little too pessimistic for the social sciences generally, because one of the social sciences, economy, has worked consistently with long-term time series. Long cycles of war and peace in history are extensively explored. For example, Fernand Braudel and his school emphasized the *longue duree* and shorter cyclical phenomena in history. Therefore, at least two fields exist from which developmental psycholinguistics could borrow methods spanning long time periods. Microanalytic conceptions in the form of stimulus-response analyses have already been central concepts for the philosophical forebears of positivist psychology, the English empiricists. These latter concerns were reflected in the emphasis on imitation in previous language acquisition research (cf. Speidel & Nelson, 1989). Presently they were rediscovered under the label of "contingencies" (Bloom, Margulis, Tinker & Fujita, 1996; Sokolov, 1993a, 1993b).

However, middle-range phenomena have been rather neglected: Once the child's responsive utterance exhibits some effect of the preceding input (which in turn might have been feedback to an earlier utterance of the child), the subsequent utterances of the mother can take this changed status of the child into account, resulting in changed input. It follows that feedback cycles entailing multiple turns and extending over many seconds and several minutes are a central aspect of the structure of the data. From a training/learning perspective such episodes should probably be considered the main units of analysis. After the immediate acquisition, the feedback cycles facilitate the short-term retention of language tokens, often including massed rehearsals that can extend over minutes. They are then followed by spaced rehearsals and long-interval reinstatements with minor or major changes. These rehearsal processes can extend over hours and days. Finally, the nature of the input and the discourse changes gradually and incrementally over periods of months and years with increasing overall levels of filial language skills, shifting from an emphasis on vocabulary to bound morphemes and diverse levels of syntax. The latter changes extend over weeks, months, and years.

This multiplicity of phenomena that require explication is subsumed in the title of the present chapter, "sequential analyses." These are contrasted with the longitudinal analyses of, for example, life-span psychology. Whereas all approaches employing repeated measures on the same participant are certainly longitudinal, the term "longitudinal"has been quite consistently associated in psychology with panel designs. That is, few—often only two—repeated measurements on the same participants, separated mostly by considerable time intervals, are labeled "longitudinal" and differentiated from "cross-sectional studies" that employ different participants for successive ages. Yet, panel designs are extremely unsatisfactory for fine-grained causal analyses. All causal events that happen in the interval between the chosen measurement points remain unknown. If a process is cumulative, depending on consistent or—in even more complex situations on unsystematically changing inputs—then the traditionally labeled "longitudinal design" is clearly not adequate for the structure of the object of study. This caveat applies fully to many past applications of this longitudinal method (measuring often only a pre and a post cross-section) to language transmission and acquisition. Few of the phenomena described in the introductory paragraphs could be captured by means of panel designs. Continuous longitudinal methods, focusing on both short-term and de-layed contingencies, are needed. This entire set is referred to here as "sequential analyses."

THE VARIETY OF PHENOMENA AND MATCHED METHODS

Table 2.1 provides a first brief overview of the variety of phenomena that must be considered and of methods that seem fit to capture them. Yet, it is not presumed that either the phenomena or the methods surveyed here cover the field exhaustively. Table 2.1 and the present chapter present the proverbial first step upon which many more have to follow, and systematically raise, rather than settle, the challenging methodological issues involved.

The left column of Table 2.1 is structured according the length of time the processes take, from seconds to years. This is self-explanatory. This same temporal structure applies to the middle and right columns.

As the major phenomena, indicated in the middle column, are generally well-known and are extensively documented below, only a brief conceptual clarification of the implications of the contrast between responses and antecedents is given here.

Responses

Traditional approaches to language acquisition research focused on responses, whether they explored filial imitations of models or the confirmations, corrections, and expansions provided by the mother. Relatively immediate contingencies are expected whose probability, that is predictability, can be computed. Yet, here lies the first problem: Should only the immediate response be recorded, and if not, how many should be recorded and after which intervals? Obviously, young children have

TABLE 2.1.
Sequential Phenomena and Matched Methods

Time	Verbal Phenomenon	Methods
A few seconds	Utterance-Response Antecedent-Utterance	Contingency analysis Zero-order Markov chains
Up to minutes	Feedback cycles Brief rehearsals Repetitions with variations	Higher-order Markov chains Lagged probabilities
Up to hours	Massed-spaced rehearsal Patterns of feedback Information density	Event series Time series
Days to a month	Reinstatements Changes in training emphases	Event series Interrupted time series
Months to years	Vocabulary size Morphosyntactic complexity	Time series

a memory span above a few seconds and could produce delayed responses. They could also be influenced by delayed feedback. Additionally, should only one category of responses, such as imitations be recorded, or multiple categories, so that the flexibility of the interlocutors and of diverse dyads can be assessed?

Extending the two-item pattern of utterance and response, one can also ask how the mother responds to a reply of a child, such as a somewhat faulty imitation, or how the child responds to a reward/confirmation. That is, sequences of three, four, or more responses are of great interest, and as indicated above, the interval between the items cannot be assumed to remain consistently minimal.

Antecedents

As discussed in Chapter 1, a major challenge for research is that of discovering the necessary and sufficient antecedents of specific utterances and of general filial accomplishments. In everyday observations of small children, the observer often asks himself: "Why did she behave this way?" "Where did this utterance come from?" In the case of missing evidence of the sources in the input, researchers in the past were prone to postulate innate knowledge and almost miraculous creativity, a mistake explored by Moerk (1980, 1981). To find all sources of acquisitions, a full record of preceding parental or filial utterances would be required, because the filial product does not need to follow immediately after a model and it can be composed of elements from diverse input utterances. Also, children often integrate parts of models with elements of their own preceding utterances in performing "without competence," as Ruth Clark (1974) expressed it. A "gradual working up to" the correct performance, as reported by Kaye (1982) is often found in the transcripts—one such sequence is exemplified below in Figure 2.6. In this search for antecedents, bidirectional, event-based analyses seem the method of choice, although they have been very rarely employed. In the case of "working up to," variations of the cumulative record and a concept of shaping seem to be needed, as the response changes in quality.

In these brief clarifications of the problems entailed in responses and antecedents, all the major methodological tools that might prove useful for handling the tasks have been adumbrated. The major ones, as appearing in the right column of Table 2.1 are briefly discussed on a conceptual (rather than a mathematical/statistical) level.

Transitional Probabilities and Markov-Chains

The concept of "conditional probability" is more widely known than that of "transitional probability" and can therefore serve as a starting point for the discussion. A conditional probability conveys the likelihood of two or more phenomena co-occurring. For example, the relationships between mental disturbances and social class could be expressed as conditional probabilities: How high are the probabilities of specific mental disturbances occurring in diverse social classes? In the present domain of language acquisition, a variant of conditional probabilities, namely transitional probabilities, is preferable because it fits the structure of the data better. The adjective "transitional"entails the temporal sequence that is so central in conversations and in learning generally. Transitional probabilities express the likelihood of one specific phenomenon occurring after one or more specified antecedents. This could be in immediate succession, or the event of interest could happen after some delay or "lag" (the label mostly employed in the field). Such transitional probabilities are the basis of Markov-chain analysis. Easily comprehensible statistical introductions and explorations of Markov-chain approaches are found in Bakeman (1978), Gottman and Bakeman (1979), Bakeman and Gottman (1986), and Gottman (1990).

Transitional probabilities are optimal for exploring interactions between persons. For example, the still controversial question of adult corrections after filial "mistakes" can be answered quantitatively by asking: What is the probability of the mother correcting an imperfect utterance of a child as compared to letting it go without comment? (e.g., Bohannon & Stanowicz, 1988). In this case, the antecedent is a filial utterance that was less than perfect and the probabilities of two subsequent maternal strategies are compared. Or, question–answer patterns, as they become established over the course of childhood could be explored: What are the changing probabilities at various ages that a child responds verbally to a maternal question? An almost infinite variety of other sequential dependencies can be selected, depending on the focus of the investigator (cf. Gottman, Markman, & Notarius, 1977).

If only two sequential items are focused on, the literature commonly refers to "first-order Markov-chains." If three-item chains are of concern and the probability of the third item is to be established dependent on the co-occurrence of the first two, then "second-order" Markov-chains are computed, and so forth. When intervals between the antecedent and the consequent, that is, "lags," are emphasized, the following differentiations are common. Immediate responses occur at "zero-lag." If one item intervenes between the antecedent and the focused-on consequent, a "lag of one" is employed; and so forth. As children react to input (or parents react to children's utterances) after varying intervals, flexible lags need to be employed in the field of verbal interactions—a problem for routine computer analyses but less of a problem for fine-grained manual analyses.

Additionally, instead of asking what the probabilities of diverse responses to an utterance are, one could inquire what the diverse antecedents of one specific type of response are. The same principle of computation, relying upon conditional or transitional probabilities, could be employed in this case, with only the direction of the sequence being reversed. This approach seems to have been minimally used in quantitative research, although it is common in hospital wards, when elicitors of specific behaviors are of interest. The same approach underlies all searches for causal antecedents in naturalistic settings.

Event-Series Analyses

The term "event series" expresses the basic principle involved in a straightforward manner: sequences of events are described numerically as to their distributions. Recent developments, as surveyed briefly by Palloni and Sorensen (1990) have added more complex approaches, such as the inclusion of covariates and of multiple response options. However, in the original and most common use, the sequence of one category of events is explored in its temporal patterning, specifying repetitions and the spacing between repetitions. "Events" are nominal variables, such as the birth of a child, breakdowns of machinery, the recurrence of a specific vocabulary item, and so forth. Event-series analyses are explained statistically for the nonspecialist in the previously mentioned works of Bakeman (1978), Gottman and Bakeman (1979), and Tuma and Hannan (1979).

Such event series are natural choices for explorations of learning phenomena where repeated events represent rehearsals. Intervals between repetitions can give some indications of memory span, which might differ with the intelligence and motivation of the learner. Long interval-reinstatements (Campbell & Jaynes, 1966) assure against forgetting. Learning research suggests that a pattern starting with some massing, proceeding to spaced rehearsal, and then to rare reinstatements, might be optimal and commonly encountered in effective dyads.

As evident from the brief remarks above, an important difference between Markov approaches and the traditional event-series analyses exists. Markov approaches focus on sequences of many diverse nominal variables, whereas each event series focuses in principle on sequences of only one type. These two methods are therefore differentially fit for diverse data sets and research questions, as discussed below.

Time-Series Analyses

Whereas event-series analyses deal with categorical variables, time-series analyses focus on quantitative variables, with the typical example being the fluctuations of the stock market. Trends in quantity-over-time are captured. These trends can be linear, a monotonous increase or decrease, or they can include more or less regular fluctuations, that is, they can be cyclic. In the first instance, the approach focuses on "the time domain" and in the second on "the frequency domain." In the latter case, a complex wave can be analyzed into its constituent cycles, and patterns in the cyclic phenomena are explored. For example, gain in height during childhood and adolescence would follow a rather linear (though not straight-line) trend, while weight fluctuations in adulthood are often complexly cyclic, being composed possibly of a yearly cycle (winter versus spring and summer) overlaid by fluctuations caused by holidays and even by diurnal changes.

In verbal interactions daily fluctuations are common, often due to changes in interaction partners or in activities (reading versus rough-and-tumble play). Yet, shorter as well as much longer fluctuations in expert–apprentice interactions are of great interest, such as intensity of linguistic information provision or varying bouts of training of specific items followed by changes in training content, respectively.

Out of the many introductions to time-series analysis, Gottmann's (1981) book appears most fit for the nonspecialist. First he surveys in brief conceptual chapters the meaning and use of diverse approaches before providing the statistical tools in a second section. The reader can therefore easily go back and forth, mastering first the concepts and then their statistical representation. In addition, extensive and well-selected background literature is provided in Gottmann's reference section.

Two special subsets of time series are dampened and augmented oscillations which appear to be important in learning and other social interactions. In dampened oscillations, the amplitude of the wave decreases gradually while in augmented ones it increases. An augmented series could be exemplified by an escalating argument or an arms race, whereas a gradual transition from massed training to increasing spacing could be modeled as a dampened oscillation. An example of a dampened oscillation in the domain of language learning is presented in Figure 2.6.

Finally, over months and years, shifts in the contents of training, from an early focus on simple vocabulary, followed by a focus on the most common bound morphemes, and shifting perhaps to more complex grammatical constructions, can be explored by means of time-series analyses (cf. Figure 2.7). The gradually increasing size of the vocabulary could be followed just like the climbing Dow Jones Average (being overly optimistic in the latter case). In brief, any items of interest that change quantitatively over the long term could be either graphically or mathematically represented by event- or time-series.

TABLE 2.2.
Temporal Dynamics of Language Acquisition

	Immediate Contingency Markov Processes	Training Episodes Bivariate time-series	Developmental Changes Bi-/multivariate t-series
Integration of component skills			x
Controlled to automatic			x
Ease of retrieval			x
Generalization		x	x
Lead-lag shift		x	x
Fine-tuning		x	x
Rehearsal	x	x	x
Correction	x	x	x
Confirmation	x	x	x
Imitation	x	x	x
Modeling	x	x	x

Practically the same interactional phenomena as found in the central column of Table 2.1, though employing slightly different terminology, are rendered in the left column of Table 2.2. The major methods are listed on the bottom of the table, and the match between method and phenomenon is indicated in the cells of Table 2.2 by *x*-marks. As the categories in the left column are well known from research on first language acquisition, this format might help to demonstrate more immediately the match between tasks and methods. Only the terms "lead-lag shift" and "controlled to automatic," both in the left column, might require brief explanations. Lead-lag shifts refer to changes in who takes the initiative. For example, with a new vocabulary item, the adult first leads in labeling and the child imitates. Soon, however, the child can be seen returning to the newly learned item by introducing it repeatedly into the conversation, whereas the mother "lags" while correcting, confirming, or integrating the item into a variety of sentence structures.

The contrast of controlled versus automatic is well known from research on skill learning. In the early stages of a skill, much intentional control is required in order to perform it well; later on, skills become more automatic, requiring little processing capacity. Similar phenomena are encountered in the field of language acquisition, where, however, the early control is largely exerted through the input of the adult expert who guides and corrects the child. Later, increasing independence from input and integration of specific items into larger routines entail both spontaneous recall and increasing automaticity of performance. Figure 2.4 presents an example of such gradual filial independence. The integration of input items is reflected in the increasing complexity of spontaneously produced constructions, as exemplified in subsequent chapters of this volume.

The reason why the *x*-marks, that is, the applicability of methods, increase across the body of Table 2.2 is that long periods of observation can be chosen for any behavior category, which then make possible and require event/time-series analyses for data reduction, without excluding in principle the simpler methods. In contrast, the topmost categories of the left column could not readily be ascertained in the case of language acquisition within short- nor within intermediate-length periods. In the middle range of time extension, generalization, lead-lag shifts, and fine tuning could be best captured within intermediate or long periods. Yet the dividing lines are not rigid and the match between method and research problem depends to a considerable extent on the ingenuity of the investigator.

Actual examples from mother–child interactions recorded in the course of early language development can clarify the conceptual principles introduced. One well-known and very effective dyad has been chosen for this demonstration with the full awareness that a large variety of interaction styles might exist, some of them resulting in equally quick learning, and others detrimental to efficient language acquisition. Methodological demonstrations and not prescriptive finality is intended in the following sections.

THE SOURCE AND NATURE OF THE DATA

All the data exemplifying the discussed phenomena derive from naturalistic inter-actions of one mother with her child. This is the famous dyad of Eve and her mother that was recorded by Professor Roger Brown and his team at Harvard university. Eve was between 18 and 27 months during the course of the recordings. The recorded and transcribed observations were analyzed by establishing categories of teaching techniques in the speech of the mother and of learning strategies in the verbal turns of Eve. Specific coding categories are briefly explained when they are first introduced. The inter-rater reliabilities in coding verbal behaviors were gener-ally in the eighties or higher, indicating that the interactional phenomena can be reliably discerned by coders who only required brief training. All details of the methodology and categorizations have been extensively described in Moerk (1983a) and only those that are important for the present purposes are specified where needed. The frequencies given below are generally per sample if not otherwise indicated. Each sample entailed two hours of interaction. The interactions mostly occurred between Eve and her mother, although brief sequences involving the father or an observer are sometimes included in order not to interrupt the continuity of interaction. For rare periods, which are be specified where pertinent, the father was the only interaction partner.

DIVERSE SEQUENTIAL PHENOMENA

First-Order Markov-Chains or Immediate Contingencies

At first, the strategy of integrating data and statistical methods more closely in order to support the above discussions through examples of applications is followed. Once some central principles of the statistical analysis have been exemplified, the emphasis will shift to sequential phenomena per se without devoting space to the detailed statistical aspects of the analyses, as these could not be covered satisfacto-rily within the scope of the present report.

Table 2.3 provides an integration of empirical results and a statistical approach. It deals with the simplest interactional phenomena: two-step sequences, either Mother–Child (M–C) or Child–Mother (C–M) sequences in the left and right field of the table, respectively. In both sections, the third column (Trp) presents the transitional probabilities of the two-step sequence for each row. For example the transitional probability from the mother employing a new or rare vocabulary item (code 29–vocabulary rehearsal) to the child doing the same is .11. For the Child–Mother pattern (codes 29-29), the equivalent value is .16. This means that whenever the antecedent is a vocabulary rehearsal, the subsequent utterance will be in 11 and 16 percent of the instances, respectively, a vocabulary rehearsal too.

TABLE 2.3.
Two-step Sequences

M	C	Trp	Sp	OF	EF	z	C	M	Trp	Sp	OF	EF	z.
29	29	.11	.04	160	62.6	15.5	29	29	.16	.05	197	62.6	24.8
51	02	.07	.02	58	18.9	11.3	29	80	.08	.03	101	35.7	12.1
61	51	.10	.03	56	17.8	15.0	51	12	.11	.04	100	33.7	16.9
27	51	.17	.03	54	10.1	30.8	24	24	.18	.06	98	29.9	28.5
53	50	,27	.01	45	2.3	56.7	51	80	.10	.03	86	25.6	15.4
54	51	.28	.03	44	4.8	58.9	02	80	.12	.03	84	19.7	21.4
61	23	.07	.02	43	12.2	12.1	25	02	.09	.04	79	32.4	12.3
60	20	.19	.01	42	3.6	38.0	22	02	.08	.04	65	29.4	10.4
61	22	.07	.03	41	15.5	10.0	51	51	.07	.03	65	24.5	10.3
61	29	.07	.04	40	14.5	10.1	24	29	.10	.05	53	26.9	15.1

To put the values of the transitional probability in perspective, the fourth column in each field gives the simple probability (Sp), that is, the probability that vocabulary rehearsal is to be expected independent of the type of antecedent. These probabilities are .04 and .05, in the case of M–C and C–M sequences, respectively; that is, around a third of the value that derives from the structure of the interaction. The contrast between transitional and simple probabilities demonstrates that the vocabulary–vocabulary sequence is an interactional structure clearly exceeding chance co-occurrences of these specific behaviors. This structural aspect is even more clearly evident from the next three columns in each field: Observed Frequencies (OF) for each two-item sequence are juxtaposed with Expected Frequencies (EF) and a z-value is given to indicate the significance of the differences. The complexities of establishing z-values are discussed by Bakeman (1978) and by Gottman and Bakeman (1979) and need not be pondered here. As a rough approximation, these authors affirm that a z-value of +1.96 can be assumed as being significant at the .05 level, higher values expressing higher significance. As seen in Table 2.3 all the z-values are far above this cutoff point, showing that the interactional structures are highly significant in the statistical sense. That they are also significant in the substantive sense becomes clear from the strategies/techniques employed, as is discussed presently.

The statistical explanations just summarized apply in identical manner for the patterns in all the rows of Table 2.3, and the respective values show that the mother and child are tuned to each other and respond to specific antecedents quite predictably (far above chance level) with specific categories of responses. Having demonstrated interaction patterns, the psycholinguistic and learning-psychological meaning of a few of these patterns can be indicated. For this discussion, the fields Mother–Child and Child–Mother are referred to as the left field and the right field, respectively. Rows will be counted from the top.

Vocabulary training (code 29) stands out as one predominant feature in row 1 for both fields and also in row two for the right field. In this latter case, the mother responds with confirmation or reward (code 80) to the child's rehearsal. For a somewhat insecure learner such an affirmation makes eminent sense: "Yes, you chose the right vocabulary item."

Also important, as far as frequencies are concerned, is syntactic training, as seen most clearly in row two of the left field and row three of the right field (the code sequences 51-02 in both fields). In the 51-02 sequence in the left field, the mother encodes a nonverbal relationship in syntactic form (code 51–syntactic mapping), and the child repeats this sentence in the form of Brown's (e.g., 1973) "reductions" (reduced imitation–code 02). In the right field, the C–M sequence of 51-02, the child produces the sentence (code 51–syntactic mapping) and the mother repeats it with expansion (code 02). As Moerk (1992) has shown and as already implied in Brown and Bellugi (1964), these expansions are mostly corrections, because the mother provides elements omitted by the child.

Browsing through the rows, it is evident that syntactic mapping (code 51) appears repeatedly in diverse contexts. From a learning perspective, this means that the mother and child exercise the equivalences of perceptual and linguistic structures extensively when they encode observed constellations into linguistic structures, repeat them, and correct them if necessary. The large variety of interactional combinations, as shown in the rows, indicate the versatility of the mother and child and functions as a counterpoint to the patterning demonstrated in the five columns of both fields that provide quantitative or statistical indices. That is, interactional structures are employed in a versatile manner. For example, in row three of the left field, the mother invites Eve to specify (code 61) one item in her linguistic construction after Eve had not specified it clearly: For example, the child might have said *That's a red* ..., with the complement noun incomprehensible). The mother would have responded with *That's a red what?* (Brown's [1968] "Occasional Question") and the child would have reformulated her utterance in a more complete manner, describing the object fully (code 51). Then, as row three in the right field indicates, the mother is often prone to repeat the child's utterance by adding some corrective expansion (code 02). For example: Child: *I lost* .... Mother: *You lost what?*, Child: *I lost teddy bear.* Mother: *You lost your teddy bear.* Rehearsal and a gradual build-up of a complex structure are combined in such or similar exercises that occur with great frequency.

Build-up sequences (code 22) reflect a pattern of exercises often identical to the one just described, only this time the focus is placed on how one of the conversation partners expands a construction by herself in repeated utterances. For example, in row nine in the left field, the mother again specified an item (code 61) that the child had not made clear in the preceding utterance, and Eve herself inserted the previously omitted item in a more complete utterance (code 22–build-up sequence). And in row eight in the right field, the mother responds with an expansion (code 02) to a filial build-up sequence, improving and correcting the child's utterance. In row seven of the same field, the mother expands and improves a filial utterance that entailed a replacement of content items in a frame (code 25). A similar analysis could continue for the other codes.

While the goal of the present discussion is not to exhaustively discuss all the forms of teaching and learning, the data in Table 2.3 show how much of this teaching and learning is going on. They also should provide convincing evidence that only sequential methodologies can capture these rich instructional interactions. If the flexibility of response patterns is to be explored, Markov-chain analyses appear to be the optimal methods. When, in this table as well as in the following sections, only selected teaching and learning principles are exemplified on the basis of sequential patterns, this does not imply that the instructional principles are the only ones encountered in the raw data. Moerk (1983b, 1985a, 1985b) has provided more extensive evidence for maternal training and filial learning that was derived from the same database. Yet, even the extensive analyses presented in these studies represent only a small fragment of the evidence found in the transcripts and of the sequential phenomena abstracted from them.

Second or Higher-Order Markov-Chains

In any conversation it is obvious that more than two elements in a sequence of verbal interactions need to be considered to capture interactional dynamics. Whether it is, for example, Question–Answer–Acknowledgment on the illocutionary level or Mistake–Correction–Improvement on the instructional level, three-step patterns are extremely common. Furthermore, as soon as the conversation does not flow completely smoothly due to misunderstandings or disagreements, longer interdependencies result from the inclusion of repair sequences. The following section provides some examples that appear most closely relevant to instructional processes. As the dynamics are getting more complex, they are depicted graphically for ease of comprehension. The principles of transitional probabilities are the same as discussed above, however now three or more items are considered sequentially.

Of great theoretical interest are the child's immediate responses to positive feedback. They can be optimally captured through second-order Markov-chains in which the pattern of: original utterance of the child–the mother's positive feedback–followed by the child's response is focused upon. The dynamics are presented in Figure 2.1. Figure 2.1 employs fan-shaped presentations to indicate some multiple paths in the flow of interactions, paths that are substantiated through high transitional probabilities in Markov-chain analyses, that is, frequent co-occurrences.

Figure 2.1 encompasses three sections: In (a) and (b) the most frequent filial responses to maternal rewards (code 80) are presented for two preceding filial strategies (code 29–vocabulary rehearsal and code 02– reduced imitation). In (c) the responses to maternal imitations (codes 01 and 02) of filial syntactic construc-

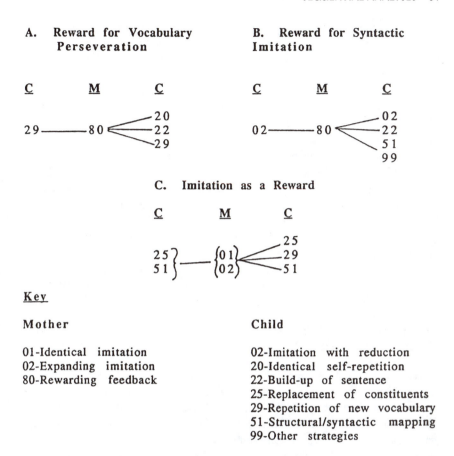

A. Reward for Vocabulary
   Perseveration

B. Reward for Syntactic
   Imitation

C. Imitation as a Reward

Key

Mother   Child

01-Identical imitation   02-Imitation with reduction
02-Expanding imitation   20-Identical self-repetition
80-Rewarding feedback   22-Build-up of sentence
                                                25-Replacement of constituents
                                                29-Repetition of new vocabulary
                                                51-Structural/syntactic mapping
                                                99-Other strategies

FIGURE 2.1.   Patterns of reward and its effect

tions are exemplified. Figures 2.1 (b) and (c) obviously reflect grammatical exercises.

Two major features are quite obvious from Figure 2.1: In (a) and (b), the child is seen to respond often with a repetition of her previous learning strategy, whether it is—in (a)— code 20–identical repetition, code 22–build-up sequences, or code 29–vocabulary perseveration. In (b), the child's chosen options include code 02–imitation with reduction, code 22–build-up sequences, and code 51–syntactic mapping, besides a category uncodable–code 99. Figures 2.1 (a) and (b) highlight either the child's vocabulary learning or the still unsuccessful struggle with minor morphemes (mostly omitted functors, code 02, as they are known from studies of "telegraphic speech"). Both endeavors are rewarded by the mother. In Figure 2.1(c) replacements of constituents (code 25) is a technique equivalent to pattern drill; and syntactic mapping (code 51) encodes environmental relations syntactically, that is, both codes reflect syntactic exercises. The mother employs a more complex response to these more complex exercises in accepting them through imitation (codes 01, 02) but also by often providing minor corrections (code 02). The child, in turn, repeats these corrected utterances, partly with variations.

In all three sections of Figure 2.1, the dyad's emphasis on repetitions, both of syntactic and vocabulary items, is obvious, as is the mother's positive feedback. The principle encountered in these structures is quite clear and is identical to two basic principles of learning theory: that rewarded behavior is repeated and rehearsed behavior is learned. The syntactic mapping (code 51) as seen in Figures 2.1(b) and (c), also often entails a repetition of a preceding statement and therefore adds one more rehearsal, while matching verbal and perceptual structures. Such a common longer pattern is: Child Mapping–Mother Expansion–Child Reduction (as shown in Figure 2.1[b] as code 02)–Mother Acknowledgment (code 80)–Child Repetition of the original syntactic mapping (code 51). In these cases, four consecutive repetitions of a sentence— often spontaneously constructed by the child—are encountered. This is obviously a valuable learning opportunity. To reflect the structure of such interactions, sequential methodologies are absolutely necessary.

Intermediate-Interval Chains of Dependencies in Extensive Grammatical Exercises

An example of complex sequential phenomena is presented in Figure 2.2. This figure gives a preliminary impression of the multiplicity of interactional paths that arise when the 38 learning strategies of the child are related to 40 training techniques of the mother, as they were coded in the underlying study. The combinations of these categories in only three-item sequences, that is 78 to the third power, would result in 474,552 different triple sequences. That is, almost half a million different patterns are possible. For longer sequences, 78 would have to be taken to the fourth, fifth, or even higher powers, and the number of combinations would soon almost approach infinity. Straightforward stochastic analyses are therefore not feasible because no sample could be large enough to assure sufficiently large numbers of occurrences of all the diverse combinations of categories to establish their expected distributions.

The microanalysis of five-step sequences as shown in Figure 2.2 relies therefore mainly on the higher than expected frequencies of the central triple patterns (M–M–C), that is, on their higher than random transitional probabilities. To these central three-element patterns are added antecedent and successor techniques/strategies that have been statistically related only to their immediately adjacent utterances and not to the entire five-element pattern. The possible antecedents of one maternal category, frame variation (code 27), are presented together with the maternal responses to the filial category, imitation with reduction (code 02). This integration results in five-slot sequences, with the multiple paths indicated by fan-shaped patterns. Similar fan-shaped patterns of antecedents could have been

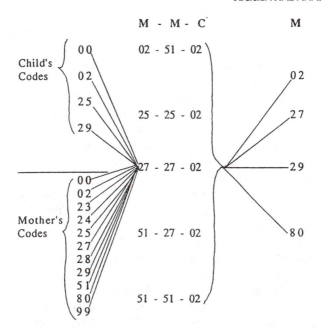

FIGURE 2.2.   Five-step sequences in mother-child interactions

presented for each of the other three maternal categories (expansion–code 02, replacement major–code 25, and syntactic mapping–code 51), as they appear in the first positions of the central M–M–C pattern. Whereas for maternal code 27, frame variation, both the child's and the mother's possible antecedents are presented, for the child's imitation with reduction (code 02) only the subsequent maternal turns are given, because no strong patterns (expressed through high transitional probabilities) beginning with filial imitation with reduction (code 02) were found that entailed a subsequent strategy of Eve.

These longer sequences represent something comparable to flow diagrams with multiple branches. At all steps in the sequence, different (but functionally often similar categories) can replace each other. A familiar analogy for this phenomenon in the domain of language would be the syntactic S–V–O pattern, wherein the slots (Subject, Verb, Object) can have a diversity of fillers. In the language training pattern, the slots are the turns of the mother and child, and the fillers are their varying training and learning strategies. This analogy is reflected in the design and structure of Figure 2.2.

Whereas Figure 2.2 provides only a few examples of an almost unlimited manifold of patterns, it can serve to highlight the value of the sequential methodology by providing insights about instructional processes. It attests again to intensive syntax training that has often been overlooked in nonsequential research. In the middle three steps of the five-step sequence, two successive maternal syntactic exercises, reflected in codes 02, 25, 27, 51 (expansion, replacement major, frame variation, syntactic mapping), precede a syntactic imitation (i.e., imitation through reduction—code 02) of the child, resulting in three repetitions of a syntactic structure while retaining the meaning almost unchanged. Two training sequences are singled out for discussion to clarify some instructional processes: First, in the first central row of Figure 2.2 it can be seen that the mother's imitation with expansion (code 02)—showing that the child had omitted some, mostly obligatory, elements in her preceding utterance—is followed by syntactic mapping (code 51)—probably of the same environmental givens which were the topic of the conversation just before. This is followed in turn by an imitation with reduction by the child and by a renewed maternal imitation with expansion (code 02 at the top of the right fan). In brief, in the underlying five-step sequence, two syntactic "corrections"—expansions (code 02)—are provided by the mother together with a renewed model (code 51), and two attempts are made by the child to master this input—the one filial code 02 shown in the figure and the other indicated by the first maternal code 02.

When the first maternal codes of the five-element pattern are included, as seen in the lower section of the antecedent fan, it becomes evident that almost all of them (with the exception of reward—code 80, vocabulary exercise—code 29, and un-codable—code 99) are codes for syntactic exercises (codes 23, 24, 27, 28—break-down sequence, minor morpheme perseveration, frame variation, and optional transformations, respectively) which refer to finer analyses and structural variations. These exercises are followed by the syntactic exercises just discussed in the middle three-element pattern and then in the right-hand fan (codes 02 and 27—imitation with expansion and frame variation)—obviously further syntactic training. The other two categories in the right fan consist of vocabulary repetition (code 29) and reward (code 80), two eminently reasonable responses to a filial attempt that was at least partially successful in utilizing the maternal training. In all these interactions, it can be demonstrated through verbatim analyses that the semantic contents remain largely the same or very similar. This results in repetitions with only minor, largely morphosyntactic changes, an ideal training opportunity with relatively low semantic information processing load.

As verbal conversations generally, and conversations between a mother and her small child specifically, are rather redundant in the themes talked about and also in the syntactic structures employed, vocabulary rehearsal over longer periods is combined with densely spaced syntactic rehearsals and restructurings. Both should facilitate language learning. Longer sequential dynamics are the focus of the next section.

Event Series in Multi-Event Sequences and Lagged Sequential Analyses

While immediate feedback might be absolutely necessary during the earliest stages of language acquisition, varying delays occur and are fruitful soon thereafter. The

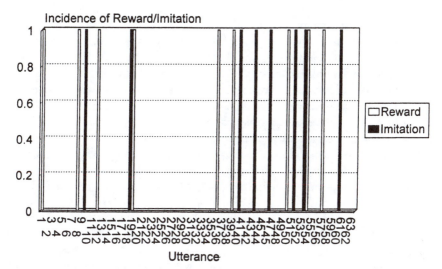

FIGURE 2.3. Intermittent rewards in verbal interactions

principle of delay applies for spaced rehearsals, reinstatements after longer intervals (Campbell & Spear, 1972), intermittent reinforcement as known from learning theory, and the delayed imitations of modeled items after varying intervals. Those varying delays imply, obviously, lagged transitions (Sackett, 1979, 1980) between the items in question. In principle, therefore, the data could be described by employing lagged transitional probabilities, yet, as the lags between items vary, while lagged Markov-analyses rely on one preselected lag, event series, as exemplified in the next major section, are more apposite to reflect the structure of the data.

Intermittent Rewards

Whereas rewards often follow a filial verbal contribution after zero or one lag, as shown in Figure 2.1, they are also spaced after varying intervals, reflecting a form of intermittent reinforcement. Such patterning would certainly be expected both from research on reinforcement and from common sense experience with learning and training processes.

Figure 2.3 presents a short and simplified, but otherwise rather random, excerpt from the transcripts reflecting patterning of rewards. The persons speaking were the mother and the child. Only three techniques are presented in Figure 2.3—reward in the form of *Yes/Yeah* that was referred to repeatedly above, and two types of maternal imitation: identical imitation and expanded imitation. The latter two are combined in the figure as "Imitation." Maternal imitation implies acceptance of the child's verbal contribution and has therefore a rewarding function, too. Independently of whether only direct reward is focused upon or whether imitation is added, it is quite evident from Figure 2.3 that Eve's mother provides rewards (or affirmations) for Eve quite consistently, though intermittently. With the exception of one brief stretch between utterances 21 to 37, the rewards seem to be relatively evenly spaced. They occur predominantly two to four lags after a previous reward or imitation by the mother. Such sequential evidence is pertinent to the motivational aspect of verbal interactions and implicitly, of language learning. Differences between dyads and social classes in reward provision could be easily ascertained with such sequential methods and might provide important suggestions for one reason of differences in filial involvement in verbal interactions and in language levels attained.

Obviously, longer segments have to be analyzed systematically to express these patterns statistically. It would be of great interest to explore how often and why stretches without rewards, such as that between utterances 21 and 37, occur, and how such patterns compare across participants of different language proficiency. In order to explore why this exceptional stretch between utterances 21 and 37 might have occurred, the original transcripts were consulted and the interaction sequence was analyzed microscopically. These microanalyses show that the mother overtaxed the child's processing capacities during these few interactions. Repair sequences were needed which disrupted the normal rhythm of reward provision. Not only a gap in rewards, but cognitive-communicative difficulties can be discovered therefore by means of such sequential analyses. Similar disturbances, if occurring frequently, might constitute one reason for problems in language acquisition.

The spacing of rewards is obviously only one of a myriad of possible topics that could be explored by means of medium-interval event series analyses. Vocabulary rehearsal, the spacing of corrections, of specific bound morphemes when the child begins to acquire them, such as the regular past tense, are some additional central topics that invite sequential analyses. One of these, vocabulary rehearsal, is presented below in Figure 2.5. The results of such sequential analyses would not only be theoretically interesting, showing extended teaching and learning processes, and cautioning against premature nativist conclusions, but could be practically useful. Previous analyses (e.g., Moerk, 1985b) have shown dyadic differences in the frequency and density of reward provision during verbal interactions of young children with their mothers, and the more ideally instructed child was also the one advancing more quickly. As many of these instructional techniques could be taught quite readily to parents of language delayed children, such insights would be directly beneficial for their children.

Changing Intervals Between Models and Imitations

Based on extensive evidence, Moerk (1989a) has argued that newly introduced items are at first either imitated immediately or quickly lost. Having been rehearsed a few times imitatively, they are employed by the child after increasingly longer lags from the model. Moerk and Vilaseca (1987) have shown this in the acquisition of the bound morpheme *-ed* of the past and the free future morpheme *will/'ll*. The changes in median lags of both over the second half of the recordings of Eve and her mother, that is, over the course of six months, are presented in Figure 2.4. Medians are focused on because means were too strongly influenced by one or two extreme outliers. The medians are given as the middle number of each of the three tiers, minimal and maximum lags are shown in the top and bottom tier. (When less

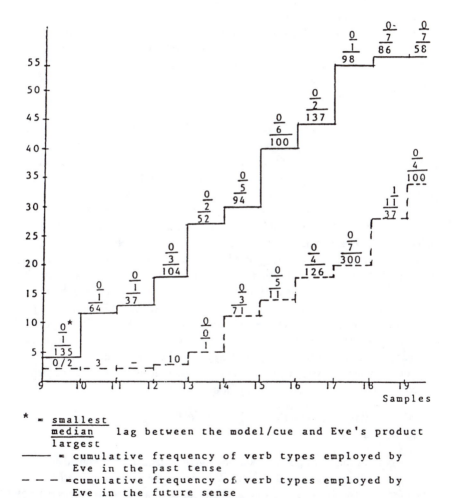

* = $\dfrac{\text{smallest}}{\underset{\text{largest}}{\text{median}}}$ lag between the model/cue and Eve's product

——— = cumulative frequency of verb types employed by Eve in the past tense

— — — = cumulative frequency of verb types employed by Eve in the future sense

FIGURE 2.4. Eve's progress from restricted formulas to generalized use of temporal morphemes and her gradual independence from input.

than three future forms were employed, as in Samples 9 to 12, the lags are presented for each occurrence.)

Although the increase in the median lags is not completely monotonic, due to small random fluctuations, in the case of the past tense the lags increase from one to seven over the recording period. For the later acquired future morphemes, an almost linear trend in median lags seems to extend from *0* to *11* in Sample 18, while the lower median (*4*) in Sample 19 can be presumed to be due random fluctuations. If correlations are employed to express the relationship between median lag and the number of the sample, that is, the time of recording and therewith the age of the child, the Pearson-Product Moment *r*'s are: *.68* and *.67* for past and future morphemes, respectively.

These correlations are impressive, especially if their squares, the variance accounted for of about 50 percent, are considered. While their statistical significance is merely borderline due to the small N, the 50 percent of the variance accounted for indicates the substantive significance of input history, as expressed in the number of the sample. Most important theoretically, the longitudinal analyses strongly suggest that morpheme mastery and increasing independence from models is a gradual process and not a rule based phenomenon. Focusing on the stepwise increase in *types of verbs* (as against tokens) employed in the past and future, as shown in the trend lines, a similar gradual increase in generalization can be noticed, from between 3 and 5 types in the first sample, to 35 and 55 types in the last, for future and past, respectively. Comparing the smallest, the median, and the largest lags, diverse learning processes are suggested as bases of these performances. Whereas one instance of the past is already employed after a lag of 135 utterances in Sample 9, that is, spontaneously, all samples exhibit uses after zero and one lag, that is, in close dependence on the preceding model. Even most of the median lags, being quite short, provide indications of the influence of preceding models, that is, of stimulus dependence. Therefore the fashionable assertions about rule following appear highly questionable because the rare delayed-uses could be due to rote formulas. In most instances rote learning and stimulus dependence could provide sufficient explanatory processes for these early stages of acquisition, as was argued in Chapter 1, and also for Berko's (1958) result. Most importantly, the present inferences about processes are based on rich longitudinal evidence and not merely on theoretical preconceptions or ease of imagination.

The Rhythmicity of Interactions as Expressed Through Their Episodic Structure

A further indication of the possible contribution of both qualitative and quantitative sequential analyses is provided in Figure 2.5, where the patterning of episodes is presented over two hours each of interactions for samples 3, 7, 11, 15, and 19 of the dyad. Verbal episodes are defined as stretches of verbal interaction that maintain the same topic. They are therefore very conducive to rehearsals as well as compari-

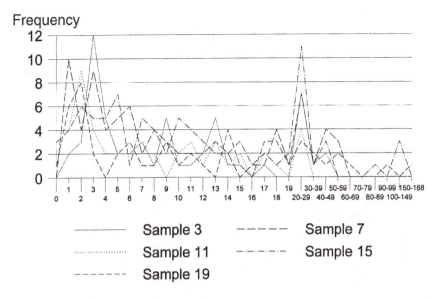

FIGURE 2.5.   **Length of content episodes, Eve and her Mother interacting**

sons of similar constructions as analyzed by Simon (1978), making it easy to extract differences between filial and adult constructions through comparisons.

Figure 2.5 shows that the length of episodes ranges widely, even within one dyad and for one age period. The range extends from single utterances (interval = 0), that raise a theme which is not even responded to, to one episode of 168 utterances in sample 19. What is more important than the extremes is the increase over the period of observation from a maximum of 48 in sample 3 to a maximum of 120 and 168 in samples 15 and 19, respectively. Sample 11 with a maximum of only 29, might indicate the impact of different interaction partners, as the mother was absent during most of this sample and the child interacted mainly with her father. This exception in episode length could, however, simply be due to random fluctuations within the range of the early samples. The means for the four samples of Figure 2.5 show perhaps even more clearly the progress of the dyad. They are: 10.9, 11.4, 7.86, 15.8, and 19.7 for samples 3 to 19, respectively. The overall linearly increasing trend and the dip when the father was the main interaction partner in sample 11 are proof of the double sensitivity of the method, capturing both age—and possibly partner— influences. This trend towards longer episodes (a length of 20 or more) and the really long ones (with 50 or more turns per partner) that are restricted to the later samples, also provide evidence of Eve's increasing attention span, an advance central to learning.

In contrast to the maxima and the means, the modal length changes only slightly, shifting mainly between episode lengths of two or three utterances. The contrast between the maxima and the modals indicates the differences between habitual processing and maximum competence, what dyads normally do and what they are capable of. The means in turn indicate the overall rehearsal and exercise intensity, a measure that could be comparable to the "on-task-time" in educational situations. Diverse combinations of these levels certainly could be a valuable cue for intervention efforts: Do adults challenge sufficiently? Too much? Or not enough?

While there might be a more or less optimal patterning of short and long episodes, preliminary evidence suggests that staccato interactions, that is, exclusively short episodes, might not be conducive to learning of more complex linguistic aspects. For example, simple directive speech that curtails episode length has been consistently found to be an obstacle to language learning. The patterning of long and shorter episodes could also be training tools to increase the attention span of children—which in turn might be conducive to faster learning of language skills. Attention span might therefore be both an effect of preceding verbal interactions and a prerequisite for maintaining longer episodes. Short attention span might therefore indirectly contribute to language delay by preventing the extensive exercises indicated above. Multiple diagnostic, remedial, and theoretical inferences are suggested on the bases of the presented sequential analyses.

Dampened Oscillations

As mentioned above, vocabulary rehearsal could be optimally captured by means of an event-series approach. The resulting patterns could also be expressed quantitatively as "rehearsal density" per time unit. Such a presentation would result in a time series in the form of a dampened oscillation. The latter presentation is exemplified in Figure 2.6. This graphic presentation is based on data from a lengthy episode of training and learning the vocabulary items *nut* and *crack* in the construction *crack nuts*.

Figure 2.6 presents both the mother's and the child's rehearsals separately as well as the summed rehearsals, first for ten-utterance intervals and later for longer ones. Massed training (seven repetitions in the first ten utterances) is followed by increasingly spaced repetitions over the next 50 utterances, followed by a second massing during the next 20 utterances (from utterance 50 to 70), a rather prolonged intermission to utterance 170, and repeated reinstatements up to 700 utterances after the first introduction of the terms. Considering the findings of learning psychology (Campbell & Jaynes, 1966; Estes, 1978), the patterning could not be more ideal to assure long-term storage. Only sequential analyses extending over almost 700 utterances could have revealed this pattern.

A Univariate Time-Series Based on Informativeness of Utterances

Not only entire episodes vary in length and therefore in the type and degree of linguistic information entailed, so do individual utterances. As already attested decades ago (Bernstein & Henderson, 1969; Williams & Naremore, 1969), dyadic

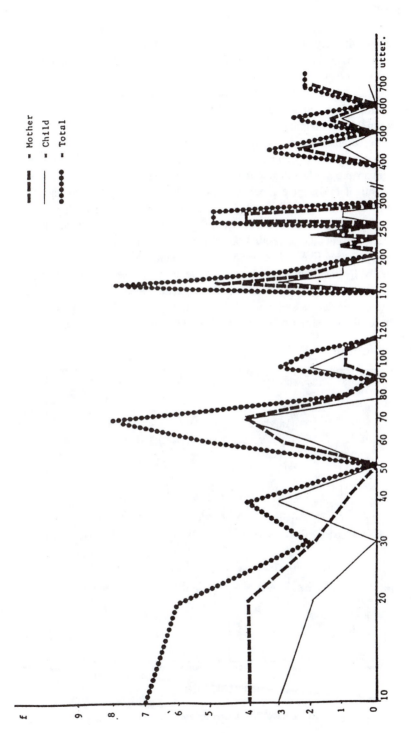

FIGURE 2.6. A dampened oscillation

styles that heavily rely on simple commands and refusals are associated with slow language progress in children. A simple *No* or *Shut up* provide minimal linguistic information. In contrast parents who employ methods of "authoritative child-raising" that entail a great deal of verbal explanation of cause-effect relationships and other conditional relations (Baumrind, 1971a, 1971b, 1980) have children who progress quickly in their language skills. This is a necessary relationship because semantically complex messages, specifying conditions and consequences, require complex morphosyntactic features for their encoding. Whereas extremely brief utterances might not provide learning opportunities, the opposite, long stretches of complex sentences, might overtax the processing capacities of young children and might therefore by disadvantageous, too. Optimal patterning of utterances of diverse complexity levels might exist and could be determining factors of differential learning.

Figure 2.7 presents the patterning of information density in one short stretch of interactions between Eve and her mother. "Information density" has been defined operationally by the number of learning strategies (of the child) and training techniques (of the mother) that were coded for each utterance. A brief precautionary note has to be inserted as to a minor distortion in these data: For each utterance, a maximum of three instructional strategies or techniques was recorded, even if in

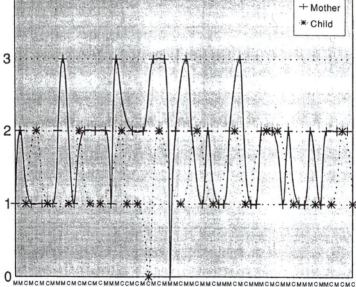

FIGURE 2.7.   A univariate time-series

rare cases four or even five could be discerned. The data in Figure 2.7 are therefore subject to a ceiling effect and the real information density might have been higher than "three" in the few cases where a maximum of three was recorded. The utterances whose informativeness is presented in the Figure 2.7 were produced in sequence by either one of the interaction partners, who is indicated below the abscissa as M or C.

With one major exception, a regular alternation is encountered in the density of information, varying generally between one and two strategies or techniques per utterance. Maxima of three strategies/techniques are rare and higher maxima would even be rarer. The one exceptional sequence of a 3-2-3 (M–C–M) strategies/techniques pattern, implying major processing demands, is preceded and followed by "zero's" on the child's and mother's side, respectively. It seems a brief period of recovery and catch-up were required after a strenuous exercise. A check of the original recordings shows that Eve was overtaxed indeed, a fact resulting in an incomprehensible utterance on Eve's side and multiple repair procedures on the mother's side. Whereas this qualitative interpretation has to be considered preliminary, Figure 2.7 suggests that time-series analysis in the frequency domain would provide information about intensity of instruction and could indicate individual as well as developmental differences through changes in the amplitudes of the cyclic process. Then dyadic time-series patterns could be related to outcome variables to differentiate the impact of fine tuned from less well tuned interactions.

Bivariate Time Series Reflecting Instructional Activities of Mother and Child

The two profiles of Figure 2.8 summarize the frequency relations between maternal imitation with expansion and filial imitation with reduction. That is, mostly correcting maternal imitations and filial reducing repetitions are presented in the two profiles of Figure 2.8 for the entire recording period of ten months. Of course, any other combination of strategies and techniques could have been presented in its temporal change. The selection of expansion was guided by the lively controversy surrounding corrections, as is discussed in Chapter 4. Even a cursory glance reveals the close parallels between maternal and filial profiles, as well as some indications of a temporal lead-lag relationship. The decline of filial frequencies begins already in sample 7, while the mother follows suit only in sample 9. Again in sample 15, the child initiates a minor decline while the mother follows in sample 17. Increases occur largely in parallel fashion without lags. Generally, as Moerk has already shown in the 1970s (Moerk, 1974a, 1975a; cf. also Moerk, 1989a), imitations decline with increasing mastery while productive uses increase. In overall frequency, the mother surpasses the child in eight out of the ten samples— she therefore leads and supports the child. She also models two principles simultaneously: imitation as a discourse strategy as well as the specific constructions she expands. This gives the child the chance of acquiring a very useful learning strategy, imitation, as well as the opportunity of hearing an abundance of corrective models to imitate. Additionally, filial imitations are rewarded, as has been shown in Figure 1 of this chapter, a form of feedback that should contribute to their maintenance.

The present brief cyclical series with only ten points of measurement does not allow the computation of the parameters of the bivariate time-series. Only a demonstration of the potential of bivariate (and by implication of multivariate) time-series analyses is intended. Yet even this graphic illustration indicates the multiple possibilities for analysis, such as degree of covariation, distance between profiles, lead-lag relationships, and rhythmicity versus linear trends in the temporal patterns. Other studies (Moerk, 1983a, 1992) have suggested that similar techniques and strategies can be employed with progressively more complex linguistic content, showing periodic increases, decreases, and renewed increases in the frequencies of specific teaching and learning procedures. Maintenance of the same strategies/techniques is often combined with change in content, similar to the beginning skier who learns to snow-plow through modeling and imitation, while later relying on the same principles to learn parallel skiing.

With the complementarity between filial learning strategies and maternal teaching techniques over time, demonstrated above, the focus of the discussion has obviously returned to mutual feedback between the mother and child, as explored

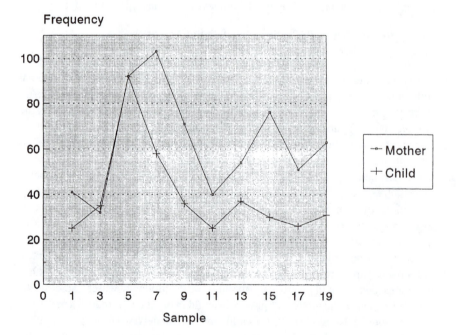

FIGURE 2.8. A bivariate time-series

in the first sections of this chapter. This time, however, the feedback is considered in a much more extended temporal framework, requiring a different descriptive and statistical approach. To do justice to the complexity of the language-learning domain, both perspectives, immediate sequential dynamics and long-term trends, including cyclical phenomena, always need to be considered together in their interdependencies. While the present database, extending over less than two years with only 19 samples already exhibited considerable complexity, changes occurring over 20 years of training and learning, including systematic educational efforts, have to be expected to be much greater and more complex. Yet, sequential methods very similar to those exemplified here should suffice for ascertaining these phenomena.

SUMMARY AND DISCUSSION

A multiplicity of sequential phenomena was sketched out and clarified through examples and preliminary analyses. The phenomena ranged from immediate contingencies, whether in first-order or higher-order dependencies, to lagged contingencies and patterns of these lags. Longer patterns were reflected in the sequence of content episodes of various complexities and in dampened oscillations of repetitions during specific training/learning endeavors.

Over still longer time spans—extending over hours—the patterning of episode lengths was demonstrated. Finally, intervals of varying lengths—up to a year—were captured in qualitative event or quantitative time series. Probable psychological implications of these temporally extended training/learning processes were suggested, such as when the increasing median intervals between maternal models and filial use of morphemes was interpreted as evidence for learning and retention of temporal morphemes.

In the time-series domain, a univariate cyclic microseries was presented, reflecting information density in one short stretch of an observation session. Then a bivariate series, extending over the entire observation period, demonstrated quite close matching of a maternal teaching technique and a filial learning strategy over nine months. Similar long-term matched performances have been demonstrated previously (Moerk, 1974a, 1975a, 1983b, 1992). With the contrast between a microseries extending over minutes and another series extending over almost a year, the flexibility of the method was illustrated.

The examples were chosen to indicate potential approaches that have been rarely, if ever, employed in past research. This was done to suggest how many training and learning phenomena have not yet been described in any detail in their temporal structures. Only when most instructional aspects have been captured by means of methods that fit the structure of "the object of investigation," and when they have been evaluated as to their efficacy in the language acquisition process, can any meaningful judgments be made about the "learnability of language" or the lack of it. As long as the methodologies necessary to capture the dynamics of first language learning processes are not employed, any conclusions are only evidence of romantic impatience, as argued in Chapter 1. It is like arguing about the nature of stars before chemistry and physics could provide well-founded models about the internal and changing dynamics of various star types.

Sophisticated descriptive methods are even more important for practical preventive and remedial applications than for mere theoretical controversies. Considering the large number of children who enter elementary school with language delays or language problems, reliable and ecologically valid methods for ascertaining the causes of these problems are needed. Once detrimental antecedents have been differentiated from successful training techniques, suggestions for remedies will flow directly from these insights. Considering the even larger numbers of children who need to quickly acquire a nonnative school/technical language in order to succeed academically, insights into optimal training and learning approaches are urgently needed, as many extensive educational efforts (e.g., Gass & Madden, 1985) prove. The present chapter provides some initial pointers and some encouragement for the remaining long journey of discovery. Most of the required methods exist and have been successfully employed in other fields. Even if databases are not yet extensive enough to employ the methods in their most sophisticated forms, the underlying concepts and principles can be adapted for trend analyses and preliminary inferences. They can also steer future data collections.

3

Input and Rehearsal Frequencies as Diacritical Criteria of L1 Acquisition Theories

> The many are guided by habit based on much experience.
> —Parmenides

> Practice makes perfect.
> —Well-known proverb

The above aphorisms might convey the impression that an agreement has existed for two and a half-thousand years across cultures and continents about the relationship between the antecedent conditions of "experience" and "practice" and the resulting outcomes of habits and perfection. The aphorisms might even implicitly suggest that the antecedent conditions are not only necessary but even sufficient. Yet precautions are called for in the application of these aphorisms to language acquisition. Catania (1992), who aimed with an open mind to integrate multiple aspects of learning psychology, emphasizes "the myriad properties of human language ...and the complexities of human learning and remembering [that] will enter into any effective account" (p. 353). Tolman (1949) postulated at least six types of learning and Gagne (1968) extended this to eight types. The contributors to Melton's (1964) volume on "categories of human learning" elaborated this differentiation even further. Additionally, not only categories of learning but diverse possible types of the relationship between practice and perfection need to be differentiated: Is input and exercise frequency a necessary condition, a sufficient one, or neither but merely an aspect that contributes to mastery? Finally, as emphasized in Chapter 1, "language" is certainly not a unitary phenomenon and many types of learning and diverse relationships between learning and acquisition might be involved in its acquisition, depending upon which of "the myriad properties" (Catania, 1992, p. 353) of language are considered. An assumption of necessity of frequent input for *all* aspects of language learning would therefore be premature.

TYPES OF LEARNING AND REHEARSAL PATTERNS

Classical learning theory does not yet provide much differential guidance about the aspects of language learning for which input frequency would be most useful, necessary, or even sufficient, as the above quote from Catania (1992) suggests. Broad evidence from skill learning and rather extensive intervention efforts in the acquisition of languages can, however, provide some preliminary guidance as to what to expect in some subdomains of language acquisition.

Motor Learning

As the aphorisms introducing the chapter suggest, the importance of exercise frequency has been recognized for motor learning, as widely substantiated in sports and industrial training. Language production certainly has a motor component that should be subject to the same principles as other motor skills. Nevertheless, as everybody knows who has listened to the accent of immigrants who have used their new language for decades, frequent use is not a sufficient condition for acquiring native-like enunciation skills. Even decades of practice do not necessarily result in perfect enunciation. More complex analyses are needed in this domain: While foreigners certainly acquire communication skills and their motor production becomes automatized—two aspects that require frequent rehearsals—something seems to be amiss in the pattern of input–output–feedback; not receiving sufficient feedback as to incorrect enunciation, the second language learner remains strongly influenced by the earlier-acquired first language skills. While exercise frequency might be necessary, it is not sufficient in this case.

Rote Learning

Experience shows that rote learning of vocabulary and of formulas is one important aspect of language acquisition. Little controversy should exist as to the necessity of exercise frequency for rote learning. Rich evidence, provided by Bolinger (1964) for "formulaic" elements in language performance makes it highly plausible that speakers rely partially on such rote-learned phrases. Following Bolinger, studies have reported on the prevalence of formulas in early speech production (R. Clark, 1974, 1977; Hickey, 1991; MacWhinney, 1982; Moerk, 1992; Moerk & Moerk, 1979; Perez-Pereira, 1994; Peters, 1983; Snow, Dubber, & de Blauw, 1982; Youssef, 1994; and many others). Rote learning and its necessary antecedent, exercise frequency, are therefore well established as central aspects in language acquisition and performance. Rote learning is generally dependent on frequent input and rehearsals.

Pattern Abstraction

It would be expected from findings on perception, especially those based on microgenetic studies (e.g., Werner, 1940) that pattern abstraction is also a central principle in language perception and language learning. Microgenetic studies have shown that global-diffuse patterns are perceived earliest, followed by differentiation and articulation of elements. This is Werner's "orthogenetic law" that has been reaffirmed in many fields of psychology. In accordance with these principles of early pattern perception, neonates already recognize the overall pattern of the mother's voice during the first few weeks of life and they even seem to abstract this pattern prenatally (Mehler et al., 1988). Generally, patterns and melodies are recognized early, before the differentiation of specific elements. In first language acquisition, a conceptualization of pattern abstraction goes back at least to Braine (1971). Because language performance is based on very few patterns, such as the Subject–Verb–Object pattern and the Copula sentence, the principle of pattern abstraction appears compatible with the structure of the object learned. Pertinent research has been reviewed by Braine (1988).

Extensive experimental research by Arbib and associates (Arbib, Conklin, & Hill, 1987) as well as Reber and associates (e.g., Reber & Allen, 1978) has demonstrated that pattern (or schema) abstraction, the equivalent of MacWhinney's (1978) "analogy," is a major principle in the learning of artificial languages. Pattern learning is also the central factor in Schmidt's (1975) "schema theory" of skill learning. It can therefore be confidently concluded that pattern learning is so basic as to be applicable to many diverse domains and employed by many species.

Pattern abstraction is greatly facilitated by massed presentations of similar patterns with slightly changing elements in the slots of the pattern (Arbib, Conklin & Hill, 1987; Baer & Deguchi, 1985; Reber & Allen, 1978). With only two major sentence types in the English language (the S–V–O and the Copula sentence), and thousands of sentences experienced per day (Moerk, 1983; Wagner, 1985), massed repetitions of the same structure are unavoidable. This unavoidability of massed rehearsal of the two basic syntactic structures would explain why these are less subject to normal input variation than vocabulary or some rather infrequent bound morphemes. The same argument applies to some sentence constituents, such as the prepositional phrase or some auxiliary-main verb constituents, such as *wanna, want to*. The abstraction of syntactic patterns should be greatly facilitated by frequency combined with temporal massing.

Rule Learning and Rule Use

A fourth acquisition principle, rule learning, has suggested itself often to the linguist and the instructor of foreign languages. From there it was generalized to accounts of the language learning of infants and young children. The problem inherent in the concept of rules is discussed in Chapter 1 and will not be repeated here. Clark (1982a), among others, already has pointed out that simple regularities should not be confused with rule-governed behavior. Habits reflect regularities, as does classical and operant conditioning, and all could be described as "rule following." This latter form of rule following is demonstrably abstracted from extensive experience—that is—based on exercise frequency. Yet, prescriptive rules could be taught as such and they could also be established relatively quickly by means of fine tuned corrections. In these cases, frequent rehearsals would not be required although they might be helpful. However, such learning presumes relatively advanced cognitive performance, which is extremely improbable in the toddler and young preschooler.

Briefly summarizing the preceding analysis, it appears that all language learning principles that seem plausible for the infant and young child presuppose input frequency. This almost self-evident postulate, combined with a presumption of greatly deficient input, resulted in the nativistic postulate of innate linguistic knowledge, as discussed in Chapter 1. In contrast to the demonstrated commonality of exercise frequency in language acquisition, as surveyed below, an almost exclusive nativistic conception of this process would require minimal input for "triggering" and "parameter setting." In principle, any frequency above zero could be sufficient (Atkinson, 1987; Meisel, 1995). Also, considerable uniformity in age, mostly the age of four years (McNeill, 1971), should be found rather independent of input, for the acquisition of the basic syntactic competence. That is, frequency of input should minimally or not at all vary with attainment. Every school teacher is aware that this assumption absolutely conflicts with empirical evidence about the syntactic skills acquired by elementary school children from diverse social backgrounds.

More specific predictions about input phenomena are rather impossible on the basis of the "Principles and Parameters Theory" of Universal Grammar (Chomsky, 1981). As Meisel (1995, p. 25) has lucidly demonstrated, the acolytes of this approach are in disagreement about virtually every relevant aspect as far as the input is concerned and "no one is able to offer independent evidence for the respective mechanisms involved as explanatory factors." Even for the basic distinction between "triggering" and "learning" the opinions differ considerably. Some descriptions of "triggering" require a "sufficient numbers of tokens" and their saliency in the input. Other strictly adhere to the old "poverty of the stimulus" argument and set input requirements to a minimum, that is > *0*, for parameter setting. Atkinson

(1992), for example, concludes that for "the setting of parameters [there is] no reason to doubt that anything other than learning, as a rational hypothesis-testing process, is involved" (p. 209). Yet, a hypothesis could be formulated on the basis of a single experience and could be rejected after a single disconfirming token. An *n* of 2 would be, in principle, sufficient for this approach. If the hypothesis is based on innate knowledge, an *n* of *1* should suffice at the margin. Other aspects of Universal Grammar, such as the X-bar principle, appear to be fully built into the genome and require no input information at all. Almost pharaonic experiments with extreme levels of language deprivation would be needed to reject such an extreme nativist hypothesis. Wherever pertinent evidence exists, from feral children or from extreme neglect (Tartter, 1986), the outcome argues totally against nativistic assumptions. Less extreme situations, as surveyed in Chapters 6 and 7 also provide evidence against such "triggering" postulates that presume great independence from frequent input and exercise.

REHEARSAL FREQUENCY AS A CAUSAL FACTOR

Due to the high level of disagreement about environmental prerequisites among the proponents of the nativistic conceptualization and the lack of detailed guidance from classical learning theory, the principle followed in the present review is to extensively survey input, as it is reported in empirical studies, and relate this input to theoretical assumptions about learning. The means for exploring cause–effect relationships are, of course, provided by covariation between the wealth of the input, combined with the frequency of productive rehearsal, and levels of language attainment, whether established observationally or experimentally. Studies focusing on the *modus ponens*, that is, high levels of attainment and rich input, can be contrasted with those focusing on the *modus tollens*, that is, low levels of attainment and input deprivation. If lack of attainment is encountered, *ceteris paribus*, poverty of input should generally be found also. The *modus tollens*, that is, effects of input deprivation, have been substantiated by abundant research on language delay of lower class and neglected children (Culp et al., 1991), and on children's difficulties with school language requirements (e.g., Feagans & Farran, 1982). Insights into the relationship between elaborated versus restricted input and advanced versus delayed language acquisition go back to Bernstein (1961, 1964). Head Start and many similar intervention programs are based on this assumption and have substantiated it. Chapters 6 and 7, exploring social class and cultural differences, present observational findings on frequency and its effects.

Even more precise evidence comes from intervention studies that first gather evidence during a *modus tollens* period of delay and deprivation (the baseline), and then supplement this during an enrichment period (*modus ponens*), resulting in swift progress (the A–B experimental design). In such interventions, language delayed children are exposed to specific enrichments which often help them catch up relatively quickly (Bereiter & Engelman, 1966; Warren & Rogers-Warren; 1985; Weikart, Bond & McNeil, 1978; Whitehurst & de Baryshe, 1989; Whitehurst & Valdez-Mechacha, 1988). Strong evidence for concomitant variation between wealth of adapted input and level of acquisition has been established in the remedial field. This domain is, however, too broad to cover within the scope of the present project.

Having indicated the link between exercise frequency and learning, fine differentiations are possible and required. Whether it is skill learning (Anderson, 1981, 1982; Holding, 1981) or classical learning theory, various aspects of input and exercise frequency have been differentiated. They are mainly massing versus spacing, as two forms of rehearsal, and reinstatement (Campbell & Jaynes, 1966) after longer intervals. Estes (1978) has surveyed evidence that the pattern of rehearsal—massing and spacing—has a strong impact on the ease of learning and the length of retention. For initial short-term retention, massed training is preferable, while long-term retention is enhanced by distributed—spaced—practice (Schneider & Detweiler, 1987). Both massed and spaced rehearsals are conducive for retention, depending on a variety of features of the learning process and the organism. As Newell (1981) summarized it: "The optimal practice distribution will depend on the unique interaction of the time available to reach the performance criterion, together with the type of skill and the age and skill level of the performer" (p. 217). The concept of reinstatement refers to the fact that, once an item has been acquired, even quite rare and brief repetitions can maintain it in long-term memory although the same rare and brief repetitions would be insufficient for acquiring the item.

ECOLOGICAL VALIDITY OF THE LABORATORY
PRINCIPLES FOR THE NURSERY

Because the technical terms: rehearsal, massing, spacing, and reinstatement have predominantly been derived from experimental laboratory research, their ecological validity for informal mother–child interactions needs to be briefly justified: Can it be expected that caretakers, who are encumbered by everyday tasks, utilize these seemingly sophisticated principles? This question is implicit in the controversy whether mere communication or language teaching occurs in the home of the young child. This question is considered first before the broader tropic of the generalizability of laboratory learning principles is focused upon.

When contrasting communication and language teaching, a false dichotomy results, as any consideration of skilled actions shows: In any type of team work between an expert and an apprentice, cooperation involves instruction. If the expert wants to include the apprentice usefully in a task, he has to guide this apprentice. In the mother–child dyad, the task is verbal communication (which intrinsically can be solved only when both participants succeed). The mother has therefore to lead her neophyte child stepwise towards mastery in each communicative situation.

Verbal communication with a novice is not possible without simplification and thereby clarification of the structure and the meaning of the message. This is most evident in the case of foreigners who are in the process of acquiring a second language. To accommodate them, native speakers engage in "foreigner talk" (Wesche, 1994; Wode, 1978) on a level they presume adjusted to the recipient's communicative abilities. One form of simplification is repetition, which provides the learner with multiple opportunities for analyzing or synthesizing an utterance, entailing rehearsals. Major forms of repetitions in their ecological settings are briefly surveyed below.

As to the generalizability of laboratory findings, rehearsal need not be seen as an intentionally undertaken teaching/learning strategy. Repetition of items or structures is rehearsal. It can logically take several forms and all are found in mother–child interaction: Repetitions could occur in input alone, they could occur in production alone, or they could occur in both input and production. The temporal sequence could be random or it could be patterned in various ways. It could be mother-initiated or child-initiated, or either. Considering the rather stable aspect of the daily routines and the restricted language skills of the child, a high degree of repetitiveness occurs naturally, as has been generally found. No specific didactic intentions need to be involved for repetitions—rehearsals— to occur. Massing occurs within one episode or routine, and spacing is given due to the repetitions of these episodes. While very intense massing could produce fatigue and boredom, this is generally avoided in mother–child interactions by the fact that the child controls the patterning, either by maintaining the topic or by shifting away from it. While long intervals between rehearsals could lead to forgetting, small children are known to enjoy repetitions of recently acquired skills and insist on routine verbal games and familiar picture books. Thus, multiple and well-known phenomena of the middle-class nursery prove that such rehearsal opportunities are common. Only the major categories are briefly mentioned.

Repetition and Variation of New Vocabulary Items

Young children, when encountering new experiences, at first show a predilection for exploring constant features, followed by enjoyment of varying aspects. Their fascination with novel objects leads initially to massing in labeling, as Moerk (1992) has shown in short-term longitudinal analyses. After some exploration, satiation sets in and new topics are talked about. Later, the child returns to the—by now partly familiar—object, which results in renewed conversations about it. This is spaced rehearsal. Because mothers are very aware of their child's increasing vocabulary mastery (Behrend, 1988; Rondal, 1981), they often "test" for recently acquired vocabulary items (Holzman, 1984a; Savic, 1977; Snow, 1977) in order to check the child's retention. Encoding specificity (Tulving & Thomson, 1973), that is, an identical context during learning and retrieval, will facilitate recall for the child in the familiar context. If the child fails the "test" the label is reintroduced by the mother and rehearsed again. The child's interest in and her eager return to familiar items is perhaps best attested in connection with picture-book reading when children insist on returning to a small selection of pictures and to specific sections of larger books (Snow & Goldfield, 1983; Snow, Nathan & Perlmann, 1985).

Although the repetitiveness that follows automatically from the routine aspects of mother–child interactions has been stressed, this is not intended to exclude more playful and exploratory activities involving a great deal of repetition. Two categories of such activities have been described: bedtime monologues of children, as reported in the work of Ruth Weir (1962), Kuczaj (1983) and Nelson (1989), and children's language play (Chukovsky, 1963; Garvey, 1977a, 1977b). They are considered briefly.

Bedtime Monologues

Recorded bedtime monologues of some children also demonstrate a strong tendency towards rehearsal of familiar items with variation, such as substitutions of elements or breakdowns of longer phrases. This can occur twice every day or even more often during the presleep period. The protocols of Weir (1962) and in Nelson (1989) show that two types of temporal patterning are encountered in these bedtime monologues. When the children repeat utterances they had heard during the day, they engage in widely-spaced rehearsals, that is, reinstatements (Campbell & Jaynes, 1966). When they then repeat their own utterances in close temporal succession, they engage in densely-spaced rehearsal, that is, massing. The massing may be interrupted by silence or a change in topic, and later the child often returns to the original topic, that is, she can alternate massed and spaced rehearsals.

It might be especially significant to note that Gerhardt (1989) reports that children encode not memories of unique events in their presleep monologues but of "generalized and schematized formats" (p. 184). That is, in the same manner as they abstract in their substitution exercises the same *general* structure underlying the varying surface strings, they also abstract a general semantic structure from their experiences of the day. Abstract schemas in both domains would therefore be matched instead of specific events, facilitating the recognition of the homology between cognitive-semantic and syntactic structure. This suggestion deserves much further exploration. Here another aspect making presleep monologues optimal for retention needs to be considered: Retroactive inhibition will minimally interfere with the stabilization of the memory traces that are established shortly before the children fall asleep.

Language Play

Bedtime monologues could be subsumed under a more general category of "language play." But the term language play will here be restricted to interpersonal verbal behavior. One partner might playfully repeated a phrase, including minor variations, and the other partner's response often provides a further set of repetitive and creative exercises. The input of parents and playmates will add some novelty to the child's exercises so that rehearsal and variation are combined. Garvey (1977a, 1977b) and Chukovsky (1963) have reported extensively on children's language games. Kuczaj (1982b) has traced the literature on intensive verbal play exercises back to the beginning of the century. More recently, Ely and McCabe (1994) have again provided impressive evidence of the repetitiveness in language play in kindergarten children. For later ages, the exercises in pig latin and a large variety of social language games are well known for diverse social groups. Play with language is therefore a widely encountered phenomenon and is also central in songs and poetry (Jakobson, 1960), that is, higher levels of language use. Although research does not yet provide conclusive evidence as to the effects of such playful exercises, from everything that is known about skill learning it is highly likely that they are conducive to language progress. The argument of Garvey (1977a) supports this hypothesis. She described language games as "practice play," a practice that ranges from the sound structure of the language to grammar and pragmatic functions.

Imitation Sequences

Many of the play exercises referred to involve longer imitation sequences of the interacting partners. From research on imitation it is known that mothers imitate their children equally or more often in most verbal interactions than the children imitate their mothers. This tendency of both partners to build on each other's utterances naturally results in rehearsals wherein both the topics and much of the verbal structure are maintained. On the mother's side, these are the "simple recasts" and "continuations" described by Nelson and colleagues (1984) or the "expansions" so famous from the work of Brown and documented by Schumacher and Sherman (1978) as well as Seitz and Stewart (1975). Moerk (1985a) has documented four-step sequences, where the child imitates a model, the mother expands upon the child's imitation, and the child imitates the expanded model. These four recurrences of the main items of the utterance are often encountered within a few seconds, providing massed rehearsals. Moerk (1985b) reported 6,939 repetitions of one mother and 4,123 of one child over 20 hours of interaction. Added together, these are over 11,000 repetitive behaviors in 20 hours or some 550 per hour, almost 10 per minute—enormous chances for rehearsals, indeed. Such imitation sequences necessarily involve the "generation effect" (Slamecka & Graf, 1978) which was also reported by the observational research of Snow and Goldfield (1983). The generation effect specifies that an item will be remembered much better if the child reproduces a model than if she encounters it only receptively; probably because imitation requires more focused attention than merely hearing an item. The more the child takes an active role in the verbal exchanges, the more often the generation effect will occur, and the higher the probability of long-term retention.

The brief discussions above indicate that the common setting of mother–child interaction during the processes of language acquisition involves many learning principles, such as encoding specificity, generation, priming, and massing, integrated with spaced rehearsals and reinstatements after longer intervals. These psychological principles, whose impact is well supported by extensive research outside language learning, indicate how optimal the conditions are in many homes for language learning. The fact that rehearsals occur as a by-product of other activities is also important because rehearsal strategies are not used by children spontaneously with the intent to assure retention until the early elementary school years (Kail & Hagen, 1982). Whatever rehearsal there is has, therefore, to occur "on the sly" and unobtrusively in the context of more pragmatic dynamics. Based on these insights from past learning research and from familiarity with the nursery setting, the empirical research on overall frequencies and on patterning of rehearsals is discussed in the following sections.

EMPIRICAL REPORTS ON INPUT FREQUENCY AND PATTERNING

Overall Frequencies

A wealth of language input has been stressed at least since Delacroix (1934) coined the phrase "*le bain de langage*" (p. 18), emphasizing that we are surrounded by language like a fish by water, that is, that we have overwhelmingly rich input. During the last decades a wide range of reports has supported Delacroix's assertion as to the wealth of the input in middle-class homes, as is shown below. Common sense experience and systematic reports from *second* language acquisition (Lambert, 1975) also suggest that the intensity and extensiveness with which a learner becomes involved with the new language to be learned is an important factor in the speed of its acquisition. Language immersion programs have incorporated this principle and have reported impressive results (Stern, 1978; Swain & Lapkin, 1982). The same principle should apply to first language acquisition, as argued forcefully by Hoff-Ginsberg (1992).

Specific frequencies of adult input seem to vary widely. Kaye (1980) reported averages ranging between 14 and 21 utterances per minute between the ages of 6 and 26 weeks, with the lower frequencies occurring at the upper age limits. That is about 1000 utterances per hour. Moerk (1983a) reported around 280 input utterances per hour for Eve, Brown's famous participant. He also produced estimates for more extended periods from Brown's transcriptions of the interactions of his participant, Eve, and her mother. Over 42,000 S–V–O sentences might be modeled for Eve per month, close to 20,000 Copula sentences, equally many questions, and around 10,000 complex sentences. For specific major sentence constituents, the estimates ranged from around 15,000 to almost 35,000 per month (Moerk, 1983a). Moerk (1983b) also estimated input frequencies for all the major sentence constituents together, both for Adam and for Eve, Brown's two famous participants. The estimates for the two children were quite similar, reaching around 250,000 per month for each. A brief calculation shows that these numbers work out to approximately 3,000,000 instances of major sentence constituents per year. Much of it must obviously be quite redundant. Wells (1986) reported between about 80 and 720 utterances per hour for children between the ages of 15 and 60 months, indicating both the wealth of the input and large variations between families. These variations in adult input should provide ideal opportunities for evaluating concomitant variations and cause–effect relationships between input and acquisition. The significance of the reported high frequencies for language learning can be appreciated from a report by Snow (1979). She found that foreign children learning Dutch heard a rather small number of Dutch utterances per day, ranging between 150 and 1,400 with a median of about 700. Yet, these low input frequencies proved sufficient for the observed children to learn Dutch.

To establish the total amount of rehearsal, not only the input but also filial productions have to be considered. Frequency-of-use data go back to the beginning of the century: Bell (1903) reported around 15,000 words per day as the production level of his two daughters who were between 3 years-6 months and 4 years-8 months old. Brandenburg and Brandenburg (1919) found almost the same frequency, that is, 14,930 word per day for their 4 year-4 month old daughter. More recently Wagner (1985) investigated frequencies for 12 children ranging in age from 1 year-5 months to 14 years-10 months. The frequencies of verbal output, in words per day, ranged from 11,700, produced by one of the youngest children, to 37,700, produced by a 3 year-6 month old child. The productions of the older children, who were between 5 and around 15 years, ranged between 21,000 and 37,200 words per day. Those are very impressive frequencies of use, indeed.

Massing and Spacing of the Input

Alternations between dense massing and spacing or "distributed rehearsal," have been discussed above and they are part of the everyday activities of the mother and child. Routines and their repetitions, nursery book reading, and the repetition of the same stories and often the same pages result in rehearsals. Weir's (1962) reported her son's bedtime monologues containing many immediate repetitions but also with long intervals between massed repetitions of related exercises. In other cultures, such as the Kaluli culture (Schieffelin, 1990) and the Kwava'ae culture (Watson-Gegeo & Gegeo, 1986) pragmatic formulas are trained extensively. In both cultures, dense repetition of a formula is observed that continues until the child repeats the item. This provides massed rehearsals. Frequent recurrences of similar settings, where the same formulas are applicable and employed, produce spaced rehearsals.

It appears that the temporal patterning between massed and distributed exercises has not yet been explored in a systematic manner. Moerk (1992) provides some examples of shifting from massing, at the introduction of a new item, to increased spacing when the item is recalled and discussed later. Chapter 2 of the present volume explored a considerable variety of temporal patterns and the methodologies that need to be employed to substantiate them objectively. Research on learning and retention has abundantly shown (e.g., Cornell, 1984), how important such patterning is. Therefore its forms in the field of language training and learning, as well as differences between families or cultures, need to be explored carefully in order to understand the language learning processes and their outcomes.

The potential impact of the frequencies described previously and of the partially massed training on language acquisition has to be related to the task faced: Only two basic sentence forms exist in English and most Indo-European languages, the S–V–(O) and the Copula sentence, each entailing two to three words at a minimum. The production frequencies discussed above might therefore translate into 4,000 to 7,000 sentences per day. Combining the frequencies in reception and production over an estimated ten or more hours of waking time, a preliminary estimate is 10,000 to 20,000 sentences per day in both modalities combined. Often groups of these sentences represent substitution sequences: the frames and most of the lexical items remain the same while one or two items are changed. *Do you want to eat meat/rice/veggies? Daddy wants to drink coffee/ water/ juice.* Such densely spaced repetitions with minor variations demonstrate not only the similarities in surface structures but also the identical underlying structure and must result in the learning of these frames. These effects, however, are the focus of the following section.

THE EFFECTS OF INPUT FREQUENCY

An exhaustive survey of the extensive literature on frequency effects need not be attempted here as the importance of extensive input has often been emphasized in the older literature (Bates, Bretherton, Beeghly-Smith and McNew, 1982; R. Clark,1977; Landes, 1975). The present focus will therefore be on the decade of the 1980s which definitely confirmed this principle, without trying to mass all the evidence up to the present which only confirms the already known. As is well known, effects of input frequency were denied vehemently for a brief period and were then generally presumed as nonexistent, even when the density of input was accepted. This denial goes back mainly to Brown and Hanlon (1979) and Brown (1973). Yet Moerk (1980) demonstrated a high covariation between input frequency and rank order of acquisition. While Shatz first questioned frequency effects (Hoff-Ginsberg & Shatz, 1982), she soon admitted that "some sort of frequency effects on the course of acquisition are commonly expected" (Shatz, 1982, p. 107). Extensive factual studies (Barnes, Gutfreund, Satterly & Wells, 1983; Wells, 1985) have in the meantime supported the early reports on input frequencies and they have confirmed that a significant relationship exists between the amount of parent–child conversation and rate of filial progress in language skills. Wells (1979) agrees with Moerk (1980) that relative frequency of items in input is more highly correlated with speed of acquisition than the relative syntactic or semantic complexity.

Ambivalence similar to that of Shatz is, however, repeatedly encountered. Wells (1985) *reported* a remarkably close fit between the frequency with which particular sentence meanings, particular pronouns, and particular auxiliary verbs, occurred in the speech addressed to children and the order in which the items in these three systems emerged in the children's own utterances. The correlations ranged from .60 to .89. He also observed the even stronger evidence of temporary contiguity between increases in input and increases in filial use. Nevertheless, he *argued against* frequency effects (Wells, 1985)—and therewith against his own evidence—and explained those covariations due to linguistic complexity. However, this argument is very probably a logical mistake. Parents adapt the linguistic complexity of their input to the child's level (as is discussed in Chapter 4 under the heading of "fine tuning"). Complexity and frequency are therefore two aspects of the same unitary dynamics, that is, simple input is provided more frequently at early skill levels. Their causal impact in naturalistic settings can, consequently, not readily be disentangled due to the high collinearity of both measures.

De Villiers (1985), too, asserted the absence of frequency effects in data from Eve and Adam, Brown's two famous participants. Yet she reported very significant relationships between the mother's and Eve's verb-use variety and she concluded that "Eve ... is tuned to her own mother's idiolect" (p. 592). For Adam as well, she found "that his mother's distribution of the verbs is an excellent predictor of Adam's own distribution ($p<0.001$) (p. 591). If "the children resemble their own mothers most closely" (p. 592), how can frequency effects be denied? When de Villiers and de Villiers (1985) provided a well-balanced discussion of the literature on frequency effects, they concluded accordingly that "for at least some classes of morphemes [Brown's dismissal of parental input frequency] seems to have been premature" (p. 73). Correlations of up to .76 from Moerk's (1980) report and of .90 and .975 from Forner's (1979) study would not easily allow any other conclusions.

Effects on Contentive Vocabulary Acquisition

The evidence for frequency effects is strongest regarding vocabulary acquisition. It goes back to McCarthy's (1930) survey report and has been continuously supported. Masur (1982) found significant associations of input frequency with noun label acquisition, and similar results have been reaffirmed repeatedly up to the present (Andrick & Tager-Flusberg, 1986; Harris, Barrett, Jones & Brookes, 1988; Hart, 1991; Holzman, 1984; Ninio, 1992; Pearson, Fernandez, Ledeweg, & Oller, 1996; Smolak & Weintraub, 1983; Tomasello, Mannle, & Kruger, 1986). The type of words, their position in the sentence, and other variables do not seem to weaken this effect. Andrick and Tager-Flusberg (1986) demonstrated that this relationship also applies to specific color terms. Harris, Barrett, Jones and Brookes (1988) focused specifically on initial use of words plus the frequency of occurrence of these words in the mother's speech and found substantial relationships. Harris, Jones, Brookes, and Grant (1986) also showed that frequency, plus a close match between maternal utterances and the children's objects of attention and their activities, were related to speed of vocabulary acquisition. Measuring very similar variables—joint attention and maternal conventional-object labeling—Smith, Adamson, and Bakeman (1988) found that about 40 percent of the variance in infants' vocabulary size was accounted for by these variables. Maternal labeling has to be meaningful for the child, that is, the referent has to be attended to, in order to facilitate learning (Ninio & Bruner, 1978). Huttenlocher, Haight, Bryk, Seltzer and Lyons (1991) reviewed supportive findings from social class differences. Demetras, Post, and Snow (1986) conclude that "the word-class formation process must be working in a frequency-sensitive rather than a categorical way" (p. 287). That is, even a prototypically cognitive categorization is shaped by input frequencies.

These studies and many more in the literature show that the impact of input frequencies pertains to all types of vocabulary investigated and to initial acquisition as well as correct usage. This finding is psychologically close to common sense.

Effects on the Acquisition of Grammatical Morphemes

For grammatical morphemes or functors, frequency effects have also been securely established. Newport, Gleitman, and Gleitman (1977) demonstrated the importance of frequency, together with acoustic distinctiveness, for the acquisition of verbal auxiliaries. In an experimental approach, Shatz, Hoff-Ginsberg, and Maciver (1989) exposed a group of children to increased auxiliary input and found that it led to significant increases in the children's use of these auxiliaries over a control group. Richards and Robinson (1993) demonstrated that increased frequencies of the Copula *to be* in initial position in YES-NO questions was related to the speed of Copula acquisition over the succeeding nine months. A combination of initial position and frequency was also shown by Garcia (1994) to lead to quicker acquisition even during the earliest stages of language development. Park (1985) reported that children were learning plurals by rote. After Moerk (1980) provided strong evidence for frequency effects on grammatical morpheme acquisition, this finding has been repeatedly confirmed (e.g., Berman, 1981; Bybee & Slobin, 1982). The latter authors argued that much of the irregular past tense is learned by rote as indicated by high correlations of acquisition order with input frequency. Shirai and Andersen (1995) reported the same covariation between input and acquisition for past and progressive inflections. Moerk and Vilaseca (1987) confirmed this principle for both past and future morphemes. Gathercole (1986) found a close relationship between environmental use and the children's acquisition of the present perfect by comparing Scottish and United States populations. She also concluded that "frequency of input played a major role in the timing and order of acquisition of the prepositional phrase" (p. 537). De Houwer (1987) concurs with this by reporting that the frequencies of occurrence of various forms largely determine the pattern of acquisition. Valian and Coulson (1988) showed that a similar frequency sensitivity still existed for grammatical markers in adults learning a miniature artificial language. Much additional supportive evidence exists in the field of remedial language training which cannot be surveyed here.

For second language acquisition, Larsen-Freeman (1976) and many other researchers found significant correlations between the order of acquisition of grammatical morphemes and frequency of use in everyday speech. Frequency is often combined with a high degree of redundancy, produced through repetitions (massed training). Hatch, Peck, and Wagner-Gough (1979) summarized the pertinent evidence of the 1970s. Krashen (1985), elaborating on his "input hypothesis," emphasizes "enough comprehensible input" and "a sufficient quantity of input" as prerequisites for the emergence of language. Frequency is implicated here at least as a threshold factor. All language immersion programs (Stern, 1978, 1983; Swain & Lapkin, 1982) have a belief in frequency effects as their rationale.

Effects on the Acquisition of Syntactic Skills

Before focusing on input frequencies of syntactic structures, their cognitive bases need to be reemphasized as they are relevant for frequency aspects: The syntactic structure of S–V–O builds upon the cognitive structure of agent–action–object, which the preverbal child and the early-verbal child have observed and performed literally millions of times. The syntactic structure of the Copula sentence reflects an object and feature relation ("The apple is red") that is even more common than the S–V–O frame in perceptual experience. The element-set relation ("You are a girl") is cognitively important for classification and extensively trained in many homes. Categorizing objects into classes is, of course, a basic function of perception even in subhuman animals. The arguments about cognitive bases have been presented already by Piaget and were reemphasized by Sinclair (1971). Rondal and Cession (1990) support this argument empirically when they report that the mothers' sentences to young children entail only nouns which are persons or things and full verbs which are actions. The homology between conceptual/semantic structures and linguistic structures is therefore close to a hundred percent.

For linguistic structures, Snow (1977b) reported from a cross-cultural perspective that the choice between a S–V–O or a S–O–V structure is "quite clearly determined by frequency in the adult language" (p. 47). Within a single language, the situation is, however, conceptually and methodologically somewhat complicated when the impact of input frequency is evaluated statistically. For broad syntactic categories, such as the S–V–O sentence and the Copula sentence, the input frequencies will be so high in most environments that the necessary thresholds for learning are assuredly attained. Accordingly, Hoff-Ginsberg (1990) found few or no correlations between input frequency and the acquisition of basic syntactic constructions. Another conceptual and methodological approach has to be chosen to find frequency effects. Those syntactic constructions for which the input frequencies are lower, and vary widely across families, have to be studied. They also have to be studied early, before cumulative frequencies have attained threshold values beyond which performance is influenced by other factors.

For the earliest stages of syntax, Garcia (1994) could show that frequency of maternal models was the main factor in the appearance of the earliest two word utterances of their children. Equally for the very early stages, Brown (1973) reported that "the pairs that become monomorphemes have as pairs very high frequency in parental speech" (p. 396). For more advanced periods, Hoff-Ginsberg (1986) reported correlations in the range of .50 between pertinent input frequencies and the children's mean number of verbs per utterance and number of auxiliaries per verb-phrase. Newport, Gleitman and Gleitman (1977) reported correlations between maternal and filial auxiliary use of about .80, and Wells (1985) found correlations in the range from .78 to .89 for several syntactic/semantic aspects. With such results, the studies do not need to be massed to also prove the impact of input frequency for the simpler forms of syntactic learning.

It could, however, be hypothesized that the situation might be different for conceptually more difficult constructions, such as the acquisition of the passive. In the past, its late acquisition was explained as due to its conceptual and syntactic complexity. Baker and Nelson (1984) could, however, demonstrate experimentally that passive constructions are learned as easily as active ones if they are frequently modeled. Slobin (1992) found in cross-cultural reports that the time of acquisition of the passive voice depends not on its conceptual difficulty but on frequency of input and its salience in discourse.

It appears that many or most cultures have noticed the requirements both for frequent input and for production (the generation effect discussed earlier). This applies especially to the training of formulas. Schieffelin (1990) reported for the Kaluli, and Watson-Gegeo and Gegeo (1986) for Kwava'ae children that teaching of routines, which are of course syntactic constructions, is common. Desired formulas are often modeled and their repetition is requested. Repeated models are often massed until the child repeats them, and the same formula is rehearsed on multiple occasions. Both massing and spacing is therefore encountered in these exercises. Since the trained formulas are consistently employed in specific contexts, the same or similar contexts will also provide priming support for recall. Once the child repeats the model, the generation effect comes into play. Optimal conditions for learning, indeed, even if in these cases surface structures are trained instead of the underlying abstract linguistic structures.

Once again a methodological caveat needs to be added even in the face of strong confirming evidence: Many effects might not have been discovered because of a methodological difficulty in the study of specific syntactic constructions—the choice of interval in naturalistic settings for ascertaining the possible effects of a certain type of input. Savic (1975) showed from longitudinal data that input frequency of specific question types increased about 6 months before the child clearly caught on to this question type. Adult–child frequencies converged only over the following 10 to 12 months. Moerk (1992) also reported temporal lags between increase in model frequency and in filial syntactic progress. However in the case he studied, the interval was only between two and four weeks. Both studies indicate, however, that prolonged increases in input frequency are needed to result in the employment of specific syntactic structures. The difference in length of the intervals in these two studies suggests that no fixed interval can be chosen for the measurement of effects, but that continuous longitudinal studies would be needed to assure the discovery of all effects. Such longitudinal studies have been, with few exceptions (e.g., Kavanaugh & Jirkovsky, 1982; Reimann, 1991), almost nonexistent until the present, while studies ascertaining cause and presumed effects within the same observation session might arrive at incorrect conclusions.

Effects of Deprivation

From the perspective of the *modus tollens*, that is, lower achievements being related to lower frequencies of language input—which is probably far from optimally spaced—even more convincing evidence for the importance of frequent rehearsals exists. This evidence derives from family and social class differences, from intermittent hearing loss of children, from studies of the language development of twins, and from cross-cultural comparisons. Only a few selected examples of the research in these fields can be provided here; Chapters 6 and 7 focus more extensively on it.

The evidence from social class differences in children's language skills and in school success is enormous. It is too well known to need repetition here. Reaching back to Bernstein's (1964) contrast between elaborated and restricted codes and the studies of Hess and Shipman (1965), such differences have been repeatedly identified. Although controversies developed later as to the justification of the concept of language deprivation, the Head Start program, with its strong emphasis on language skills, provides a strong indication of the validity of the early reports. Continuing high academic failure rates of children from backgrounds with less language input are another indication of the validity of these conceptualizations. For more complex language skills, such as narrative skills, Peterson and McCabe (1994) could show a relationship between level attained and social class membership. The relationship for academic language skills is supported by the high drop-out rates of students from lower socioeconomic status (SES) backgrounds during their first year in college.

Focusing on a more extreme type of deprivation, Allen and Oliver (1982) found that child neglect causes language delay. Although many causal factors will be involved in this situation, including emotional and motivational ones, neglect certainly also implies a low degree of enriching verbal stimulation. Christopoulos, Bonvillian, and Crittenden (1988) have provided specific evidence about the causal variables by showing that neglecting parents spoke much less to their children and produced by far fewer complete grammatical utterances. Tartter (1986) provided a rather comprehensive survey of cases of extreme neglect, including feral children, and its disastrous impact on language acquisition.

Organic disturbances can also result in lower intake and consequent language delay. Geer and Schick (1988), in a study of hearing impaired children, stress the need for consistent language stimulation throughout the child's development. A report of Friel-Patti, Finitzo-Hieber, Conti, and Clinton (1982) about the language deficits of a group of children prone to otitis media demonstrates this delay most impressively. This group had a 71.5 percent incidence of language delay, with 42.9 percent delayed more than six months. The organic difference of blindness has also fascinating effects on language input and acquisition, as discussed by Brumark (1989) and most recently by Andersen, Dunlea, and Kekelis (1993). While the dynamics are more complex in this case, due to the visual deprivation, accompanying relative language deprivation and relative linguistic delay commonly go hand in hand.

An almost necessary relative "neglect," that is, lower linguistic input, is found in the case of twins because parents have less time to allocate to each sibling. Papousek, Papousek, and Bornstein (1985) as well as Tomasello, Mannle, and Kruger (1986) confirm the widely shared impression that twins' language development is delayed in conformance with their lowered speech input. Similarly, Stafford (1987), by comparing large samples of twins and singletons, found that twins receive less responsive and less conversation-eliciting maternal speech and are also significantly delayed in their language development.

Such a *modus tollens* perspective could be extended to cause-effect relationships in diverse cultures. Lower levels of verbal stimulation during early childhood, such as in the Chinese and Japanese cultures, results in slower sound and slower language development compared to American middle-class children (Caudill & Frost, 1973; Ho, 1994). Many studies on environmental deprivation in cultures and subcultures furnish similar indications, even if the focus in these studies was not exclusively on language acquisition. Chapter 7 focuses on these studies.

SUMMARY AND DISCUSSION

First, some qualifications of the implicit argument presented above might be in order: The emphasis upon input frequency does not entail the stronger argument that high frequency would be a necessary precondition for the learning of all items at all times and in all situations. Carey (1978, 1982) found almost one-trial learning, or "fast-mapping" of new vocabulary items in somewhat older children. Similarly, the report of Dollaghan (1985) on rapid vocabulary acquisition would be another example against such a universal assertion. Rice, Buhr, and Nemeth (1990) demonstrated fast-mapping of labels even in language-delayed preschoolers. Nelson's (1987) proposal of a "rare-event cognitive comparison theory of syntax acquisition" would be—if valid—a counterargument in the case of syntactic learning. The impact of rare-events and fast-learning at certain times and on the acquisition of specific items does not disprove a general reliance on high frequencies of rehearsal. Additionally, rehearsal is almost certainly needed for the maintenance of even the rapidly acquired structures.

Therefore it can be concluded that wealth of input is a prerequisite for effective language development. The previously suggested "poverty of the input" was a misconception in the case of middle-class children and it is a misconception in all known cases where language development resulted in high levels of mastery. Input is enormously rich and dense and stretches over decades of the language learning process. While it would nevertheless be premature to argue universality for the provision of frequent rehearsals, a high degree of generality for those items acquired early is suggested by the reported findings. Since there is strong evidence that not all children of all cultures attain the same high levels of language skills, a uniform level of input and rehearsal frequency should not be expected across cultures and subcultures.

An analogy from a very different field, the report of Chase and Simon (1973) about chess masters, can put this argument into perspective. The chess masters had spent between 10,000 and 20,000 hours studying chess patterns, and they remembered between 10,000 and 100,000 different patterns as a result of this extensive commitment. (Interestingly, this number is closely equivalent to the number of words an average reader recognizes.) That is, even highly gifted persons largely learn due to extensive exposure, and they largely rely on memorized patterns in establishing their expertise. This is increasingly recognized for all levels of expert mastery (Glaser & Chi, 1988).

After the extensive survey of factual research, a survey which is certainly not all-encompassing especially as far as foreign-language publications are concerned, the evidence can be briefly related to the theoretical question of the title and the first part of the paper. First, recapitulating the logical argument: If based mainly on innate knowledge, language should develop uniformly, rather quickly, and without much evidence that environmental support influences the speed and end product of the acquisition processes. It also should be based largely on the testing of hypotheses whether features of the native tongue accord with innate knowledge. Progress should therefore be saltatory and not gradual. If on the other hand, language is learned as a complex skill, it should be acquired gradually, take considerable time, and much environmental support. As rote learning and pattern abstraction appear to be the predominant mechanisms of learning in many species, and in young children, these simpler mechanisms would be expected to predominate in infants and toddlers. Input should therefore be adapted to these learning mechanisms. These adaptations would be reflected in fine tuned, frequent, and often densely spaced rehearsals.

It need not be demonstrated that language acquisition proceeds gradually, extending over the first decade and, for more complex constructions (Chomsky, 1969; Ingram, 1975), into the teens and twenties. Environmental support is immense, as has been partly demonstrated above, even if only two general principles, frequency and spacing/massing, have been covered. Most of the more specific training and learning processes have been dealt with in another publication (Moerk, 1996). Although *modus tollens* phenomena could only be adumbrated, common sense knowledge affirms (and every elementary school teacher can confirm) that delay in language acquisition and low levels of final accomplishment commonly occur together with environmental deprivation. The rather autonomous developmental progress based on innately guided blossoming of a language organ, buffered against environmental vagaries, is nowhere to be found.

When considering the speed of language development, it is surprising that the only case where strong evidence for speedy learning, labeled "fast mapping" (Carey, 1978, 1982; Rice, 1990), has been repeatedly established, pertains to vocabulary learning; a type of knowledge even the most extreme nativist would probably not assert to be innate. On the level of syntax, the nativists' focus, progress is painfully slow, even when progressing from the first word to the simple correct S–V–O sentence a year or more later. This slow progress is observed even though the syntactic constructions can build upon homologous sensory-motor structures. For the abstraction of the linguistic structure a great deal of massing of substitution sequences has been reported. More specific details of teaching and learning interactions that train abstractions have been presented in Moerk (1985a, 1992, 1996). Hundreds of thousands of opportunities exist therefore for the learning of the latent structure as repetitions of the structure with diverse surface fillers are encountered. Abstraction is even necessary since the brain could not handle this mass of experience other than by abstracting the commonalities. Such abstraction is a generally established principle of perceptual learning.

Whether rules are acquired and employed by young children was not explored because the concept of rules remains undefined (Baker & Hacker, 1984). As Lakatos was fond of saying: "A fish may well be able to swim with not the slightest knowledge of hydrodynamics." Fortunately, the research community has produced abundant evidence of simple learning. The empirical evidence is supplemented by powerful conceptual models that are fully sensitive to input, whether it is the Competition model (Bates & MacWhinney, 1987; MacWhinney, 1987, 1989) or the Skill-Learning model (Fischer & Corrigan, 1981; Moerk, 1986, 1989b; Sonnenschein & Whitehurst, 1984). Additional fine-grained research on language acquisition across diverse language-delayed populations, social classes, and cultural groups (e.g., Slobin, 1985, 1992) is needed, with careful attention devoted to input (e.g., Schieffelin, 1990), to the concomittant variations in the speed as well as forms of acquisition, and to the level of the end product.

Such explorations of input and processes can then provide the basis for causal inferences and for optimal early interventions in cases of language delay. They can also provide the rationale for didactic school programs intended to remedy such delays. For the millions of language delayed children, empirical interactional learning research can provide the means to alleviate or eliminate such delays.

Before such effective intervention can be contemplated, additional aspects of the input in its relationship to the processing tendencies of children need to be explored. Chapter 4 focuses on a further feature of the input, fine tuning, that appears necessary for effective training. One specific aspect of fine tuning, corrections, is explored in Chapter 5.

4

Fine Tuning in Communication and Language Training

> ...a benign environment can provide precisely the information that will facilitate the acquisition of the next increment of skills.
> —Langley and Simon (1981, p. 375)

Input adaptation to the child's language level and learning needs has generally been referred to as "fine tuning" in the field of first language development. Outside this field, a large variety of terms have been employed for very similar principles. It is therefore desirable to relate fine tuning to other commonly employed concepts and principles and thereby to clarify its meaning and implications. Such an exploration of conceptual ties will also integrate the relatively recent concept of fine tuning (conceived about 1975) with principles of psychology and education that have been employed for hundred years or more.

FINE TUNING BY MANY OTHER NAMES

Kagan's (1970) "optimal level of discrepancy," while focusing mainly on a feature that arouses and maintains attention in young infants, also defines optimal stimulation in relation to the infant's preceding experiential history, that is, to his/her readiness or level of competence. Hunt's (1961) "problem of the match," which implies an optimal level of discrepancy, and Bruner's (e.g., 1983) "raising the ante" in the process of "scaffolding" are functionally equivalent concepts.

75

Vygotsky's (1962) "zone of proximal development" (ZPD) entails a level of readiness of the child and constraints on the capacity of mastering new tasks. The zone encompasses the distance between the level of performance that children can reach unaided and the level of performance they can attain when guided by another, more knowledgeable, individual. In this manner, the ZPD also incorporates the social support that is central in fine tuning. When adult experts lead the child while staying within the zone of proximal development, this is closely equivalent to Bruner's (1984) "scaffolding" and "raising the ante" previously mentioned. Bruner (1978, p. 44) also formulated a "fine tuning theory of language acquisition: "the mother's interpretation...is guided by a continually updated understanding of her child's competence."

Burton, Brown, and Fischer (1984) have suggested an ICM (increasingly complex microworlds) paradigm, wherein the student is exposed to a sequence of environments in which his tasks become increasingly complex. The increase is calibrated to the level of increasing competence of the learner. More broadly in the field of cognitive problem solving, Simon (1978) formulated a "difference-by-comparison heuristic" in which one "compares the current node with characteristics of the desired state of affairs and extracts differences from comparison" (p. 278). If the differences are small enough to be manageable, progress is achieved, otherwise failure threatens.

The educational concept of "readiness," the cornerstone of all educational programs that involve age-grading, is conceptually equivalent to fine tuning. Readiness focuses on students' level of performance from the perspective of planned educational interventions. These interventions are to be adjusted, that is, fine tuned to the students' levels of competence in order to be most effective. A well-known practical application of this principle was employed in programmed instruction (Gagne, 1962; Holland & Skinner, 1961) which emphasized minimal steps between levels of accomplishment. These basic ideas are now widely integrated into computer-assisted instruction. As Atkinson (1972) has argued, "powerful instructional strategies must necessarily be adaptive; that is, they must be sensitive on a moment-to-moment basis to a learner's unique response history" (p. 929).

Linking education and cognitive psychology, differential readiness is presumed in Gagne's (1968) eight levels of learning. In Gagne's system the lower levels are necessary prerequisites for "cumulative learning" and for progress to higher levels. In cognitive psychology, the best known theory relying on readiness and fine tuning, even if employing a different terminology, is Piaget's theory. Stages of cognitive development are achieved by means of equilibration processes that utilize environmental "aliments." These aliments are close enough to the established level of mastery, but also incongruous enough from the preceding levels of cognitive functioning, to produce a disequilibrium. Accordingly, Inhelder, Sinclair, and Bovet (1974) emphasize that training effects depend upon the child's developmental level, that is, on the competence that the child has at its disposal. Fischer and associates

(Fischer, 1980; Fischer, Kenny, & Pipp, 1990; Fischer & Pipp, 1984) have built on Piaget in developing a skill theory in which an upper limit of complexity or optimal (maximal) level is contrasted with a usual level of performance. Social scaffolding is useful both for functioning at the upper limit and especially for transcending it. In this theory, more than in Piaget's, cognitive development and social influences are interwoven as they are in Vygotksy's system.

Whereas Gagne integrated cognitive and educational perspectives, Bruner (1973) and Burton and associates (1984) focused on motor skill learning, which integrates cognitive and behavioral aspects. Studies of behavioral learning obviously simplify empirical analyses of fine tuning of input to levels of readiness since both aspects are easily measured. Therefore the behaviorist paradigm should also entail pertinent principles. Two concepts that are closely related to fine tuning are those of shaping and of transfer. Shaping proceeds in small incremental steps that are designed in accordance with the preceding performance, and it relies on successive approximations toward a goal response. Parallels to fine tuning are obvious in the emphasis on small increments and in the iterative conceptualization of the learning process. The well established concept of transfer entails similar features. Transfer was explained by Thorndike (1903) as being based on identical elements, with more identical elements resulting in more transfer. According to this interpretation, in transfer most elements are identical to previously learned ones (the readiness) and only one or a few new element(s) need to be acquired (the discrepancy aspect). Therefore relatively little additional processing capacity is required. Osgood (1949), building on Thorndike, suggested a process-based interpretation for the phenomenon of transfer that focused on the similarity of "cognitive processing characteristics" instead of on the similarity of components. More recently still, the Osgood's "processes" became rules, concepts, or "productions" (Anderson, 1987) that accounted for the transfer of learned skills in the process of cognitive skill acquisition. In all these explorations, whether of behavioral or cognitive skill acquisition, preceding skills are necessary prerequisites for later, more complex ones, and the training process follows an incremental pattern.

Practical applications of the concept of fine tuning as well as theoretical arguments go back much further. The entire apprenticeship system, whether in the learning of a trade in Western culture during the Middle Ages, or the learning of any skill in pretechnological societies, entails fine tuning. These phenomena are often described by employing the term "task sequencing," as, for example in Greenfield and Lave's (1982) report on the training of weaving skills in the Zinacanteco culture. The anthropological literature contains many similar reports, as surveyed by Greenfield and Lave (1982) and Rogoff (1990).

In education, concepts that are now represented by the term readiness go back to Comenius' (1592–1670) *Didactica magna*, (1628–1632) and to Pestalozzi (1746–1829). There is a straight line of conceptual transmission from Comenius to Pestallozi, through Froebel (1782–1852), the founder of the kindergarten movement, to Maria Montessori, to Piaget, and to recent cognitive theories. All of them involve emphasis on a natural order of development and an optimal gap between established mastery and new demands. As is well-known, Montessori's method consisted of breaking down complex tasks into smaller behavioral components that were manageable for young children, that is, she explored subroutines, that have been emphasized so heavily by Bruner (1984) and by Anderson (1987) in cognitive skill acquisition. Montessori's components already mastered could also be labeled identical elements as per Thorndike or identical processes as per Osgood. In Piaget's (e.g., 1936) system, sensorimotor schemas are subroutines that gradually become automatized and can then be "reciprocally assimilated" that is, "compiled" (in Anderson's terminology, 1987).

The above conceptual network, as sketched out in broad strokes, is intended to serve two purposes. First, to anchor the concept of fine tuning broadly in psychological theory and research, and second to indicate how generally, perhaps even universally, the principle of fine tuning has been employed in diverse fields and in diverse paradigms of teaching, training, and learning.

In the following section, empirical reports of fine tuning in first language acquisition are surveyed. Then studies that dispute fine tuning are scrutinized. After that, conceptual and methodological principles that explain and resolve the debate over the evidence and theories are explored. Further on, psychological and interactional principles are specified that make such fine tuning possible. Building on these evaluations, recent reports are surveyed that present a more differentiated concept of tuning, showing how it varies—not only across dyads, but even within single dyads. Finally, available reports are integrated on effects of fine tuning and of rough tuning; with the latter presenting varying degrees of challenge to the child's processing capacity.

EMPIRICAL REPORTS OF FINE TUNING
IN LANGUAGE TRAINING

It is common knowledge that children progress incrementally in their language skills. They proceed from single words, or brief formulas that are processed like single words, to two and more word utterances that permit the substitution of elements. They then gradually add some minor grammatical morphemes until they acquire competence in the more complex constructions of their mother tongue. It takes up to the end of the teen years (Chomsky, 1969; Ingram, 1975) to achieve this. In this lengthy process, they are continually guided and supported by their social environment, whether parents, older peers, or teachers.

A more comprehensive survey of the diverse features of adult guidance has been provided in Moerk (1996) and is also discussed throughout this book. This chapter focuses on evidence of fine tuning in normal L1 transmission. The extensive research on language delay and the differential adjustment of parents to the language skills of normal and delayed children (e.g., Rondal, 1995) is largely excluded. Related principles that are encountered in the field of second language training and learning (e.g., Krashen, 1985; Swain, 1985) including "foreigner talk" (Hatch, 1983), that is, the simplification that native speakers employ when speaking to not yet accomplished nonnative speakers, will be mentioned but not comprehensively surveyed. However, the first (preverbal) year will included. It entails fine tuning of suprasegmental features and phonological simplifications, while gradually including vocabulary provision, rehearsal, and grammatical simplifications. That is, fine tuning is first only aimed at the acoustic-perceptual adaptation to the attentional propensities and memory restrictions of the preverbal infant, and then becomes more directly linguistic and semantic when the child begins to comprehend and produce speech. Menyuk, Liebergott, and Schultz (1995) have emphasized those changes most recently. They demonstrated how different types of maternal tuning accounted for variance in gain scores among children at various points of their development.

Variation has to be expected not only across developmental stages but also across dyads. Considering what is known about temperamental differences between infants (Chess & Birch, 1970) and stylistic differences between mothers, as well as between social and cultural groups (Moerk, 1985a; Snow et al., 1976), such variations might be quite extensive. Additionally, chance variables might be important for individual dyads: What worked best the first time for one mother and was retained by the infant will not be the same for another dyad. Each dyad might be prone to repeat what worked well and move on in somewhat different directions from this basis. A combination of probable universal principles of early attention (Kagan, 1970), of perception, and of memory with such idiosyncratic factors, will produce logical and analytical challenges. Seemingly different maternal adaptations might serve the same process, such as when long-term storage might be achieved primarily through manipulation of attention variables or primarily through extensive rehearsals. Such differences have to be expected across dyads, social classes, and cultures.

Yet, in spite of some cross-linguistic variation, Cruttenden (1994) reported in a literature survey that "every language that has thus far been studied has a special register for speaking to infants" (p. 149ff), that is, every culture takes into account the special requirements of the neophyte language learner, even if in different ways. This universality of some form of baby talk has been consistently confirmed since the early work of Ferguson (1964). Harkness (1976), for example, reported that Guatemalan mothers did not only employ a slow rate in speaking to their language-learning children, thereby facilitating acoustic analysis, but they repeated themselves as often as necessary for the child to repeat the model or understand the message. The same intensity of repetition has been reported by Schieffelin (1990) and by Watson-Gegeo and Gegeo (1986) from two other preindustrial cultures. These findings, although not fully included, are partly surveyed in Chapter 7.

Even within the short time span of infancy and the preschool years, extensive changes occur in children's cognitive and language development. Related changes should occur in the input if it is matched to the changing informational needs of the children. In accordance with the logic of the assumption that parental input is tuned to the child's developmental progress, it has to be expected that changes in input will probable not be monotonic. During periods when certain features of children's speech *cannot* change, such as the MLU (mean length of utterance) during the first year, and then again during the approximately six months of the one-word stage, when they *do not* change, minimal change should be expected prima facie in the equivalent input features (i.e., maternal MLU), if productive "language ability of the child is a powerful determinant of variation of many aspects of maternal speech and conversation style" (Cross, Nienhuys, & Kirkman, 1985, p. 286). If on the other hand, the main causal variable is the receptive ability of the infant, then maternal MLU changes should appear only around the age of nine months when first single-word comprehension has been plausibly demonstrated (Benedict, 1979). Anticipating these developmental analyses, Phillips (1973) and Lord (1975) have reported that parents only shift to baby talk around the end of their child's first year of life.

The principle of qualitative and quantitative tuning implies, for the period before infants have acquired language abilities, that their attentional/motivational, their perceptual, and (in part) their conceptual capacities, should predominantly determine the input features. The principles underlying early maternal fine tuning should therefore be quite different from those underlying the later linguistic adaptations. Therefore a close consideration of perceptual development, as provided, for example, by Gibson (1969, 1984), should accompany the description of the early input. This development, from wholistic and global to differentiated, articulated, and later to integrated perception (Colombo, 1986; Gibson, 1969; Goodman, Lee, & de Groot, 1994) cannot be described in detail here. Yet, drastic changes need to be pointed out in acoustic analysis and storage of patterns at about 7 to 8 months of age (Colombo, 1986), that is, briefly before the first evidence of comprehension of single words is recorded (Benedict, 1979). When input is analyzed into multiple elements which are then integrated in productions, at the beginning of the more-word stage between about 16 and 18 months, changes in fine tuning should also be related to this important developmental advance. Further changes with the beginning of metalinguistic awareness (Sinclair, Jarvella, & Levelt, 1978) are then mainly utilized in instruction in elementary schools. These relatively late phenomena will, however, be excluded here.

Suprasegmental Features of the Preverbal Period

For the period up to about eight months of age, the main task of the caretakers is to catch and maintain the attention of their infants as well as to motivate them to engage in vocal and gestural exchanges. Adaptations in suprasegmental features, such as intonation contours, pause length, and pitch changes have been widely reported for the first year of life (Ferguson, 1964, 1977; Fernald, 1984; Papousek and Papousek,

1983; Cruttenden, 1994). What the Papouseks (1983) called "intuitive parenting" clearly implies fine adaptation to the immature attentional, perceptual, and memory requirements of the infant. A motivational component is implicit in many of these input adjustments which maintain the infant's involvement in the interactions and thereby necessarily contribute to learning and retention. Input phenomena are discussed separately for these four process characteristics.

Specific attention-arousing techniques have been documented by Blount and Padgug (1977), by Fernald (1984), Papousek and Papousek (1983) and by Stern (1983). They generally consist of a higher pitch of maternal speech together with exaggerated changes in intonation contour. Vowels are elongated and pleasant melodic contours are maintained together with increased rhythmicity (Papousek, Papousek, & Bornstein, 1985). Infants orient longer to such speech (Kemler-Nelson et al., 1989) than to adult–adult speech.

Perceptual facilitation is provided, in accordance with the wholistic perceptual tendencies of the young infant, by means of the prosodic features of maternal speech. Fernald and Simon (1984) found slow articulation in speech directed by mothers to infants as young as three to five days. Utterances were short, containing few syllables, and lengthy pauses between utterances clearly marked the boundaries. Infants show greatest sensitivity to prosody at around four months. This is also the time when utterance–medial pauses are shortest in adult input (Stern, 1983). This means mothers maintain the prosodic contours without interruptions. Karzon (1985) could show immediate effects of such simplifications in that infants between one and four months could differentiate three-syllable sequences only when produced with *motherese* prosody. Werker and MacLeod (1989), too, reported accordingly that four month-olds devoted longer attention time and showed more affective responsiveness to baby talk than seven month-olds.

More specific musical and rhythmic patterns are added to the general adaptations. A dominant trochaic pattern of parental input and of filial production (Wijnen, Krikhaar, & Den Os, 1994) is widely encountered. Such a trochaic bias, that is a strong–weak predilection (e.g., *Mommy, Daddy, doggie*) might be combined somewhat later with an iambic pattern (Kelly & Bock, 1988), such as in simple Copula sentences: *The man is nice. The tree is high.* Trochees and iambs are some of the most basic patterns in poetry and they are closely related to the pattern of the heartbeat. The learning of language structure might therefore even be based on, and facilitated by, prenatal learning of a biological rhythm. Related to these rhythmic patterns is the fact that "syllabic sequences are sung in short structured melodies with distinct patterns of rhythm and accent" (Papousek & Papousek, 1983 p. 210). du Preez (1974) commented on the same phenomenon from a different cultural background. It is known that musical qualities are motivating for all of mankind.

Blount and Padgug reported for somewhat older children between eight months and one year-six months: "younger children received a higher rate of features that marked affect; older children were addressed with more features that marked semantically meaningful speech" (p. 67). As long as the infant does not analyze the

verbal input in its grammatical and semantic aspects, specific syntactic and semantic fine tuning is not yet needed and would be useless. It is evidence *for* fine tuning
and *not against* it if linguistically motivated grammatical adaptations are not found
in input provided to preverbal children (Snow, 1977; Kaye, 1980). As long as the
infant's processing does not change on a specific feature, fine tuned interactions
should not change in the same feature either.

Analytic Support During the One-Word Period

With important attentional and perceptual changes occurring around seven to eight
months of age, changes in input are expected and found (Snow, 1977). As the infant
begins to analyze the input, simplifications that help in processing finer aspects of
the sound structure of the mother tongue are required. Additionally, when infants
provide evidence that they have begun to master the sound structure of some words,
the relationships between words and their referents need to become a focus of the
dyadic interactions. These new emphases do, however, not imply that the input
features from the earlier period are suddenly discontinued. The degree of change
is mainly gradual and somewhat additive.

Attention-Focusing Techniques

Responding to the infant's increasing capacity for differentiation and articulation
of acoustic stimulus patterns, *motherese* stresses specific syllables and makes them
highly salient (Gleitman & Warner, 1984). As infants produce more clearly recog-
nizable learned sound patterns (Colombo, 1986; Crystal, 1987), mothers can follow
the infant's lead by imitating—and refining—these productions. The ratio of
maternal to child imitation is reported as about four to one (Pawlby, 1977; Uzgiris,
1983). Yet, in accordance with the increasing familiarity of the infant with the
regularly repeated sound patterns, the mother also introduces variation in the
repetitions to produce the degree of variability that helps to maintain attention but
also to abstract regularity (Kagan, 1970; Kaye, 1980, 1982). However, at about
seven months the mother also "raises the ante" (Cazden, 1979) by insisting on more
language-like interactional contributions from the infant.

As infants need to attend to the relationships of the learned sound complexes to
the nonverbal context, mothers increasingly integrate familiar objects into mother–
child interactions and thereby provide the opportunity for the child to relate sound
patterns to referents. This goal is achieved when mothers comment predominantly
on items on which the infant's attention is already focused (Moerk, 1983b, 1985c;
Snow, 1995). As Moerk (1983b) reported, "the mother employs mostly a theme
proposed by the child and repeats it with minor and major variations" (p. 28). As
infants return often to the same objects in their play activities, many opportunities
for the association of words and referents occur. Focused words appear predominantly at the end of utterances and they are produced with an exaggerated terminal

rise, features that attract attention and facilitate processing plus storage through the recency position.

Perceptual Clarifications

Clarifications are offered by reducing the length of maternal utterances as compared to the preverbal period (Murray, Johnson, & Peters, 1990). The processing of the verbal input is also simplified by the mother's endeavors to make individual words stand out (Murray, Johnson, & Peters, 1990; Ruke-Dravina, 1977; Sherrod, Friedman, Crawley, Drake, & Devieux, 1977; Stern, 1983). As Gleason (1981, p. 292) explains: "as infants begin to comprehend speech, adults switch on a modification program that cleans up fuzzy phonetic distinctions, segments the stream of speech into short clauses, highlights important words, and, in general, makes the system clearer and clearer." Hirsh-Pasek and associates (1987) also emphasize the prosodic features that serve as cues to the parsing of the input, features that the infants can utilize effectively. The same phenomenon was reported by Kemler-Nelson, Hirsh-Pasek, Jusczyk, and Wright Cassidy (1989).

Motherese first clarifies content words through vowel modification and only later function words (Ratner, 1984). Gleason (1981) has shown pitch matching (p. 290) and clear distinctions in voice onset-time (p. 291). Malsheen (1980) has summarized the overall principle concisely: "It appears that as soon as the child attempts to articulate phonological segments that contrast in voicing, the mother begins to issue phonological instructions through a special set of phonetic cue-enhancing rules. Consequently, the mother is presenting her language-learning child with an idealized corpus of voiced and voiceless phonetic segments—one that contains fewer less carefully articulated, categorically ambiguous segments than does normal A–A speech" (p. 184). Perceptual simplifications are added by means of consonant harmony, wherein, for example, *doggie* becomes *goggie*, lowering the analytic tasks for the infant.

Integrative Support During the Early More-Word Phase

Beginning at about 16 months, but with wide individual and cultural differences, the third phase of training/learning comes increasingly to predominate. This is the phase of hierarchic integration in Werner's terminology, wherein the mastery of more complex linguistic structures is gradually achieved. Differentiation and articulation of functors and bound morphemes certainly do not end with the new phase. In contrast, such differentiations will provide the elements for further refined integrations. This phase might be described as continuing until the dawning of metalinguistic knowledge around the age of four years or even longer; but the end point is of no relevance to the present discussion.

Attention-Focusing Techniques

Attention to linguistic contents is maximized when the mother continues to follow child's lead. Moerk (1983b) specified numerically that "whereas the mother introduces a new topic less than 5 times per hour on the average, the child introduces new topics around 20 times" (p. 25). Then the mother responds reliably to the topics introduced by the child. In addition to adapting to the interests of the child, Garnica (1977) reported even for five-year-olds that the mothers maintained higher pitch and larger pitch ranges. The focus of the message is reflected by means of a peak in frequencies at the end of phrases (Fernald & Mazzie, 1991). Therefore, both cognitive-semantic and simple perceptual means are maintained in order to retain the attention of easily distractable and very active toddlers and preschoolers. In many homes, routines have also been established, whether bedtime stories or picture book reading, that are almost optimal for focusing the attention of the child on linguistic contents.

Perceptual Clarifications

Clarifications are especially needed now to provide reliable cues as to sentence boundaries (Broen, 1972). In *motherese*, prosodic and syntactic boundaries almost invariably coincide (Fernald, 1984). Kemler-Nelson and associates (1989) reported furthermore that "the prosodic qualities of motherse provide infants with cues to units of speech that correspond to grammatical units of language" (p. 55). Also, as mentioned above, Bernstein Rattner (1984) has shown that vowel clarification is now also provided for functors and not only for contentive words. During this period, mothers are prone to employ sentence fragments in some of their turns, thereby simplifying the complexity of the analytic task, when the child is attending to the entire maternal utterance and not only to stressed elements. Most of the relevant clarifications are discussed below.

Although this is not a complete survey of the information available now, and even less of the probable cultural variations in language and interactional features yet to be ascertained, the fact of fine tuning to the acoustic-perceptual and attentional tendencies of the infant can barely be doubted for the early period of language development. Gleason (1981) has summarized the changing aspects of fine tuning: "Speech to very young infants contains modifications that are primarily affective and tuned to infants' perceptual preferences in such a way that they help establish preverbal communication. As infants begin to comprehend speech, adults switch on a modification program that cleans up fuzzy phonetic distinctions, segments the stream of speech into short clauses, highlights important words, and, in general, makes the system cleaner and clearer. Still later, after children have acquired the basic phonological and grammatical distinctions of the language, these language-teaching modifications dropout" (p. 292). Cruttenden (1994) agreed that "we possess a limited amount of evidence that BTPh (Baby Talk Phonetics) and BTPr (Baby Talk Prosody) are fine tuned .... Fine tuning for solidarity, for affect and for attention (as shown by BTPh1 and most of the BTPr effects) is at its peak in the prelinguistic stage; fine tuning for clarification and possibly for segmentation (as shown by BTPh2 and some of the BRPr effects) is at its peak in the holophrastic stage" (p. 149). (Cruttenden's BTPh1, Baby Talk Phonetics 1, refers to *simplifying* modifications in adult speech that occur during the prelinguistic period, BTPh2 refers to *clarifying* modifications to increase the contrast between morphemes, which occur during the holophrastic stage, BTPr , Baby Talk Prosody, refers to attention arousing and maintaining modifications.)

Fine Tuning Supporting Advanced Vocabulary Acquisition

Having surveyed maternal fine tuning to the processing requirements of the infant, the emphasis will be shifted to more advanced language instruction in contentive vocabulary and morphosyntactic skills. Whereas there is abundant research on vocabulary development and also some on vocabulary input, little of it was focused directly on the fine tuning of vocabulary. The available evidence is often indirect, established when other topics of input and filial productions were explored. Also, the situation is conceptually more complex in the case of vocabulary than in prosodic/phonetic adaptations and it therefore deserves a brief logical analysis before empirical findings are discussed.

Whereas some bases for fine tuning, such as immediate filial attention or productive MLU, are relatively easy to observe, the criteria of linguistic complexity are less obvious in the domain of vocabulary acquisition. On the one hand, difficulties of word length or acoustic complexity are resolved by simplifying complex words into baby talk form. Therefore these features do not function as decisive variables. Cognitive factors, such as abstractness of concepts or references to temporally and spatially distant referents (the distancing operations) (Sigel, 1986) exert some influence. But these criteria are not fine enough for fine tuning. Mothers certainly have to be concerned about the processing load and need to take precautions not to teach too many vocabulary items at once, if they want to fine tune their input to the capacities of the child. They select therefore labels on the "level of usual utility" (Brown, 1958), that is, those employable in many contexts. Yet, all these are relatively rough criteria.

Finding little secure guidance as to features of vocabulary difficulty that might guide fine tuning, it appears advisable to employ a bottom-up approach and to survey empirical reports as to which principles mothers actually employ in order to keep vocabulary input adjusted to the learning capacities of infants.

Whole Objects and Pointing Strings

Quine raised the philosophical question of how the learner would know what the expert is referring to when relating a sound complex to a pointed-at object. Does the expert refer to the whole object, a specific feature, an activity, or does he utter a personal evaluation, such as "pretty"? Research provides a clear-cut answer to this question: In accordance with Werner's orthogenetic law, the child first focuses on the whole object, and most mothers have caught on to this basic law and provide a whole-object label. Ninio (1980b) reported that 95.3 percent of all ostensive definitions in a picture book situation referred to the whole object. Only after objects are labeled, might differentiations be added by means of "pointing strings," (Murphy, 1978; Murphy & Messer, 1977; Wheeler, 1983) or by adding a well-known verb in order to describe an activity. In the subsequent utterances, the object label is mostly repeated, and object-plus-feature messages are therefore trained.

The Basic-Object Level

Even if caretakers have gotten used to providing a whole-object label, they still need to decide which of the possible labels for the object to choose: the name of a pet, the label "kitty," "feline," "animal," or any other category term. They employ the general principle of providing the label on the "basic-object level" (Anglin, 1977; Brown, 1973; Mervis & Rosch, 1981; Ninio, 1980). That is, mothers provide terms that can encompass a wide range of members of the set but which nevertheless allow the child to make necessary differentiations between sets. For example, a terrier is "a doggie," and no animal is primarily labeled "an animal" for the young child. Some items are even mislabeled in order to stay within the familiar basic-level category. Mervis and Mervis (1982) reported that mothers named a leopard "kitty-cat" and a toy truck "car" in accordance with this principle. Later, superordinate and subordinate terms are carefully introduced in interactions that are structured almost like conscious teaching lessons.

The described strategy lowers the memory load the child faces when learning, for example, only one word for all types of four-wheeled vehicles. That is, parents provide noun labels on the "level of usual utility" (Brown, 1958). Although less explored, transcripts show that the same principle applies for verbs: People are described as "walking," or children as "running," and neither as "shuffling," "waddling," or "strolling." Lucariello and Nelson (1986) demonstrated fine differentiations in labeling according to context, whether during play, routines, or novel situations. Correlations between mother and child usage in the various contexts were generally above .50 and reached .86. Therefore both the child's language level and the type of context affect fine tuning, as would be expected: new contexts require more information processing and require more support in training and learning than routinized ones.

Finer Differentiations and Distancing

With the child's increasing age, mothers use more diverse vocabularies (Phillips, 1973) and add linguistic elaborations after having simply labeled items (Wheeler, 1983). As the findings of Wheeler (1983) indicate, fine tuning is perhaps more clearly evident in what is *not* talked about. Labels for objects and activities occur before labels for more finely differentiated features. Cognitively complex aspects are avoided. Brown, Cazden and Bellugi (1969) considered input from both perspectives: items that are generally *not* employed and those that are found commonly. Some of these contrasts are: Whereas *where* questions are common, *when, how,* and *why* questions occur very rarely. That is, discussions that include vocabulary about spatial aspects occur very early, since obviously children have to orient themselves in space and in relation to the objects they encounter. As children spend most of their time in familiar surroundings, many opportunities for rehearsals exist. In contrast, discussion about time and causality appear a good deal later (Moerk & Vilaseca, 1987). Continuing with Brown and associates' report, some modal auxiliaries, such as *may* and *must* are seldom heard, whereas the catenative auxiliaries *wanna* and *gonna* are very frequent. These contrasts indicate both cognitive readiness and pragmatic factors as bases for the input. The observable here-and-now in the case of where-questions and the focus on intentions (*wanna*, *gonna*) by both conversation partners, respectively, require the pertinent vocabulary. Probabilities (*may*) or deontic aspects (*must*) are far above the grasp of the toddler and are avoided.

More specialized fine tuning for vocabulary was also found by Hayes and Ahrens (1988) and Sokolov (1993). Fine tuning even pertains to such specific aspects as the correspondence between mothers and their children in the use of mental terms (Furrow, Moore, Davidge, & Chiasson, 1992). But it extends to overall discourse topics (Wanska & Bedrosian, 1986) as well as overall isomorphy in either expressive or referential style (Goldfield, 1987). Bruner (1983) has concisely summarized the maternal alertness to the child's level: "the mother appeared to be operating on a freshly updated, detailed 'inventory' of his knowledge of objects and events, of the words he had previously understood, and of the forms of expression of which he was capable" (pp. 81–82). Of course, parents do not need to rely exclusively upon their memory. Infants and toddlers provide ongoing guidance for their parents as to their readiness for new items. They often imitate rare and novel words (Moerk & Moerk, 1979) and therefore give indications of their readiness to learn them, whereas parents, in turn, respond to these imitations by constructing (often lengthy) feedback loops.

Feedback Loops

Closely contingent feedback loops are most conducive to fine tuning. Whether it is the controversial "corrections" (see Chapter 5), "expansions," "extensions," or "recasts," most of the elements in the preceding utterance of the child are retained so that the child's processing load is light. The few items that are changed or added stand out from the unchanged background in a figure–ground relationship and elicit special attention and active processing. As these feedback loops are so effectual, the mother often employs "feedback productive techniques" (du Preez, 1974) in the form of "testing questions" to establish occasions for such loops. After mere recognition tests, the mother asks recall questions: "What is that?" or more complex ones, asking for features and activities of an object. The child's partially successful response then provides the opportunity to give fine tuned feedback.

Picture Books as Graded Teaching Tools

First of all, as every librarian can confirm, picture books are written on greatly differing levels of complexity, that is, they can be developmentally ordered. When selected with reasonable care by parents, they are already rough tuned to the child's level. The child's own predilections and rejections then contribute to fine tuning together with the parents memory. A more extensive discussion of the topic of picture book reading in its instructional aspects is found in Moerk (1996). Only some aspects that are central to fine tuning will be selected here.

Picture books are tuned first of all by introducing a "symbolization gradient" (Moerk, 1977) that provides a bridge from the real object and action to analogically symbolized object referents, the pictures, and to the arbitrary symbols of language. Picture books also present a "tailored environment," by simplifying the complex real-world stimulus and mainly depicting the critically distinctive features of the represented objects. As mentioned, the book itself and also the pages to be read are often chosen by the children and are therefore on a level that is meaningful and manageable for them. Once the book reading has begun, there is a well established sequence in label provision, as discussed in answering Quine's question (Goodsitt, Raitan, & Perlmutter, 1988; Snow & Goldfield, 1983). After basic-object labels and similar basic-activity labels have been mastered, descriptions of differential features increase sharply from 16 percent to 25 percent of the verbal input over the period of one to two years. It has been discussed in Chapter 3 that picture book reading is also fine tuned to the rehearsal needs of children. In Chapter 5 it is shown that the same principle applies in respect to corrections, which are provided in practically 100 percent of vocabulary mistakes (DeLoache & DeMendoza, 1987; Snow & Goldfield, 1983).

In the course of the second year of life, an important shift is initiated by the mother from mere labeling and imitations to tutorial questions *Were is...?* and *What is that?*. Snow (1978) reports this shift occurring between 12 and 18 months, whereas Wheeler (1983) finds it extending from 18 to 29 months. It is likely that even within the tutorial questions fine tuned mothers would shift from *Where is ...?* questions, checking recognition vocabulary, to *What is that?* questions, checking recall memory. This sequential appearance of tutorial questions needs to be further evaluated empirically for individual words and possibly as a general tendency in the course of development.

From the 1970s on, Schumacher (1976), Dunn and Wodding (1977), Moerk and Moerk (1979), Howe (1981) and Sachs (1979, 1983), have shown progressive elaboration, so that this fact can be considered well supported. Moerk and Moerk (1979) have demonstrated for one child the inclusion of rare grammatical morphemes, borrowed from picture books, in the child's immediate and delayed imitations, leading to generalizations in the context of the child's own activities.

Finally, and perhaps most importantly from a developmental perspective, the "distancing function" (Sigel, 1986; Sigel & McGillicuddy-Delisi, 1984) can be trained effectively in the picture book situation. Picture books are uniquely progressive in leading conversations away from the familiar context of the dyad to spatially and temporally displaced, or even fantasy, contexts. Even within one book the distancing is incrementally progressive: First the distancing is short-interval. As

Goodsitt, Raitan and Perlmutter (1988) have shown, the dyad moves from an initial exclusive focus on the picture in view to references to preceding and subsequent pages. Later, picture stories are related to the child's own past experiences or even to future plans (Peterson & McCabe, 1994). That is, from simple labeling of present objects, to recall of temporally proximate discussions of other pages, to temporally and contextually distant personal experiences, and to future possibilities, a gradual extension of distancing occurs. Because the child provides consistent feedback by maintaining or losing interest and by his level of comprehension of what is said, fine tuning is easily possible.

Conclusion

As the above survey indicates, the evidence for fine tuning is extensive. There is basically no disagreement as to the fact that changes in input vocabulary occur with the development of children. Snow's (1977) summary from one study can represent the field: "The speech of Ann's and Mary's mothers did change strikingly between 3 months and eighteen months in terms of what they were talking about. ...the mothers were attuning their speech to their children's growing interest in objects and activities outside themselves, and their need for information about those objects and activities" (p. 7). The bases for such fine tuning are also common knowledge: Speakers are very alert to signs of noncomprehension or loss of interest in the listener. And infants are quite brusk in providing this feedback. In addition to this immediate feedback, mothers also remember, of course, what they read before with their children and what the children knew. Therefore their selection of stories and their shift from modeling to tutorial questions can also be guided in a roughly tuned way by their own memory. As Wertsch (1979), Wood (1980) and Rogoff and Gardner (1984) have demonstrated from many forms of skill training, the adult monitors the child's level and supports the child's extension of skills to higher levels of performance and competence. As the mother raises the ante, the child's development proceeds (Cazden, 1983). The mother would not raise the ante if she could not surmise that the child is ready for it. In accordance with these findings, Moerk (1975) reported a cluster of "primitive" interactional forms and a cluster of "more mature forms," each of them entailing high intercorrelations between the variables contained in the cluster. He concluded from multiple high correlations between maternal and filial forms of verbal interactions that these "provide striking proof of the high level of calibration achieved between the partners" (p. 792). Therefore evidence for fine tuning has accumulated for more than twenty years.

Morphosyntactic Tuning

There exists broad, almost general, agreement as to the existence of morphosyntactic tuning. In a field as controversy-prone as developmental psycholinguistics, this indicates a very robust phenomenon. Evidence for such tuning goes back to the earliest studies of Broen (1972), Moerk (1972) and Snow (1972). It was confirmed by Phillips (1973), by Moerk (1975a), and by Cross (1977). Snow, Perlmann and Nathan (1987) provided an extensive, though by far not complete listing of pertinent studies. Snow (1995) followed this up with a concise summary. The present discussion can therefore be brief and does not need to present a comprehensive survey of almost 30 years of literature.

Acoustic-Perceptual Tuning

Discussion in preceding sections has shown how mothers adapt their prosodic input to the perceptual needs of the child. Whether it is the slower presentation of utterances, the extended pauses between constituents, the even more extended pauses between sentences, and the exaggerated intonation contours stressing the most important elements, all are adjustments to the processing limitations and inclinations of the young infant. They make perceptual segmentation easier and in this manner provide many chances for initiating semantic-syntactic analyses.

Quantitative Fine Tuning

Quantitatively, the relationships between the children's and the mother's syntactic complexity have generally been expressed through comparisons of their MLUs (Mean Length of Utterance). Early studies were in quite close agreement as to the existence and closeness of this fine tuning. Cazden (1972, p. 106) therefore already felt justified to conclude: "Where some aspect of mother's speech has been tracked over a period of time, it has been found to increase gradually in complexity as the child's speech does." Phillips (1973) added a descriptive refinement by specifying that mothers become more consistent in the complexity of their utterances at the transition from the preverbal to the verbal period, that is, from the infants' age of 8 months to 18 and 28 months. This specification is important regarding arguments against syntactic fine tuning, as it demonstrates that mothers are aware of the infants processing needs and capacities. This conclusion was confirmed by Cross and Morris (1980). Quantitative syntactic fine tuning would be of little use before infants begin analyzing the input. Moerk (1974a) added another feature in reporting not only an increase in maternal MLU but also an increase in the mother's lead over the child's level. That is, when children become more able to face greater linguistic challenges, mothers provide these. This finding also indicates that both maternal tuning and maternal lead in MlU have to be considered in the evaluation of the degree and timing of fine tuning. Bohannon and Marquis (1977) and Bruner (1975, 1978) supported empirically and argued theoretically the fact and the importance of syntactic fine tuning. Confirming studies could be massed; but it is evident that even in the 1970s the evidence was overwhelming.

Qualitative Fine Tuning

The most central qualitative feature of morphosyntactic fine tuning is that educated adults make almost no mistakes when talking to their small children (Broen, 1972; Brown, 1973). No false starts or ungrammatical sentences occur—

though sentence fragments are not uncommon, simplifying the analytic task. Neither do adults produce numerous passive or other complex constructions when speaking to their babies. The few complex constructions that are encountered in well rehearsed formulas of everyday pragmatic utility do not need to be syntactically analyzed by the young children to be understood.

Semantic-syntactic correspondence, as documented in detail by Rondal and Cession (1990) in the mother's models, aids syntax learning. For example, in maternal utterances addressed to children, agents are almost always in subject position. This simplifying technique of the mother makes it easier for the child to see the equivalence between semantic and syntactic categories, as was argued by Schlesinger (1971). More sophisticated syntactic simplifications and clarifications have been demonstrated by Moerk (1985a) by showing how mothers analyze and synthesize syntactic structures for their children and how they train the abstraction of underlying schemas from surface strings. He demonstrated several thousands of these exercises in the 20 hours of mother–child interaction studied. As analytic, synthetic, and abstracting processes need to be performed by children to master language productively, it is seen that the mother/expert models these skills in the manner that a master guides an apprentice in the performance of complex tasks.

When mothers increase the complexity of the input, they do this gradually for specific sentence constituents also. Moore (1965) already specified features of this increasing complexity: He reported that from periods I–V, as categorized by Brown (1973), the mothers of the children Adam, Eve, and Sarah, gradually increased the length of their predicate noun phrases. Fraser and Roberts (1975), studying children in the age range of one and a half to six, found increases in both grammatical complexity and vocabulary diversity. Moerk (1975a) demonstrated "a high level of calibration" both quantitatively and qualitatively (p. 792) even in cross-sectional studies.

When parents expand, extend, correct, or recast filial utterances, this almost necessarily entails fine tuning. They add one or a few items while maintaining the message content and most of its form. Whereas the topic of expansions, extensions, and corrections, or negative evidence has never been specifically explored in respect to its features of fine tuning, it is almost self-evident that most forms of immediate feedback, whether expansions (McLean & Vincent, 1984; Moerk, 1983b; Scherer & Olswang, 1984), corrections, negative evidence (Farrar, 1992; Moerk, 1991, 1994; Saxton, 1993), or substitutions (Sokolov, 1993), generally presume multiple aspects of fine tuning, especially morphological fine tuning. This research is surveyed in Chapter 5, when corrections are discussed.

More complex syntactic constructions, such as those involving multiple adverbials, complex verb phrases, and more intricate subordinate sentences, are not included in the present survey. All of these advances only become common during later developmental periods, including the primary and secondary schools. Developmental progress in these constructions is again incrementally achieved through systematic educational endeavors. However, the enormous educational literature surpasses the scope of this review.

MAJOR OBJECTIONS TO FINE TUNING

Objections to the existence of fine tuning became common during the later 1970s to the early 1990s. They took two forms, one based only on logical arguments, the other on presumed empirical counterevidence. The logical arguments seem to be based on two rationales that can be dealt with quite succinctly.

The Logical Arguments

First, it is asserted that mothers are intent on communication but not on any form of language teaching. It is asserted that mothers, who are busy with many practical tasks, could not be expected to attend to the exact level of the child in order to fine tune their speech to it (Pine, 1992). Communicative tuning might be acceptable but not linguistic tuning. The second rationale asserts (e.g., Shatz, 1982) that an "omniscient mother" would be needed to know how to adjust to her child's level. Durkin (1978) went even further in mystifying the dynamics by arguing that the "caregiver is innately tuned to the emergent abilities of the infant" (p. 109). However, far less mystical principles are required.

The logical answer to the first argument is straightforward, as Moerk (1986) for first and Krashen (1985) for second language learning have shown: Instead of a conflict existing between communication and instructional fine tuning, effective communication requires attentive tuning to the processing capacities and needs of each communication partner. The principle underlying fine tuning is very prosaic: Speakers mainly fine tune their communication based on the fairly immediate feedback they receive from their particular listeners as to the latters' comprehension of the preceding message or the lack of it. This has been repeatedly confirmed by investigators (e.g., Bohannon & Marquis, 1977; dePaulo & Coleman, 1986). Speakers therefore follow the general rule "to behave so as to be understood"(Franco & D'Odorico, 1985), that is, they follow Grice's (1975) Cooperative Principle of speaking in a manner to be understood.

A certain degree of fine tuning to the level of the communication partner is therefore a necessary and unavoidable aspect of successful communication. For communication partners of unequal proficiency, the expert wanting to convey a message has to help the apprentice to understand its form and elements. That is, she (mostly the mother) has to simplify, analyze, and clarify its elements and relations. The same applies to any shared activity between an expert and an apprentice: If an apprentice is to cooperate with an expert, the latter has to simplify the task structure for the former. In contrast to the arguments of Shatz (1982) regarding an "omniscient mother" and of Durkin (1978) pertaining to an "innately attuned caregiver," the mother only has to be somewhat alert to the child's signal of noncomprehension in order to maintain adequate levels of fine tuning in her verbal input.

A minor, but theoretically important, shift in the argument is entailed in the word "adequate" in the preceding sentence. The term adequate is employed to signify that a principle of "satisficing," in Simon's (1990) terminology, is sufficient—that is, reaching good-enough solutions. "Optimizing" (again in Simon's terminology) is not needed and mothers do not and need not always remain fine tuned to their children. Sometimes they increase the linguistic lead—whether accidentally or because they can rely on the nonverbal context to disambiguate the message, and sometimes one or two messages overtax the capacities of the child, whereupon repair sequences are mostly instituted (Bohannon & Stanowicz, 1988).

The logical and practical implications of the above arguments deserve explicating: If the main goal is effective communication, then the linguistic complexity of the utterances can vary with the familiarity of the message and the amount of contextual support. For example, picture captions and conversations about pictures can be more complex because the picture disambiguates the message. The complexity of a specific message might also have been built up over weeks and months of repetitions. Even apparently complex messages might therefore be easily decoded, based on such a learning history. In such cases, the investigator who studies only a brief section of interactions would be puzzled by the apparent lack of fine tuning in such cases and would come to incorrect conclusions—due to his methodological choice. This points again to the pitfalls of brief cross-sectional recordings, as explained in Chapter 2.

Whereas filial comprehension as the basis for fine tuning has been emphasized above, a second principle is perhaps even more strongly suggested by the extensive literature on filial imitations and maternal expansions/extensions, as summarized most comprehensively in Speidel and Nelson (1989). Children are prone to imitate relatively new elements in adult models and they regularly omit minor elements when they have to deal with utterances that are too complex for their present level. Parents rather consistently expand or extend those imitations, showing thereby their awareness of the omissions. As the children show their level of readiness through their imitative productions, the mothers can barely avoid being aware of it. Brown and Bellugi (1964) have already reported on the quasi-compulsion adults experience to provide the completions and corrections. Again no mystical principle is needed to explain this second basis of fine tuning. Both these well-supported phenomena undermine the logical arguments against fine tuning.

The Presumed Counterevidence

Next, the supposed empirical evidence against fine tuning needs to be considered. In comparison with the broadly employed arguments against fine tuning, it is astonishing how few empirical studies are quoted in support of these arguments. One single study, that of Newport, Gleitman, and Gleitman (1977) (NGG in the following) is almost universally relied upon. It therefore deserves closer attention. One interpretive sentence of this study, especially, is quoted repeatedly: "There is no compelling evidence in our data that mothers tune their syntactic complexity to the growing language competence of their children through this crucial age of syntax acquisition, the period from one to two and a half years" (pp. 123–124). This statement needs to be related to the numerical evidence the authors provide.

As to mother to child speech, the authors report that its MLU is much smaller than adult–adult speech; the speech is "highly intelligible," and it is "unswervingly well formed" (p. 121). All the measured differences between M–C and A–A speech are highly significant statistically. These reports of NGG indicate at least considerable rough tuning to the child's level. Some specific correlations are worth mentioning: Correlations between M imperatives and C language complexity are negative and range from −.35 to −.72; between M declaratives and C mean number of noun phrases per utterance they range from .33 to .69. The authors conclude therefore "these maternal speech features are apparently adjusted in detail to characteristics of the listener" (p. 125), that is, the child!

The following correlations suggest even cause–effect relationships by indicating that maternal input was well adapted to the children's learning needs and capacities: Maternal deixis correlated with the children's estimated vocabulary: $r = .62$; exact imitation plus expansions with C's vocabulary: $r = .79$. For partial imitation with expansions and "every measure of child sophistication" r ranges from .52 to .88. Finally, measures of M self-repetition and C age $r = −.55$ (all these data on p. 129); M self-repetition and measures of child sophistication: $r = −.68, −.69$ (p. 130). In Table 5.3, on page 132 the authors summarize measures of child growth in their relation to measures of maternal speech. In one of the columns, that for C auxiliaries/verb phrase, out of 10 correlations only two are below .20 and several are in the fifties and one is .88. The child's MLU shows similarly close relationships with maternal input. On page 133 the authors conclude therefore that "certain language-specific aspects of the child's speech seem to be influenced rather dramatically in their rate of growth by aspects of the mother's usage." This last interpretation of the authors is obviously not just restricted to fine tuning but extends to the much stronger inference of cause–effect relationships.

The contrast between the often quoted "no compelling evidence" (pp. 123–124) and the quote just given is impressive, even if the two quotes do not directly contradict each other. While one might be cautious regarding the strong causal conclusion of the last quote, all the above correlations suggests close interdependencies between mothers and children. That not more of the substantial correlations are statistically significant is a function of the small N of 15 dyads. The r-squared, as indications of effect size, provide strong evidence that the interdependencies are functionally important. This, even brief, reanalysis suggests that Rondal's judgment (Rondal, 1985) from a decade ago still stands: "that Newport et al.'s . . . implications regarding the lack of significant middle-term effects of mothers' speech on children's speech are not valid" (p. 118).

Can the contrast found in NGG be resolved? Whereas space constraints do not permit this fully, a solution can be briefly indicated. The authors presumed an expected instructional curriculum (pp. 122–123), based on common sense and on foreign language teaching, but did not find exactly this curriculum employed by the mothers. They concluded therefore there was no maternal tuning, even if there was much what they interpreted as maternal effect. Also, it should be noted that as early as pages one and three of their report the authors insist on nativistic interpretations of first language acquisition. Fine tuning has always been seen as one central factor, together with corrections, that invalidates nativistic postulates. Nativists and NGG insist on "a haphazard, disorganized sample of sentences [that] is partly degenerate (containing false starts, mumbles and ungrammatical sentences) and is only loosely tied to referents and situations the child observer could perceive " (NGG, p. 111). With these assumptions, it is not astonishing that the authors came to the conclusion seen in the first quote, even in spite of their own empirical evidence. What might be astonishing is that researchers over almost 20 years repeated the conclusion without checking the empirical evidence that accompanied it.

Two further studies are sometimes quoted that seem to refute a fine tuning hypothesis. These two studies, of seemingly secondary importance, one by Snow (1977) and the other by Nelson, Denninger, Bonvillian, Kaplan, and Baker (1984) can not be evaluated in the same detail as the one of Newport and associates (1977). Yet a brief description is in order to assess them:

On page nine Snow (1977) presents unquestionable trends in maternal linguistic input within the age range between three months and eighteen months. She therefore correctly summarizes that "the speech of Ann's and Mary's mothers did change strikingly between three months and eighteen months in terms of what they were talking about" (p. 7). Yet, Figure 1 shows no consistent trends for the MLUs for the same age range. But why should MLUs change (if mothers are tuned to their children) during a period when the children were producing either no words or were in the one-word stage? If the mother follows the lead of the child, as reported in many studies (Menyuk et al., 1995; Moerk, 1975a), then lack of change in the children's MLU should be accompanied by lack of change in the mothers' sentence complexity. Only clearly demonstrated changes in comprehension of longer linguistic constructions, of which Snow provides no evidence and which at this age could not be based on syntactic analyses, would suggest that maternal MLU should have increased. Snow's finding of a lack of change in maternal MLU therefore suggests maternal fine tuning—in contrast to the conclusion that was drawn by some authors.

Nelson and associates (1984) correlated maternal and filial MLU not longitudinally but across dyads and admitted that "mothers varied enormously in how widely their utterance lengths exceeded their children" (p. 32). This admission implies that the low correlations they found reflect the confounding impact of dyadic style variables and little else. The authors report that maternal MLU did not differ (4.00

and 4.02, respectively) at 22 and 27 months, while the children's MLU differed: 1.48 and 2.19 words per utterance at 22 and 27 months. This unchanging maternal MLU is especially astonishing because the authors also reported a considerable difference for both mothers and children in auxiliary use: .218 and 2.46 for the mothers and .024 and .067 per verb for the children. If auxiliary verbs are more frequent at the later age, it would seem sentences should be longer too, if the increase was not compensated by some other decreases—none being mentioned. In accordance with the reported maternal difference, the authors draw "a conclusion of maternal adjustment to the child's increased production of auxiliaries" (p. 33). They even reported that maternal use of auxiliaries at 22 months predicted child auxiliary use at 27 months (r = .62), a seemingly causal relationship. Generally the authors demonstrated "contingent maternal replies as predictors of children's syntactic growth" (p. 36), that is, not only fine tuning but effects of such fine tuning. That Nelson and associates (1984) would have been cited in the subsequent literature as evidence for lack of fine tuning can certainly not be due to their findings.

Kaye (1980) is also sometimes cited as showing lack of tuning. Yet this author would certainly not agree with this interpretation, as indicated by the data he reports and even more by the "apprenticeship metaphor" developed in Kaye (1982). Apprenticeship implies, of course, fine tuned adjustment of the expert to the learning needs of the apprentice. Kaye is therefore clearly a proponent of fine tuning and he (1980) specifically concludes that mothers adjust their language in accordance with their expectations of the infants' competence.

It can be concluded—and the writer challenges the field to falsify this conclusion—that none of the studies providing presumed evidence against fine tuning stands up to careful scrutiny. In contrast, most of these studies provide evidence for fine tuning, if the latter is taken literally, that mothers tune their behavior to the lack of change, or the change, respectively, in their children's pertinent linguistic productions; and only production variables were measured in these studies.

A RECENT CONSENSUS ON FINE TUNING?

The decades from around 1975 to the early 1990s were replete with the controversies described above. Towards the end of this period, however, it appears that positive relationships between filial language level and input phenomena are again becoming, at least tacitly, accepted. Wells (1985) provided rich and convincing evidence for a broad array of fine tuning phenomena which include syntactic, morphological, as well as vocabulary aspects. Hayes and Ahrens (1988) reported very similar findings. Moerk (1992) found fine tuning in the course of the acquisition of various syntactic constructions as well as changes in this fine tuning for each specific construction over the course of the acquisition process. Farrar (1992) and Moerk (1991, 1994), while focusing on corrections, provided strong support that this feedback, provided predominantly in the form of grammatical morphemes, is well tuned to the learning needs of the child. Shirai and Andersen (1995), too, found that the speech of caretakers has the same distributional patterns as the speech of the children for tense-aspect morphology, that is, it is adapted to the children's speech. Specifically for the training of the future and past morphemes, Moerk (1992) has presented abundant data on maternal fine tuning and argued for a cybernetic model to understand the training and learning process. Similarly, Sokolov (1993) could show for modals, pronouns, and nouns that fine tuning is developmentally sensitive. In general, the more carefully investigators look, the more evidence they find for fine tuning.

Speidel (1987) discussed verbal interactional tuning for second language training in educational settings, where, since it cannot be individualized, it necessarily has to appear more as rough tuning. She correctly emphasized that the "fine" in fine tuning needs to be defined more circumspectly, yet she generally confirmed the principle of tuning in these contexts. Of course, the entire grade progression in school, and the readiness concept underlying it, reflects such a system of tuning that has its roots in Comenius (1592–1670), as mentioned in the Introduction. Lack of sufficient tuning results in failures and dropping out, as is well known from practical experience.

Both fathers and mothers adopt *motherese* in speaking to their children (Ratner, 1988; Rondal, 1985), that is, both adjust their speech to changes in the child's language, although fathers might do it less consistently as the child's language mastery increases (Tomasello, Conti-Ramsden & Ewert, 1990). A combination of fine tuning by mothers and rough tuning by fathers, peers, and teachers might present an ideal opportunity for linguistic progress because it combines support with challenges. With this last conclusion, iterative increases in input complexity are indicated. Increases can involve syntactic complexity, morphological completeness, and shifts in processing requirements as well as in cognitive demands. When mothers change from modeling items to testing them, they shift from reliance on recognition memory to recall memory. And when they shift semantically from the here-and-now to the there-and-then, that is, the training of the "distancing function" (Sigel, 1986), both recall memory and abstraction are involved. Menyuk and associates (1995) emphasize therefore correctly "the mothers' knowledge that more can be given and asked of the baby in terms of conversation" (p. 158).

Power (1985) reported from a broad semantic and cognitive perspective how parents adapt their teaching to the age and competency level of their children. From sensorimotor interaction in the here-and-now, they shift to verbal behavior and pretend play, and to complex relational play behavior. Parents therefore follow a "training curriculum" in response to their children's level of competence. Fine tuned adjustments are also attested to across organic differences in children. Only a few examples of the extensive literature shall suffice: Nienhuys, Cross, and Horsborough (1984) compared maternal speech styles to deaf and hearing children and found that mothers made adjustments of linguistic variables, of interaction style, and of syntactic complexity. Gallaway and associates (1990) found a similarly high correlation between children's and mothers' utterance length in hearing impaired children. Such adaptations to the child's level are also found when mothers interact with their Down's syndrome children (Mahoney, 1983; Rondal, 1978).

From this recent evidence, and following from the nature of the information processing demands, it must be concluded that various degrees of fine tuning are quite securely established for diverse populations of language-learning children (Cross, Nienhuys & Kirkman, 1985). Otherwise, of course, mother and child could not communicate effectively. While many unresolved problems regarding specific measurement operations remain, the focus can be turned to the effects of fine tuning.

EFFECTS OF FINE TUNING

A strong causal claim was made when fine tuning was postulated as a prerequisite for second language learning in Krashen's (1980) "input hypothesis" which focuses on "comprehensible input." In order to be comprehensible, the input has to maintain a certain degree of tuning. In this general postulate, multiple aspects and effects of fine tuning are still undifferentiated. Quantitative and qualitative aspects of fine tuning need to be differentiated as to their effects. On the quantitative side, Heckhausen's (1987) "step-ahead strategy," what Krashen (1985) labeled an "$i +$ 1 level" have to be differentiated from tuning on the same level or even on a simpler one. In accordance with Heckhausen's and Krashen's conclusions, Silverman and Geiringer (1973) showed that the positive influence was greater when the model calibrated the input one stage above rather than two stages above child's level.

This last report raises the question as to the optimal level of tuning and variability or stability of this level. Indications for the advantage of larger gaps, but still within the range of rough tuning, are found in reports of picture book reading. Whitehurst, Falco, and associates (1988) have developed the dialogic reading method, which guides parents to transcend the simple labeling and to proceed to comments about pictures and about related personal experiences. Extensive research on the impact of picture books in language learning (Moerk, 1985c; Whitehurst et al., 1988; and the contributors to Dickinson, 1994) have shown how parents proceed from training mostly simple labels, to descriptions of activities, then to descriptions of minor features, or even the explanation of causal relationships. Yet, as mentioned repeatedly, the swift progress in picture book reading is made more feasible because the pictures support the interpretation of the verbal input.

After providing models on a level of complexity the child has already mastered, mothers might (repeatedly) maximally challenge their children in specific but changing language aspects and this challenge seems to lead within a period of a few weeks to a spurt-like progression in the children's homologous verbal productions (Moerk, 1992). There are also multiple reports of differential tuning of fathers and mothers, with fathers being more challenging and therefore contributing a special challenge. These questions remain largely unanswered and represent challenges for the optimal design of interventions.

Besides instructional effects, emotional and motivational consequences of fine tuning, or its lack, are perhaps even more important than purely linguistic aspects. Lack of fine tuning will result in frequent miscommunications and the need for repair processes. Such frequent breakdowns probably produce frustration and avoidance reactions, if one can generalize from L2 learners. Lack of satisfactory tuning in some families might therefore also explain the negative attitudes toward language and verbal interactions children acquire.

For the present concern, L1 acquisition, immediate effects of fine tuning can usefully be differentiated from long-term effects. Immediate effects are easier to substantiate, although they require relatively unfamiliar statistical approaches, based on transitional probabilities or Markov-chain models. A methodologically adequate evaluation of long-term effects would need to employ multivariate longitudinal methodology and require large samples. Because most methodological and substantive improvements remain an unfulfilled challenge, as indicated in Chapter 2, the conclusions presented below have to be considered as preliminary, almost certainly underestimating the effects of fine tuning that could be demonstrated with more advanced methods.

Immediate Effects

Immediate effects are implicated whenever feedback cycles are discussed. Such immediate effects have often been reported, though diverse terminologies were employed for the maternal or experimental interventions: "Expansions" (Brown & Bellugi, 1964), "extensions" (Cross, 1977), "recasts" (Nelson, 1977) are some of the best known concepts. All these labels implicate a similar principle of fine tuning because the adult retains the child's topic and makes only minor improvements or changes in the form of the preceding utterance of the child. Because adults make *improvements*, immediate positive effects on filial language learning become probable and can be ascertained. The entire topic of "corrections" or "negative feedback" and its effects fall under this heading, but this has been dealt with previously in Moerk (1991, 1994, 1996) and is surveyed more extensively in Chapter 5.

A considerable numbers of studies have shown that such contingent fine tuning, whatever the label employed, very often results in contingent improvement in one of the child's subsequent utterances. From Slobin's (1968) report it is known that about 50 percent of such expansions result in immediate improvements in the child's subsequent utterance. Accordingly, Snow, Dubber and de Blauw (1985) summarized from many studies (Cross,1978; Furrow, Nelson, & Benedict, 1979; Wells, 1978; Wells, Barnes & Gutfreund, & Satterly, 1983) that children learn to talk more quickly if their mothers provide a large proportion of conversational responses that are semantically contingent on the children's own utterance and that fall within limits of complexity matched to the child's own level. Semantically contingent utterances are, by definition, optimally semantically matched. Most processing resources can therefore be focused on the linguistic aspects of the utterances and are not required for deciphering the meaning. Moerk (1983b, 1985b, 1990) has provided many detailed demonstrations of the varieties of fine tuned feedback and of their effects on subsequent filial utterances. Scherer and Olswang (1984) did this specifically for expansions. Bonvillian, Raeburn, and Horan (1979) could show that models spoken near the children's rate of speech (another aspect of tuning), and level of complexity were imitated more successfully than more dissimilar models. Sokolov (1993) more recently has confirmed such contingent fine tuning with many correlations between parental and filial variables reaching .90 and above.

Long-Term and More Global Effects

Long-term, global effects of fine tuning per se are more difficult to prove unambiguously since multiple causal factors that are highly intercorrelated might produce the effects. Mothers who are motivated and attentive enough to fine tune their input and feedback will very probable produce multiple additional adjustments to the child's language learning needs that facilitate progress. Even if high correlations are found, or high percentages of variance are accounted for by a selected antecedent variable, caution as to the causal interpretation is desirable.

To establish concomitant variation, studies of lack of fine tuning and the resulting effects are perhaps the clearest sources of information. Bee and associates (1969) and Hess and Shipman (1967, 1972) have provided the earliest evidence for the negative effects of lack of fine tuning. Much of the discussion in Chapter 6 is relevant to this topic, even if the diverse authors often reported mainly on input deficits, and lack of fine tuning is only indirectly demonstrated. A very defective input is, however, also probably not fine tuned. Some transcripts mentioned in Chapter 6 reveal the astonishing phenomenon that a mother was not only unable to get a message across to her child over pages of a transcript, but even unable to elicit any verbal response: certainly an extreme lack of tuning between mother and child. As to be expected, even toddlers in such situations were already greatly delayed in their language skills.

On the positive side, the reports on long-term effects of fine tuning are numerous. Cross (1975) reported correlations of .72 and .84 between maternal MLU and filial MLU (of the 50 longest utterances) and filial receptive level, respectively. She concluded therefore that "mothers of accelerated children are sensitively tuned in" (p. 126). In a later report, Cross (1977) found correlations of around .50 between measures of maternal length of utterance and filial measures of language production. Furrow and associates (1979), by reporting large cause–effect relationships of fine tuning at the age of 18 months on language levels at 27 months and negative effects of lack of fine tuning, provide additional support for these dynamics. The same authors found simplicity of input to be an effective teaching strategy for young children. They obtained many correlations in the range of .70 to .80 and higher between simple maternal speech, provided at the age of 18 months, when the child's language mastery is still quite rudimentary, and filial language development nine months later. Hampson and Nelson (1993) specified that 79 percent of the variance of child MLU at 20 months could be accounted for by maternal fine tuning in the form of referential repetition seven months earlier. Moerk (1992) graphically demonstrated how maternal fine tuned modeling resulted in steep filial advances in the specific language skills trained. For such young ages an almost minimal gap is an optimal gap and produces long-term effects fairly reliably. Watkins (1988) reported that even preverbal fine tuning is predictive of child's later receptive language development. Murray, Johnson, and Peters (1990) found also that the mother's fine tuning during the preverbal period accounted for 86 percent of the variance in the child's receptive ability nine months later. Furrow, Nelson and Benedict (1979) recounted impressively high correlations between fine tuned maternal speech at 18 months (still in the one-word stage) and child language mastery nine months later. Effect sizes for factors of semantic and syntactic complexity, computed from squared correlation coefficients, were largely around 50 percent and up to 64 or even 81 percent.

Experimentally, Baker and Nelson (1984) and Nelson and associates (1984) have demonstrated the long-term effect of recasting, which is a form of fine tuning. The effects are especially evident in their intervention approaches with children who had previously been relatively deprived of this maternal teaching technique. In educational settings, which are broad-based interventions, Speidel (1987) could demonstrate statistically significant improvements in grammatical mastery for elementary school children following fine tuned conversational interventions.

Even these few reports, which could be massed, indicate multiple positive impacts of fine tuning on language acquisition from the preverbal period to the school level, whether immediately or long-term. Such a cause–effect relationship could have been expected from established knowledge of skill learning and from the field of education. It could almost be considered a tautology that effective teaching has to be fine tuned to the processing capacities of the learner. The progress in language skills shown by many children prove that such effective teaching is common; the complementary failures of others, as discussed in Chapters 6 and 7, can be related to its absence.

SUMMARY AND DISCUSSION

The wide range of phenomena reflecting fine tuning, independent of the labels they have been assigned, was reviewed in a brief introductory section. This review showed that in many domains of training and learning, but especially in apprenticeship situations, fine tuning is considered a prerequisite for success. Then, the conversational evidence, from the preverbal period to morphosyntactic training and learning, was briefly summarized. It could be shown on the basis of many studies that diverse forms of fine tuning extend from the acoustic-perceptual level to the highest layer of language, morphological and syntactic skills. Several puzzles encountered in the literature pertaining to lack of maternal changes over some time periods were clarified by emphasizing that changes in input need to be matched to changes in filial performance in order to be fine tuned. If no clear changes in filial performance are observable, such as during the preverbal period, no changes in maternal verbal behavior should logically be expected, presuming fine tuning to filial language level and not just to age.

A critical evaluation of the methodological and conceptual issues can be condensed in three points: (a) a biased use of evidence, (b) a confusion as to what fine tuning is tuned to, and (c) a neglect of the level of the aimed-at end product: simple formulaic training with much repetitions might require much less fine tuning than training for optimal progress to high levels of language skills.

The Use of Evidence

Major clarifications also seemed required in regard to both logical objections to fine tuning and even more to presumed counter-evidence to it. It should be a matter of course, that in the evaluation of a controversy *all* evidence is considered and evaluated quasi in a meta-analysis. What often happened in the studies surveyed was that only the evidence that supported a nativistic ideology was selected and contrasting evidence was neglected. The problem often lay not so much with the authors but with those who eagerly and frequently quoted one interpretive statement and completely neglected the evidence provided. Some authors were even cited as witnesses against fine tuning although they had emphatically argued for fine tuning. Such biased selection from previous research is useful in defending an ideology but not in providing the basis for scientific falsification (Popper, 1962) of hypotheses.

The data, in contrast to the interpretations, often indicated considerable fine tuning and quite often also effects of this fine tuning. Both immediate effects and more long-term global ones could be made plausible on the basis of many studies. Especially impressive is the evidence from the *modus tollens* perspective, that lack of fine tuning (certainly combined with other factors, as discussed in Chapter 3) seems to result in extensive language delay.

The Diverse Comparison Standards for Fine Tuning

Logically, the basis of effective fine tuning have, of course, to be the processing needs of the infant and child. Two questions arise from this logical principle: (a) How can and do untrained mothers know those needs, if even researchers might differ greatly in their evaluations? (b) Can those needs be presumed to change monotonically with age to justify concepts and correlational methods based on rectilinear assumptions? It was seen that such a monotonic, age-based presumption was the basis from which some authors inferred lack of fine tuning when no maternal change was found over a specific age period. In answer to the first question, the behavior of the children should be considered a much more plausible causal factor that guides mothers than age per se. Filial behaviors could consist of indicators of comprehension or they could be, more clearly and less ambiguously, the immediately preceding productions of the child. From almost all the studies cited it appears that filial productions mainly resulted in fine tuned maternal feedback. This principle explains how most busy and preoccupied mothers could be mostly fine tuned: Just a second before their reply, they had listened to the child's somewhat imperfect utterance, and they adapted their reply to it. (This argument does not deny that some tuning could also be based on memory of more remote performances and on more general criteria—especially in the case of adults encountering unknown children. The various bases of tuning still need to be explored.)

Maternal changes should therefore be expected together with filial changes in production. This logical conclusion is in close accord with the findings, both that maternal input changes little in purely linguistic aspects during the preverbal period, and that later changes shift from vocabulary to diverse morphosyntactic aspects when the infant starts producing some of them.

When emphasizing filial productions as the most immediate guide for the mother, the changes in principles over the developmental period need, however, to be reemphasized. The early tuning to the perceptual and emotional needs of the young infant is well documented and might be of great importance for the development of "social communion" (Malinowski, 1923), that is, the enjoyment of first vocal and then verbal interactions. The principles and the immediate effects of fine tuning change profoundly when the interactions become increasingly verbal. Then the tuning would be more directed to informational efficiency, making sure children learned that they could "do things with words" (Austin, 1962) and gain rewards effortlessly. This is the typical situation of skilled performance when an expert and an apprentice cooperate in solving a task. It is most clearly seen in "foreigner talk" (Wesche, 1994) which is adapted to the comprehension constraints of the foreign interlocutor. With the dyadic goal being to be understood and to understand, the communicative function intrinsically entails an instructional aspect—for the expert to clarify his message sufficiently to get it across and also to disambiguate the learner's message to understand it. The more complex the intended messages, and the less they are supported by nonverbal contextual cues, the more the language code has to be mastered.

The Aspired End Product Impacting Training

The emphasis on varying task-complexity leads directly to a further consideration, the intended end product or the level of language skills striven for. As very simple tasks require little teaching, so very simple goals, such as effectively transmitting routine commands, require little fine tuning. Frequent repetitions in standard situations, with responses modeled by older siblings, might suffice for such rote learning. Wong-Fillmore's (1976) descriptions of immigrant children learning formulas on the playground provides good pertinent evidence. If a narrow range of standing formulas suffices for most adult functioning, then extensive rehearsal of these formulas in consistent contexts might suffice. Therefore fine tuning should vary between social classes and probably also between cultures of differing technological-bureaucratic levels of development.

Regarding social class differences, as focused on more extensively in Chapter 6, Hess and Shipman (1967, 1972) reported that the teaching of some mothers reflected a failure to understand the child's needs and limitations, that is, that it was not well tuned to the child. Similarly, Bee and associates (1969) found middle-class mothers to be generally more in tune with the child's individual needs and qualities than lower-class mothers. Many conceptually related reports about the negative impact on language acquisition of maternal directiveness (e.g., Nelson, 1973; Pine, 1992; Rocissano & Yatchmink, 1983) entail similar principles. A directive style, found more in lower SES families, entails simple and rather unchanging input that is tuned to the wishes of the adults but minimally tuned to the informational requirements of the children. Considering longer-term effects of this lack of tuning, it is only too well known that many lower-class children have difficulties in mastering those school requirements that require increasingly CALP (cognitive-academic language proficiency) aspects of language.

Cross-cultural differences are presented in some detail in Chapter 7. Only the general principle is stated here: Often universality of fine tuning is implicitly presumed and then argued against based on scanty evidence. Yet, the standard of Western middle-class families and the learning needs of their children entail, obviously, different goals and therewith instructional methods that differ from those in extremely dissimilar cultural settings. While some aspects of baby talk, those reflecting the attentional and perceptual tendencies of young infants, might be more generally found (as long as there is an interest in early interaction), more advanced aspect should differ with cultural needs. The available cross-cultural evidence does, therefore, seem to support the efficacy of fine tuning as well as its necessity for producing high-level language skills.

In the field of skill training, the relationship of fine tuning to goal levels has been regarded as self-evident. Burton and associates (1984), for example, argue for skill learning: "clarifying the top-level goal may imply a different standard of measurement for the hierarchical ordering of the subskills and a corresponding change in the sequence of microworlds" (p. 145) that are designed for training purposes. In any skill and especially in competitive sports, the training is, of course, fully designed or oriented toward the goals to be attained and also tuned to the changing competence levels of the learner. In a gradual and incremental fashion each advance of the learner is followed by a change in near-term goals, in training contents, and consequently also in training methods. Yet, these promising insights from skill-learning have only rarely been employed for a clearer conceptualization of language learning (Moerk, 1986).

While the preceding remarks were intended to elucidate controversial domains and hopefully to present new vistas, the practical implications deserve repetition: With large numbers of children in the United States who are neither linguistically nor cognitively prepared for elementary school, and with most developing countries intent on increasing the educational level of their populations, problem formulations are needed that accord with the complexities of real-life phenomena. Life's demands are not relativistic but elitist. As rapid technological and cultural change require increased language skills for large segments of the population, the optimal training methods should be expected to change with these demands. Fine tuning is probably one of the most effective training methods in an age when children should not only be heard but should develop into partners ready to engage in complex verbal interactions, as Baumrind (1971a, 1971b) described it so well.

5

Do They Learn From Corrective Feedback? Epistemological and Empirical Perspectives on 25 Years of Research on Corrections in L1 Transmission

> The adult glosses the child's utterance as just that simple sentence which, in view of all the circumstances, the child ought to have said and presumably did mean.
> —Brown (1973, p. 106)

The approach in this chapter is somewhat different from that employed in the other chapters. In the previous ones, the emphasis was mostly placed on the older literature, indicating how much could already have been known decades ago if investigators would only have searched disinterestedly. Once the point was well supported it was unnecessary to add all the most recent literature. In the present chapter, after a brief overall introduction to the controversy surrounding this topic, the emphasis is on the last two decades and specifically on the study of Morgan, Bonamo, and Travis (1995) (henceforth MBT). The reasons for this change deserve a brief explanation: First, Moerk (1991, 1994, 1996) has already presented three discussions of corrections. It would not be too meaningful to repeat everything that was said in these publications, especially as they are readily accessible for anyone. The second reason is that only in the later 1980s did the field begin to take account of the evidence for corrections to at least question the old dogma. The third reason is that MBT have presented a careful study, employing a method rather new in psychology, time-series analysis, which was recommended in Chapter 2 as an almost ideal approach for language acquisition research. Since this could be the beginning of important progress, a careful analysis seems advisable. Because their main methods, contingency analysis and time series analysis, are relatively little known, the danger exists that readers might accept trustingly the interpretations of MBT, whether they are correct or not. Therefore an attempt is made to clarify how misleading some of MBT's interpretations are and to show how interpretations and evidence contradict each other. The discussion is structured so that the cursory reader finds a summary of the evidence of MBT which strongly supports the existence and effectiveness of corrections. For the specialist in the field, exact tables and figures in MBT will be indicated where misinterpretations occurred so that independent evaluations are possible by going back to the original article. As causal time-series analyses encounter interpretative challenges generally, and especially in L1 acquisition, the causal interpretation of the interactions will be scrutinized carefully to clarify pitfalls and help avoid them in the future. It is shown that serious conceptual flaws mar the analyses of MBT, whereas the factual evidence proves both the existence and the impact of corrections on first language learning. Additional (mainly statistical) counterarguments to MBT's analyses are found in Bohannon, Padgett, Nelson, and Mark (1996).

The title of this chapters questions whether "they learn from corrective feedback." The referents of the "they" has intentionally been left ambiguous since this essay refers to two sets of learners, that is two sets of referents: One set is children learning their first or second language. The second set is researchers studying children learning their language. How readily do these researchers abandon cherished beliefs when disconfirming evidence suggests that they were incorrect?

The cherished old belief, the denial of the existence of corrections in the input provided to children learning their first language, is well known as is the resulting denial of learnability of language (Wexler & Culicover, 1980). In contrast to these denials, much factual evidence demonstrates both the existence of corrections and their impact on first language learning, as surveyed extensively by Moerk (1994). It is very briefly revisited in the first part of this chapter. After prolonged resistance to this evidence, the latest—and possibly the last, if researchers prove able to learn—of these denials is found in Morgan, Bonamo, and Travis (1995) who utilized an impressive array of approaches to bolster their arguments.

Because researchers are the second set of persons whose readiness to learn is questioned, a few words of epistemology are in order. It was already well known to Lavoisier (1745–1794), to Darwin (1859 reprinted 1966) and to Planck (1950), and many other scientists that researchers often find it difficult to accept evidence refuting their theories. Two conditions seem to contribute to this difficulty: (a) The more of their reputation scientists have invested in a position, the more difficult its abandonment becomes. Rare is the scientist who has the courage to recant his own previous pronouncements. (b) The more an individual's position is part of a larger ideology or a general paradigm, the more a refutation would threaten not only one specific hypothesis but the entire superstructure of the paradigm. Multiple denials and auxiliary hypotheses are employed in this case to protect the established ideology from new evidence. Popper's (1959) optimistic reliance on falsification as the major road to progress in science is therefore confronted with serious obstacles in these instances. With the presently dominant antiempirical paradigms, as surveyed in Chapter 1, a rejection of empirical counterevidence is even ideologically sanctioned.

Three versions of the cherished beliefs rejecting corrections have to be considered. They have been labeled: (a) the existence question, (b) the generality question, and (c) the effectiveness question. That is, (a) Are corrections provided? (b) Are they provided for all children and for all categories of mistakes? And (c) Are they effective by contributing to learning when provided? It is quite obvious, that questions (b) and (c) are fallback positions, in case the denial of the existence of corrections, which is the original position, cannot be maintained. These denials and their refutation will be briefly discussed below.

Before the argument is further developed, the concept "corrective feedback" in the title needs to be conceptually grounded. Multiple terms are employed in the field of first language acquisition when referring to corrective feedback. They range from "corrections," to "negative feedback," to "negative evidence" and to "negative instances." All these terms have the idea in common that children are shown that some of their utterances are incorrect or imperfect. Because the concept "incorrect" in the educational or linguistic sense is, of course, foreign to the young child, it would be more precise to say that children are shown that the adult's formulation, the presumed standard, is different from the utterance they had produced themselves. Other terms, such as "expansions" and "recasts," though entailing additional aspects, generally also refer to corrections of the child's incomplete formulations. MBT employ the term "corrective recasts" in order to more precisely specify this subset of "recasts." The present discussion mainly employs the terms "corrections" and "corrective feedback," largely disregarding these terminological variations. Only when specific arguments and findings pertaining to the differentiated subsets are referred to are the pertinent terms employed and explained.

A brief logical analysis is also required pertaining to the theoretically important concept of "negative instances." It is often asserted that learning—in the hypothesis testing sense—would be much easier if negative instances, that is, sentences that are not in the language, were available. But the almost unanimous assertion is that the child never encounters negative instances. This consensus appears astonishing if basic principles of skill learning and cognitive psychology (Simon, 1978) are considered. In these fields, learning often results from a comparison of a current state with a desired state by means of a difference-by-comparison heuristic (Simon, 1978). This principle appears directly applicable to dyadic interactions in first language acquisition. When children produce reduced or incomplete English, adults often expand and correct them, thereby designating the child's utterance as a negative instance. This feedback conveys the message: "This is not how one does it. Let me show you how to do it better." The child's own utterance is thereby characterized as a negative instance. Such a type of feedback is very familiar to the child from other domains of training since he is told very frequently: "Don't do it this way, let me show you the right way." From this consideration it follows that many utterances of children that are followed by expansions and corrections can function as negative instances. As children are very familiar with such interactional formats, they know how to interpret them, and could learn from them through the difference-by-comparison heuristic. If this argument is accepted, it follows that children are flooded with self-produced negative instances, which are characterized as such by adult feedback.

THE THEORETICAL CONTROVERSY IN RELATION TO ANALOGICAL LEARNING SITUATIONS

It is common sense knowledge that people (and animals) often learn from failures or errors. This principle applies across a wide range of species and learning contents, from operant conditioning of lowly animals to states and their governments ("No more appeasement," "The Vietnam syndrome"). Howard (1991) as well as Neustadt and May (1986) have extensively discussed such governmental historical learning from negative feedback. Certainly in any type of skill learning, feedback to incorrect or suboptimal performance has a very important function for the achievement of improvements (e.g. Newell, 1981, 1991). Similarly in second and foreign language instruction, corrective feedback has been provided almost universally (Faerch, 1985; Kasper, 1984; Schachter, 1984; Speidel, 1987, 1993). It would therefore be expected that this broad principle should also be applicable in first language acquisition. And so it seemed at the beginning.

In 1958, when describing the original word game, Roger Brown strongly emphasized the existence of corrections. Since much of the later denial is based on two of Brown's later statements, this earlier stance of Brown deserves brief documentation: Brown (1958, p. 194) argues : "the tutor ... improves the fit (between the tutee's label and the tutor's standard) by correction." Brown repeats the same argument about correction on page 220. Later Brown and Bellugi report that "a reduced or incomplete English sentence seems to constrain the English-speaking adult to expand it into the nearest properly formed sentence" (Brown & Bellugi, 1964, p. 140). Brown's (1973) description of "expansions" and their functions also appear to emphasize their corrective functions "the adult built up the child's utterance into a well-formed sentence by adding words, mostly but not exclusively functors," (p. 105) and "the adult glosses the child's utterance as just that simple sentence, which in view of all the circumstances, the child ought to have said" (p. 106) and "expansions (could be) a potentially valuable training technique" (p.106). Note that Brown describes, with the exception of Brown (1958), morphosyntactic corrections by referring to a standard ("ought to have said"), and thereby to a technique for syntax training. Even more affirming of corrections and their possible impact is Brown and Hanlon's (1970) assertion that "repeats of ill-formed utterances usually contained corrections and so could be instructive; repeats of well-formed utterances would not be corrections" (p. 43). Brown's position regarding corrections was therefore quite accepting and positive. But this admission of corrections was almost never referred to by later investigators: an interesting case of selective attention.

The turnabout came with two statements of Brown and associates (Brown, Cazden, & Bellugi, 1969; Brown & Hanlon, 1970) where Brown and Hanlon assert that "in neither case is there a shred of evidence that approval and disapproval are contingent on syntactic correctness" (p. 47). The denial of contingent approval seemed to imply for many researchers a denial of the existence of corrections—which it does not. Note that Brown and Hanlon denied here the contingency of "approval and disapproval," leaving the option open in principle that corrections could be provided as *approving* expansions (e.g.: Child: "Here kitty." Adult: "Yes, here is a kitty.") Moerk (1992, 1994) has shown extensively that sensitive mothers provide mostly such approving corrections, relying on a "Yes-but" principle—as do most experts when training apprentices.

Admittedly, Brown (1973) extended the denial quite specifically to corrections—in the same work where the above-quoted specifications of "expansions" as syntactic corrections appeared. Two formulations appear worth quoting: "In general the parents seemed to pay no attention to bad syntax nor did they seem to be aware of it," and a few lines later: "But syntax ... seems to be automatically set right in the parent's mind, with the mistake never registering as such" (Brown, 1973, p. 412). These statements imply that corrections are nonexistent—although parents could provide correcting expansions without being intentionally aware of it. (The writer, being a nonnative English speaker, quite often hears corrective reformulations of his utterances from adult interlocutors who would be much too polite to do this intentionally.). The fact is, as shown and argued by Brown himself, that parents set the utterance right in their expanding responses—if not in their own mind. This was strongly emphasized by Brown and Bellugi (1964) in a conclusion deserving repetition because of the almost universal misinterpretation of Brown's ideas: "a reduced or incomplete English sentence seems to *constrain* the English-speaking adult to expand it into the nearest properly formed sentence" (emphasis added). Brown (1973, p. 106), when emphasizing the adult's guess of what "the child ought to have said," stresses the adult's contrasting of the obligatory structure with the child's faulty one. While there are seeming contradictions in Brown's changing interpretations, it needs to be reemphasized that Brown extensively reported syntactic corrections, even if under the label "expansions." The examples of expansions Brown provides show that they provide multiple grammatical corrections, including syntactic ones.

To assess the astonishing change in Brown's reports, the selective attention of investigators, and the impact of the subsequent denials, these developments have to be related to the tidal wave of nativism unleashed by Chomsky (1965). This nativism resulted in the denials of the learnability of language (Wexler & Culicover, 1980), as is well known. Because the argument of Gold (1967) made corrections a precondition for learnability in hypothesis-testing conceptualizations of language learning, corrections had to be denied in order to be able to deny learnability. It is therefore a plausible assumption that Brown's own later ambivalence might have been caused by Chomsky's nativism, as the close temporal contiguity between Chomsky's (1965) first major work and Brown's change of mind suggests. Brown's strong denials thereafter provided optimal support for the dogma of nativism that was sweeping the field. (This dogma in turn would make learning from negative evidence, that is, refutations derived from empirical findings, difficult for those scientists who had accepted it.)

A minor qualification of the above account that exclusively emphasizes Brown's impact is, however, required: In addition to the statements of Brown's there were two brief anecdotes which were unendingly quoted in arguments against corrections. They came from Braine (1971) and from McNeill (1966). They deserve quotation to clarify their import:

> Child: Nobody don't like me.
> Mother: No, say "nobody likes me."
> Child: Nobody don't like me.
> (Eight repetitions of this exchange follow).
> Mother: No, now listen carefully, say "NOBODY LIKES ME."
> Child: Oh! Nobody don't likes me.
> —McNeill (1966)

> Child: Want other one spoon, Daddy.
> Father: You mean, you want THE OTHER SPOON.
> Child: Yes, I want other one spoon, please, Daddy.
> Father: Can you say "other spoon?"
> Child: Other ... one ... spoon.
> Father: Say ..."other."
> Child: Other
> Father: Spoon
> Child: Spoon
> Father: Other ...spoon.
> Child: Other ...spoon. Now give me other one spoon?
> —Braine (1971, abbreviated)

Considering that the predominant denial in the literature pertained to the *existence* of corrections, it is simply astonishing that those supporting these denials would have wanted to publicize these two quotes. They show not only the existence but an almost extreme intensity of corrections. Braine even reports (Braine, 1971, p. 160) that he tried to correct his child "over a period of a few weeks."

Even the fallback position regarding a presumed ineffectiveness of corrections is partly compromised by the anecdotes. As is obvious in the last repetition in McNeill's anecdote, the child had incorporated the third person singular -*s* into her utterance. The only aspect that proved resistant to change was the formula *don't like*, a formula the child had probably heard and used thousands of time. Also, because the child probably had not analyzed the negation *No-* as a separate semantic element in *Nobody*, she needed an element to negate the intended message, that is, the *don't*. Almost the same argument could be repeated for Braine's corrections: Their extensive provision, their approximation to success (*Other ...spoon* uttered by the child as imitation), and the correction being overridden by a formula that was certainly trained thousands of times (*Do you want another one?* asked by adults.) Both quotes therefore certainly prove the existence of syntactic corrections and also, to some degree their effectiveness, even against overwhelmingly over-learned formulas.

Yet, when considering the effectiveness or ineffectiveness of corrections, the language level of the child needs, of course, to be taken into account. To respond efficiently to the corrections, they would have needed to analyze these words into their elements. Corrections certainly need to be matched to the mastery level of a learner in order to be effective. The matching principle (Simon, 1978) is central to the difference-by-comparison algorithm, as is fully known from all areas of learning. A large contrast between the learner's level and the information proffered in the correction militates against the utilization of this information. This requirement has been totally disregarded in the reliance on the random anecdotes from McNeill and Braine. It is highly probably that the words *nobody* and *other one* were unitary elements for these children. Arbitrary anecdotes without providing any evidence as to the match or mismatch between the child's level and the corrections can therefore be very misleading and should not have been used as bases for encompassing arguments against corrections.

As already indicated, the denial of corrections took three major forms during the last decades: the denial of their existence, their generality, and their effectiveness. The denial of the generality of corrections sometimes takes two forms, stressed variously by diverse authors: The denial of generality for all forms of language mistakes, from phonology, to vocabulary, morphology, and syntax; and the denial of generality for all children of the world past, present, and future. This last formulation is, of course, not falsifiable in principle (in Popper's 1959 sense) and is therefore not a scientifically meaningful argument. Neither is it an important proposition as long as language learning is not seen exclusively as an hypothesis-testing process. For any rote learning process, or a process based on analogy

(MacWhinney, 1978), neither corrections nor negative instances are a necessary condition. Yet they might be highly conducive to speedier language learning and to attaining higher levels of perfection. (The fact that many adults go through life consistently employing incorrect grammar suggests much uncorrected rote learning. The writer finds formulations such as "I would of thought ..." in compositions of his college students!)

The Denials of Corrections After Brown

Brown was, as is known, "the father" of the present wave of L1 acquisition research and his judgment had profound influence both through his publications and perhaps even more through his students who soon occupied most of the chairs on L1 acquisition in the best universities of the country. Through international contacts, this influence spread widely outside the United States. Due to this strong, almost single-source influence, precaution in the evaluation of the resulting unanimity is suggested.

Denials of the Existence of Corrections

From Brown and Hanlon (1970) on, the absence of corrections was either presupposed or forcefully asserted. Only a few examples of this denial can be provided: Platt and MacWhinney (1983, p. 413) express this denial very definitely: "Not only has it been shown that parents tend not to make grammatical corrections of children's language...." Atkinson (1986) reports on "the standard view that the primary data contain no negative information" (p. 99) and he makes "the standard assumption that the primary data contain no negative information"(p. 100). After several repetitions, this assumption acquired increased significance—and truth-value: "Common to all arguments and, therefore, especially significant, is the assumption that the learner receives no negative information" (p. 105). Arbib, Conklin, and Hill (1987, p. 145) state: "Thus the child appears to learn his language from positive evidence alone. Negative evidence, that is, corrections, are not available to him in general and are not used if available." Note here a double denial of the existence and the impact of corrections. The impact is focused upon below.

Similarly, Bowerman (1987) takes "the no negative evidence problem" as given and comes to the conclusion that "the 'no negative evidence' problem is not a myth but a real and serious challenge for the construction of an adequate theory of language acquisition" (p. 457). She cites many authors from the mid-1980s who agree with her position. Book reviews in the *Journal of Child Language* (e.g., Freeman, 1989) and in *Applied Psycholinguistics* (Leonard, 1989) take the absence of negative evidence or corrections for granted. Gordon (1990) still denied the generality of corrective feedback and proceeded from this denial to argue against the learnability of language. Freeman (1989) can serve as an example of the utter neglect by these theorists of factual evidence. As quoted above, Brown (1973) described his concept of expansions as "the adult glosses the child's utterance as just that simple sentence, which ... *the child ought to have said*" (p. 106, emphasis added). Yet Freeman asserts "Unfortunately ... it seems to me that the condition which the rule dictates for learning that there is information how an entity *ought to have been represented* is psychologically implausible. When children learn, they do not have such information" (p. 469, emphasis added). Here Freeman, obviously, denies what Brown had demonstrated two decades earlier. If counterevidence, supplied even by the most famous investigators, is simply ignored, then obviously the research field can not benefit from this empirical evidence and the theory has become a dogma.

Denials of the Generality of Corrections

As explained above, two aspects need to be differentiated: the generality for all types of linguistic error, and generality for all children. The later will be labeled here "universality" to avoid confounding these two types of denial.

A large body of literature exists on the availability of vocabulary corrections, and it seems this type of corrections has never been denied. The above quoted denials were almost exclusively tied to Chomsky's nativism and therefore to the denial of syntactic corrections. Most authors are silent on corrections of bound morphemes, but they appear to tend to presume them as available. Bound morphemes are obviously language specific and acquiring them through learning could not be denied. As quoted above ("adding words, mostly but not exclusively functors" Brown, 1973, p. 105), expansions are largely corrections involving grammatical morphemes, whether bound or free, and nobody, to my knowledge, denied the existence of expansions. Surveying past literature, it therefore seems that the denials pertained implicitly to grammatical corrections only in accordance with the belief in innate syntactic knowledge (although the above two anecdotes entail compounded denials).

As to the denial of the universal provision of corrections, authors averse to learning approaches, such as Morgan and Travis (1989), are at last forced, very reluctantly, into ambivalent admission that "negative feedback may occasionally be available." They follow this admission immediately with a strong denial: "the contention that language input generally incorporates negative information appears to be unfounded" (p. 531). In this argument, the existence of corrections is granted, but the generality of corrections is—somewhat cautiously ("appears to be") denied. The results of Morgan and Travis themselves suggest a constructive answer to the question of universality: They studied Adam, Eve, and Sarah, Brown's famous participants, and found that corrections were most frequent in Eve's dyad (up to 50 percent), fewer in Adam's, and almost absent in Sarah's family. Probably not coincidentally, Eve was also fastest and Sarah slowest in language acquisition. In trying to deny the universality of corrections, the authors have therefore provided preliminary data, that is, concomitant variations, as to its effectiveness.

One year later, Gordon (1990) was even more cautious in denying the universality of corrections: "there are cases of language acquisition in which feedback *does not appear* to occur" (p. 27, emphasis added) and "it *would seem* ...in various cultures (and *probably by several* parents in our own culture" (p. 219, emphasis added) that children do not receive feedback. After these last hesitant assertions, the denial of universality seems to have been dropped in the subsequent literature. Note, of course, that such denials cannot be supported in principle, as an exhaustive recording of all the input a child receives would be impossible and certainly has never been attempted. Neither can a universal-existence assertion be supported, for that matter. Yet, concomitant variations with effective learning would seem a promising research avenue.

Denials of the Effectiveness of Corrections

A very interesting shift happened during the last decade, as already indicated when quoting Arbib and associates (1987) above. It becomes clearer when the entire quote of Platt and MacWhinney (1983, p. 413, emphasis added), whose first clause was quoted above, is considered. The entire quote reads: "Not only has it been shown that parents tend not to make grammatical corrections, but also that *such corrections, when made* have little observable effect." Interestingly, the second part of this assertion logically contradicts the first part, yet at the same time it reinforces the rejection of corrective feedback. One must ask: Do parents make grammatical corrections or don't they? How can one meaningfully deny the effectiveness of corrections if they are nonexistent? And how can one deny the existence while admitting in the same sentence that corrections are provided ("when made")? Similarly, MacWhinney (1987b), in the introduction to the edited book in which Bowerman's restatement of "the no-negative evidence problem" appeared, emphasizes that "the papers are all remarkably unanimous in the conceptualization of the 'negative instances problem.' This problem focuses on evidence indicating that children do not learn by correction or 'negative instances'" (p. xii). Note here too the change from nonexistence of corrections to a presumed lack of any effectiveness while their existence seems to be assumed. Most of the subsequent literature is divided according to the paradigms accepted by the diverse authors. They either repeat the unexamined denial or, in contrast, provide strong supportive evidence for the short-term effectiveness of corrections. This has been shown in some detail in Moerk (1991, 1994, 1996).

Positive Evidence Supporting Corrections in Language Acquisition

As opposed to the quoted facile denials that are generally quite devoid of evidence, the empirical studies have to be considered very carefully. If evidence exists, it has to be given special attention as it goes clearly against the predominant fashion and could serve to refute an ingrained belief.

The Existence of Corrections

A considerable number of studies, such as those of Bohannon and associates (e.g., Bohannon, MacWhinney, & Snow, 1990; Bohannon & Stanowicz, 1988), Farrar

(1992), or Snow and associates (e.g., Demetras, Post, & Snow, 1986; Saxton, 1992, 1993) have demonstrated the existence of corrections. Moerk (1994) has surveyed 50 studies that report the existence of corrections in several language communities. The table presented in this previous study is included here as Table 5.1.

Although the studies included in Table 5.1 end with 1993, the evidence is so overwhelming that it would be redundant to follow it up to the present. More extensive recent literature searches suggest that probably close to one hundred such studies exist supporting the existence of corrections. It will be seen below when MBT's study is discussed that these authors, too, provide strong evidence for the existence of corrections. MBT (1995) focused on two grammatical structures: the provision of the article and the auxiliary in *Wh*-questions where it is obligatory and demonstrated that corrections occur with considerable frequency (abstract and passim). This is certainly an important admission since they thereby reject the nativistic *no negative evidence assumption*. Moreover, the pertinent corrections are

TABLE 5.1.
Studies Reporting Corrections

#	Author(s)	Date	#	Author(s)	Date
1	Brown	1958	2	Brown & Bellugi	1964
3	Slobin	1968	4	Brown & Hanlon	1970
5	Moerk	1974	6	Soderbergh	1974
7	Harris	1975	8	Moerk	1975
9	Seitz & Stewart	1975	10	Moerk	1976
11	Cross	1977	12	Nelson	1977
13	Ruke-Dravina	1977	14	van der Geest	1977
15	Wellman & Lempers	1977	16	Lieven	1978
17	Moerk	1978	18	Schumacher & Sherman	1978
19	Holzman	1983	20	Moerk	1983a
21	Moerk	1983b	22	Platt & MacWhinney	1983
23	Snow & Goldfield	1983	24	Baker & Nelson	1984
25	Goldstein	1984	26	Hirsh-Pasek et al.	1984
27	McLean & Vincent	1984	28	Nelson et al.	1984
29	Scherer & Olswang	1984	30	Schachter	1984
31	Moerk	1985a	32	Moerk	1985b
33	Demetras, Post, & Snow	1986	34	Nelson	1987
35	Pemberton & Watkins	1987	36	Penner	1987
37	Becker	1988	38	Bohannon & Stanowicz	1988
39	Tomasello & Heron	1988	40	Whitehurst et al.	1988
41	Bohannon & Stanowicz	1989	42	Reimann	1989
43	Farrar	1990	44	Moerk	1991
45	Farrar	1992	46	Moerk	1992
47	Reimann & Budwig	1992	48	Saxton	1992
49	Furrow et al.	1993	50	Sokolov	1993a

reported by MBT as occurring contingently (p. 183) and being provided in a differential manner (p. 191). Contingency and differential provision of feedback certainly should be conducive to learning. It appears therefore that the existence of corrections cannot and is not denied anymore by most empirical researchers.

The Generality of Corrections

As discussed above, two aspects are differentiated: whether corrections are provided for all categories of language mistakes and whether they are provided for all children. Since the MBT (1995) studied only three children and two constructions: article use with singular count nouns and auxiliary use in *Wh-* questions, no strong conclusions about generality can be drawn from their study. Yet it is important that the authors report frequent corrections of these two syntactic mistakes, because the existence of syntactic corrections had been most adamantly rejected since Brown and Hanlon's (1970) denial of them (though they had provided factual evidence for it—as shown above). Additionally, Moerk (1991) and Farrar (1992) have shown frequent cases of morphological corrections, and Brown (1958) himself and most investigators have accepted the existence of vocabulary corrections. It has therefore been shown that corrections are supplied by caregivers for all three major categories of language skills: vocabulary, morphology, and syntax. Phonological corrections seem to be tacitly admitted as they are so obvious as to be undeniable. The exact forms of this provision would, however, deserve closer study—especially considering the problems L2 learners have.

MBT report that corrections were supplied to all three children, in spite of SES and age differences, though with different consistency. Moerk (1994) surveyed studies from multiple languages demonstrating corrections, and Watson-Gegeo and Gegeo (1986) found extensive corrections in a nonindustrial society also. Their report deserves a verbatim quote: "two-person use of repeating is primarily associated with correcting and didactic drills. In addition to correcting phonology, morphology, syntax, or word choice, caregivers use dyadic repeating to teach social behavior such as table manners" (p. 27).

Generality across time and space appears probable even if not provable. However, as argued above, for most observational learning conceptions (e.g. Whitehurst & de Baryshe, 1989) corrections are not a necessary, but only a conducive, condition for language acquisition.

The Effectiveness of Corrections

A summary of 14 studies reporting on positive effects of corrections was provided by Moerk (1994) and is also included here as Table 4.2. The extended discussion of this table is readily accessible in Moerk (1994) and need not be repeated here in detail.

Only the size of the effects, as far as they can be discerned on the basis of the widely diverging statistical indicators given in the diverse studies (see the right column of Table 5.2) shall be emphasized. Fifty or more percent improvements and

TABLE 5.2.
Evidence as to the Effectiveness of Corrections

Author(s)	Setting	Statistical Indicator
Becker (1988)	Parent-Child Pragmatic error	59% Improvement
Chapman *et al.* (1986)	Home Word usage	% Improvement: Production = 38 Comprehension = 65
Farrar (1990)	Experiment Gram.morpheme	Plural + r = .75 Progressive r = .81
Farrar (1992)	Experiment Gram.morpheme	Imitations = 12:6 correction Repetition 14:4 vs. recast
Goldstein (1984)	Experiment Syntax, Lexicon	Corrections - 100% effect Modeling: 0% to 100%
McLean and Vincent (1984)	Naturalistic Expansions	Significant increase after 400' of training
Moerk (1983)	Home, Expansions Corrections	Proportion imitated = .225 Proportion rehearsed = .536 Proportion improved = .305
Moerk (1990)	Home Expansions	Observed vs. expected frequencies offilial utilization 4 to 6:1
Nelson *et al.* (1984)	Mother-child Growth 22/27 ms	r = .34 to .43 p < .05 and p < .01
Pemberton & Watkins (1987)	Head Start	Lexical gain t = 5.75 p < .001 Syntactic gain t = 3.16, p < .01
Scherer & Olswang (1984)	Home + Experiment	Slope imitation 3.0–6.0 Slope spontaneous .5–3.0
Slobin (1968)	Home Expansions	About 50 percent
Sokolov (1993)	Naturalistic Mother-Child	R^2 = 53 corrections R^2 = 57 corr. + errors
Tomasello & Heron (1988)	College Foreign lang.	Rules + Exceptions, Proportion correct = .92; Surpass controls p < .05/.001

effect sizes of 50 and higher are quite common—even after often relatively brief interventions. Such findings are almost common sense in the domain of skill learning and can be also easily documented in verbal skill learning, both regarding first (Moerk, 1992) and second language (Gass, 1997; Tomasello & Heron, 1988) acquisition.

Similar to the studies of corrections, the extensive research program of Nelson and associates on "recasts" has also demonstrated the effects of this form of feedback—which mostly entails corrections (Nelson, 1977; Nelson, Carskaddon & Bonvillian, 1973). The extensive evidence on the impact of expansions, clarification requests, and confirmation checks—all of them indicating some flaw in the preceding utterance—is closely analogous to the results of the studies on recasts. Considerable evidence exists therefore as to the effectiveness of corrections.

Nelson, Welsh, Camarata, Butkovsky and Camarata (1995) have more recently presented the valuable observation of a "recast gap" in language-impaired children. That is, otherwise normal, but specifically language-impaired children received fewer recasts than children without language impairment. This evidence from the *modus tollens*, that is, relative deprivation, perspective suggests that recasts (or corrections) might even be a necessary form of input for normal language acquisition in average homes. Such *modus tollens* perspectives are discussed in Chapters 6 and 7. They provide information from the perspective of deprivation as to effects of input generally and about specific features of the input.

In the following discussion, the focus is centered on MBT (1995) who explored negative feedback in multiple ways, reported several data sets suggesting its effectiveness, but argued against such effectiveness. The conclusions of MBT contradict not only their own numerical evidence but also the verbatim examples of extensive impacts of maternal corrections that Moerk (1991) has provided partially from the same data set (the interactions of Brown's Eve and her mother). Verbatim evidence is, of course, closest to the actual observations and therefore least distorted by theoretical biases. A finding similar to Moerk's was already reported by Slobin (1968) also from the same data set: In 50 percent of the provisions of maternal "expansions" (the term employed by Brown's group), children incorporated some of the corrective linguistic information into their own subsequent utterances. That is, in contrast to MBT's conclusions, research extending over thirty years has substantiated the effectiveness of corrections—and an immediate effectiveness of 50 percent is certainly not negligible.

The Study of Morgan, Bonamo, and Travis

The major focus of the MBT article is centered on the effectiveness question, which is also the case for the present reevaluation. When considering effectiveness, the prerequisite evidence for the existence of corrections, which was so frequently denied, has necessarily to be included. MBT provide three sets of data to judge effectiveness: (a) A set of contingencies between mistakes and corrections as well as between corrections and improvements, with chi-square values of significance. (b) Correlation coefficients between corrections and improvements. (c) Lagged time-series analyses of the relationships between the same variables. These three sets of analyses will be evaluated separately.

Contingencies and Chi-Square Computations

MBT found high percentages of corrections of article omissions for Adam, Eve, and Sarah: 34.8 percent, 41.4 percent, and 35.3 percent, respectively—which demonstrated that filial mistakes certainly have an effect on the caregivers. Concerning possible effects of corrections on children's subsequent grammaticality, the authors report impressive impacts of corrective recasts, leading to improvements of 23 percent for Adam and of 29 percent for Eve (p. 185) and to self-corrections of 25 percent for Adam and of 60 percent for Eve (p. 186).

However, there are glaring contradictions between the facts reported and the conclusions drawn by MBT. When the authors report 3 self-corrections for Eve after 5 corrective recasts and then conclude: "we failed to find any evidence that recasts prompt self-corrections" (p. 186), they obviously contradict themselves. The same contradiction is found between the report of 23 percent and 29 percent of article use (p. 185) after target recasts—corrections—and the authors' conclusion "we found no evidence to support the contention that recasts provide negative evidence and serve as corrections." In contrast, 23 to 29 percent immediate improvements after such corrections is a respectable success rate, even if lower than the 50 percent reported by Slobin (1968) for all types of expansions. In accordance with the authors' numerical evidence, several of the chi-squares between corrections and improvements were significant for Adam and Eve. For Sarah, growing up in a home with a much lower educational level, the dynamics are different, as Moerk (1980) demonstrated long ago.

The high percentages of instances when corrections where effective do, however, probably reflect not just the impact of corrective recasts since many other—unanalyzed— antecedents could have contributed to this impact. While MBT therefore probably overestimate the effectiveness of corrections (in their data only, not in their conclusions!), they are to be congratulated for this impartial reporting of effects that go against their theoretical outlook.

This effectiveness was found even on the basis of still unsatisfactory methodology. MBT selected only the immediately following instance of filial noun-use in their chi-square analyses for the ascertainment of effects, although we know, at least since Kaye (1982), as well as from all skill-learning, that children and all learners often work up to the correct construction, using multiple supports if available. Multiple corrections and multiple subsequent trials would need to be studied to capture such working up to a goal response. Such an appropriate methodology would probably show even higher impacts of corrections.

While the methodology has only minor flaws, the logical flaws of the design and the argument are significant: The authors contrast the effects of corrections with the behaviors following parental move-ons. Here lies the first flaw: By employing the categories of corrective recasts and move-ons, the authors switch the level of discourse without noticing it. Corrective recasts pertain to the instructional level of discourse, whereas move-ons pertain to the conversational and functional level. The latter category is neutral regarding instructional aspects. An unlimited variety of instructional features could be involved in move-ons. The authors therefore contrast corrections, an instructional category, with a mere conversational category whose potential instructional functions are not even considered. The problem is fully evident in MBT's definition of move-ons. A move-on "was coded if none of the other categories was applicable" (p. 183). Move-ons are therefore a waste-basket category entailing all other teaching interventions besides the set of various corrections. One variable is compared with an unknown multitude.

MBT find somewhat more improvements after this undifferentiated multitude of instructional techniques, the move-ons, 34 percent and 37 percent for Adam and Eve, respectively, than after pure corrections: 23 percent and 29 percent for Adam and Eve, respectively. They draw the completely wrong conclusion from this comparison—that corrections have no impact. A practical example might clarify the error of this argument.

It is as if a medication has proven its effectiveness in curing an illness. Then another company comes out with a similar product of similar or higher effectiveness. If the effectiveness of this latter product were used to argue that the first product is ineffective, this would clearly be a non sequitur. In the present case, MBT's argument would just be slightly relevant if corrections had been argued as the only intervention leading to improvement. However, even then it would not disprove the effectiveness of corrections, only the multivariate nature of the cause–effect relationships. No proponent of corrections as a training tool has ever argued that corrections are the *only* training tool. Therefore MBT's comparison of corrective recasts with move-ons is both irrelevant and logically incorrect.

The only conclusion the authors can draw from their comparison is the following: One category of training devices, that is, corrective recasts, is approximately two thirds as effective (23 percent/29 percent versus 34 percent/37 percent, p. 185) as all the other training and learning devices combined. Again, this is impressive evidence of the effectiveness of corrections. If MBT wanted to establish a rank order of variables leading to improvements, they would have had to exhaustively ascertain all or most of the possible antecedent variables and compare their impacts alone and in combination. They obviously did not do this, and any comparison is inadmissible since they do not have equivalent items to compare.

Correlational Evidence

The second set of data focuses on long-term effects of the corrections and consists of correlations between the cumulative number of recasts and proportional grammaticality. Taken at face value, the correlations of $r = .71$, $r = .87$, and $r = .80$, for Adam, Eve, and Sarah, respectively are striking. Squared, to calculate the percentage of variance accounted for by the cumulative corrections, this would indicate that more than 50 percent and up to 80 percent of the variance in improvements is accounted for by cumulative recasts/corrections.

But this would almost certainly be an overestimate. Many other training and learning aspects are accumulating simultaneously with the corrections. These would need to be partialled out to separate the diverse influences on the regular use of the article and the auxiliary in *Wh*-questions. Since the authors did not record any other training procedures, such partial correlations could not be computed. The above indications of very high effects of cumulative corrections should therefore be considered as very preliminary and inflated estimates.

MBT elected a univariate analysis of the cause–effect relationship although they are fully aware that any dependent variable is potentially a function of multiple determinants. Their highly inappropriate example (the cumulative number of animal crackers eaten being correlated with language acquisition but not being a causal factor), intended to discredit a causal interpretation, (p. 187) demonstrates this awareness. MBT's attempted solution to their problem of omitted variables—partialling out age—however, is not the solution to the multiplicity of causes. It is a serious logical and methodological mistake. This procedure has also been employed by other authors in the past and has led to incorrect conclusions. A brief conceptual clarification will therefore be attempted.

As is generally understood, partial correlations are employed to differentiate the impact of multiple *independent* variables on a dependent variable. It is additionally agreed upon, as Baer (1970) has cogently argued, that age is not a causal variable by itself. It is mostly employed in two ways in developmental psychology: either as a measurement variable (She became seriously ill at the age of 3; The intervention lasted from ages 3 to 5), or as a rough index variable for cumulative environmental impacts, when, for example, relations between cognitive development and age are ascertained. MBT employ age in this second sense as an index variable for cumulative experiences.

Here lies the crucial problem: Age (as they use it) is equivalent to the cumulative aspect of their cumulative corrections. Controlling for age is therefore "tantamount to partialling the relationship (between cumulative input and acquisition) out of itself" (Gordon, 1968, p. 593). Or in other words, since cumulative corrections and age are roughly equivalent (they would be fully equivalent if the corrections were provided in equal increments), controlling for age amounts to controlling for the cumulative aspects of the input, that is, for the single independent variable ascertained. (From the purely statistical perspective, these topics are discussed for multiple independent variables under the label "multicollinearity;" (e.g. Blalock, 1963; Gordon, 1968; Kenny, 1979).

In actual observations, age and accumulated frequencies do not exhibit perfect correlation. In the cumulative curves of MBT (cf. their Figure 3 and Figure 7), the accumulation is negatively accelerated. The partialling out of the age (measured in equal increments) removes cumulative corrective recasts as if they had occurred in equal increments. The remaining partial correlation between corrective recasts and proportion correct then reflects the negative acceleration in the accumulation, that is, the declining number of corrective recasts per time period/sample. Figure 1 clarifies this relationship between Proportional Grammaticality (PG) and negatively accelerated provision of corrections (CSAMPLE = corrections per sample) with data estimated for Eve from Figures 1 and 3 in MBT. The principles, even if not the exact curves, would be the same for Adam and Sarah in the same two figures.

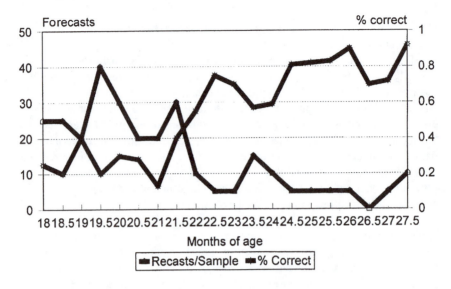

FIGURE 1. Corrective recasts/sample and percentage correct

The dynamics underlying the negatively accelerated provision of corrections over the developmental period result from a straightforward principle: With higher correctness for the later samples, in the case of Adam and Sarah between 80 percent and 100 percent correct, fewer corrections were required or even possible. An almost necessary negative correlation results therefore between level of perfection and corrective recasts provided per sample. The more effective the early occurring corrections, the quicker the improvement, and the steeper the decline in needed and applicable corrective recasts in later samples. The partial correlations obtained by MBT ranged between −.40 and −.55 for the three children studied (p. 187). The negative correlations therefore only reflect the conceptually obvious; but they certainly do not show that training or corrections are not effective in the learning process. Formulated more generally: MBT confound the causal effect of corrections, that is, the mother to child direction of causality (corrections affecting learning and level of mastery) with the child to mother causal direction that resulted in a decline of maternal corrections due to the child's improvements—achieved because of the earlier corrections (learning results in fewer mistakes and therefore fewer chances for corrections). The decline in number of corrections provided per sample should therefore be the dependent variable and not the independent one in their analyses.

In the more idealized example of Figure 1 above, which is built on averages, the negative correlation between corrections per sample (CSAMPLE) and proportional grammaticality (PG) would even reach −95. Yet, if interpreted causally (with all the usual precautions), it still would only show how effective corrections had been in necessitating fewer corrections down the road.

Time-Series Analyses

As time-series analyses (in the time-domain, that is, presuming linear changes) are based on cross-correlations, the same principle as that just discussed also applies to the time-series approaches of MBT and even more to the lagged relationship. The corrections decline with age, that is, with the level of perfection evinced by the children. This inverse relationship is logical and necessary. (The only exception would be if the parents steeply raised the ante and became more demanding—which is not easily possible in the case of providing the article and the Copula, when the child approaches perfection).

Similar dynamics underpin the learning of any skill: In the early stages the learner will have to employ much time and energy to master the rudiments. Later when the skill is mastered better, the learner will be able to perform it more efficiently with less time and energy invested. A negative correlation would therefore be found between level of mastery of the skill and time and energy invested during the successive periods of acquisition. This does not mean obviously that time and energy invested in learning the skill is a negative predictor for its achievement; just the opposite: The more time and energy invested, the quicker mastery will increase and the quicker the level of time and energy invested can decrease across successive periods, that is, the more negative the correlation between teaching/learning strategies and mastery level will be.

Since MBT provide an economic example (economic examples come most easily to mind because time-series have been employed most extensively in economics), another economic example might help clarify the logical mistake made by MBT in their time-series analyses: It is generally the case that the higher the percentage of the working-age labor force that is employed, the smaller the number of claims for unemployment compensation will be. That is, there is a clear inverse relationship between claims for unemployment compensation and the percentage of working-age people employed. If a consistent change is observed in both trends, and if compensation claims are chosen as the leading indicator, then lagged bivariate time-series, with *any* lag chosen, would show that decreasing claims for compensation are followed by increasing percentages of employed workers. But nobody would claim that the declining claims cause the increase in the employment. The cause–effect relationship is just the opposite, that higher employment results in fewer claims, in the same manner as better language mastery results in fewer corrections.

Applied to the causal structure of the present case, if proportion correct were chosen as the predictor, then a real causal relationship would have been captured since lack of mistakes precludes corrections. (Additionally, the dyad might have progressed to new categories of focused training and a few slips of attention, resulting in mistakes, might not be attended to, as suggested by Figures 5 and 7 in

MBT.) If on the other hand, declining corrections are taken as the predictor variable, then the misinterpretation that MBT committed follows, that declining corrections would seem to *cause* improvement. That is, MBT completely misconceived the causal structure of training processes: With every effective training process, the intensity of training will decline with increasing mastery of the trained item. Negative correlations, as MBT found them. are therefore evidence for effective training—and not the opposite, as they imply. In this way, MBT confounded the causal impact of corrections, with a presumed causal function of the *decline of corrections*.

MBT provide by far fewer exact data for the learning of auxiliary inversion in *WH*-questions, and what evidence they present has to be culled from Figures 5 and 7, two graphic time series of Proportional Grammaticality with increasing age and Cumulative Corrections over age. Since the exact values in the figures are unclear, the following numbers can only be approximate, as estimated from the figures. But these figures provide impressive indications for cause–effect relationships: For Eve, the cumulative frequencies of corrective recasts progress almost linearly between the ages of 23 and 26 months (ms), flatten out at 26.5 ms and 27 ms and increase again at 27.5 months. Her proportional grammaticality shows—with one exception close to the beginning (23.5 ms) a similar steady increase to 26.5 ms, declines briefly at 27 ms, that is, during the second session when she received no corrections, and increase again at 27.5 ms with the renewed provisions of corrections. The correlation between these two series must be in the .90s, and it is regrettable that the authors did not provide it. Such cause–effect relationships are even more clearly indicated for Sarah who received quite minimal corrective feedback. When Sarah was performing very poorly between 35 and 35.5 ms, she received the first bunch of corrections and increased her proportional grammaticality from .1 to .6 between 35 and 36 ms. With no additional corrections, Sarah had one relapse to zero grammaticality at 36.5 ms, recovered somewhat, and relapsed again to .2 or lower at 45 ms. This high error rate seemed to be a signal for the parents and they again provided corrections at 45.5 ms—whereupon Sarah jumped to levels of proportional grammaticality around .8 and even 1.0. When the parents discontinued their corrections between 47 and 51 ms, Sarah declined precipitously between 51 and 56 ms. Only a relatively reliable provision of corrections between 51 and 55 ms enabled Sarah to regain—after a short lag—levels around .9 and higher between 57 and 61 ms. A quite tight concomitant variation over time is observable in these bivariate time-series in the frequency domain, reflecting cyclical phenomena and resembling closely the A-B-A-B-A-B designs of experimental interventions.

Adam's two profiles combine first the steady increase seen in Eve and then the decline in proportional grammaticality in response to the lack of further corrections after 45 to 60 ms. With further absence of corrections, Adam does not regain his previous higher levels, analogous to the A-B-A design in experimental interventions.

As is evident from these abbreviated descriptions, the bidirectional cause–effect relationships between the parents and their children seem to be especially close with respect to corrections and grammaticality in auxiliary inversion in *Wh*-questions. It is therefore extremely regrettable that the authors neither provided the exact data nor the correlations. Ideally one would want bivariate time-series analyses in the frequency domain to capture the fluctuations and their—somewhat lagged— dependencies. For this, however, there are not enough data points. It is also regrettable that MBT provided unequal end-points for the ages in the curves for causes and effects of Adam and Sarah. The proportional grammaticality curves, that is, those for effects, end at around 57 and 63 ms, respectively, whereas the curves for corrections, the presumed causes, end at about 54 and 55 ms respectively. It would have been of great interest how the parents reacted to the decline in Adam and the improvement in Sarah during the last three or eight months for which data about corrections are not presented.

One overall word of caution has to be added to this somewhat detailed discussion: In these descriptions of lack of corrections, and so forth, the reference was, of course, only to the brief observation sessions. Absolutely nothing is known about the 10 to 12 hours per day, and the many intervening days, when no observations were performed. Extrapolation from the observation sessions to the other periods is fraught with problems of sample selection and external validity, although it might be implausible that children and parents would systematically alter their verbal behavior in respect to these minor grammatical aspects. Therefore while the cause–effect relationships described in the recorded data are probable, what is needed are microanalytic and extended investigations of the impact of corrections. More systematic rendering of data than what MBT provide, both against and for a favored hypothesis, would be an absolute precondition for objective evaluations.

SUMMARY AND DISCUSSION

MBT (p. 184) have shown how extensively caregivers provide corrections (34.8 percent for Adam, 41.4 percent for Eve, and 35.4 percent for Sarah) when they are called for. The existence question for grammatical corrections has once again been answered affirmatively. Since the corrections studied were provided for syntactic mistakes, the generality question has also been confirmed to some degree; the existence of vocabulary and morphological corrections being more generally accepted. MBT have thereby confirmed the assertion of Furrow and associates (1993) that "grammar of children's utterances per se has eliciting powers" (p. 374) and disconfirmed some of Brown's earlier denials. MBT can therefore be added to the 50 studies surveyed by Moerk (1994) proving the existence of corrections.

Pertaining to the effectiveness question, the correlations between cumulative number of recasts and proportional grammaticality in the children's utterances in the range of .68 to .87 suggest a strong impact of corrections. The estimated 50 to

80 percent of the variance accounted for by corrections are, however, almost certainly an overestimation since other training variables were not included in MBT's analyses and could therefore not be partialled out in the analyses. This indication for the effectiveness of corrections is reinforced by MBT's report that Adam and Eve incorporated these corrections in up to 60 percent of the instances into their subsequent utterances. The probabilities of corrections provided by caregivers (p is about .37; the average of 34.8, 41.4 and 35.4 percent) need to be multiplied with the probability of incorporating corrections ($p =.60$). This shows that about 20 percent of mistakes result in immediate improvements due to corrections, a considerable percentage, indeed.

MBT failed to explore other training aspects that could contribute to grammatical advances. For the exploration of contingencies between multiple training techniques and learning strategies, microanalytic, multi-lagged Markov-chain methods would be more appropriate than the authors' chi-square approaches. Using less than adequate methodology, the authors left the question of multiple factors in immediate contingencies unanswered. In MBT's correlational and time-series analyses the following central point was overlooked: If a learner gets close to perfection in a specific skill or subaspect of it, then there is little opportunity and need to provide further corrections. The two-step causal chain, of effective correction resulting in fewer mistakes and therefore in fewer corrections at later times, confounded the authors and lead them to deny the impact of corrections which they had shown by means of their data.

Most fascinating is the further evidence in MBT's data that the authors have failed to analyze. It pertains to the decline of filial performance with the decline of parental corrections, the A-B-A patterns as discussed above. Therefore corrections seem to be required not only for learning but also for maintenance, a phenomenon well-known from second-language acquisition under the rubric "language loss," and as discussed extensively in Chapter 3 under the headings of rehearsals and reinstatements. Simple time-domain time-series analyses, however, cannot capture such cyclic phenomena. Frequency-domain analyses, employing cross-spectral density functions or cross-spectra, instead of the cross-correlation function, would be needed, as Figures 4 and 5 of MBT suggest. Figure 4 especially shows how much cyclic variation is still left in the residuals.

It can be concluded that Morgan and associates' data—as against their interpretations—provide impressive evidence for the existence, density, and effectiveness of corrections. They also confirm their generality as far as syntactic phenomena are concerned. MBT's *methods* are a promising improvement over previous research, although they still fall short of what is required. Yet much more careful attention has to be paid to the *logical structure* underlying these newer methods and to the cause–effect dynamics in lengthy and multivariate learning processes.

Research on corrections generally parallels the MBT study in exhibiting full-scale contradictions between findings and the conclusions draw from them. The timing of the pertinent publications suggests the dynamics underlying these contrasts: In Brown's early—pre-Chomskyan—publications, the corrective force of maternal feedback was consistently emphasized, but labeled in its most common form "expansions." After Chomsky's (1965) nativism and Gold's (1967) stress on corrections as condition for learnability, the unwelcome evidence of corrections, now hidden behind the labels of "expansions" or "extensions" (Cross, 1977), remained invisible even in full view. When, over the next quarter century, the evidence for the existence of corrections became overwhelming enough to obviate any plausible deniability, the fallback positions of denying its generality and its effectiveness became dominant. This tendency is still strong in MBT and the field more generally, as reviewed above.

Having surveyed the history of the controversy, the second question—whether researchers learn from negative feedback (or from "anomalies" in Kuhn's [1962] terminology), can be considered. The answer can be a reassuring, even if guarded "yes"—although their learning proceeded much slower than that of the children. During the last ten years, the existence of corrections has become increasingly accepted. As MBT's study shows, even their linguistic generality is now at least implicitly acknowledged; otherwise MBT would not have studied syntactic corrections, whose existence had been categorically denied, as shown above on the basis of verbatim quotes. There is still considerable confusions regarding both aspects of generality: Whereas generality as to linguistic forms is increasingly substantiated, generality across cultures and times will have to remain indefinitely open. Yet, as is shown, especially in Chapters 6 and 7, obvious corrections might not be needed for all levels of language learning. Rote formulas and simple patterns might be learned predominantly on the basis of frequent correct models, similar to the reversal shift learning of lower animals and young children, as mentioned in Chapter 3.

Parallels between children's and scientists' learning are also discernable. For both, a tendency might exist to learn gradually based on cumulative corrections, as evident in the correlations ranging in the .80s, as reported by MBT, as well as in the gradual acceptance by many scientists of corrections over the last ten years. Children, of course, have it easier. They do not need to defend either a dogma or a personal reputation related to the formulation of the dogma. They do, however, sometimes have ingrained formulas, as in the examples provided by McNeil and Braine, which interfere with immediate intake of corrective information. (Basically, dogmas and habitual formulas are rather similar, a dogma being a conceptual formula.) Scientists exhibit considerable resistance against responding immediately to corrective feedback. This resistance was exemplified by MBT and many others in their denial of the effectiveness of corrections despite the large number of studies reporting it.

This resistance is part of Lakatos' (1970, 1978) insight that even scientific rationality works much slower than most people would expect. Cautious changes appears very sensible from both an evolutionary and information-processing perspective. In the evolutionary domain, with many random changes facing the organism, quick abandonment of proven behavior patterns in response to a random contingency would prove maladaptive. From an information-processing perspective, patterns (whether formulas such as *other one* or *don't like* or those based on frames, such as Verb–Noun without the unstressed determiner) have been built up over a long learning history and reflect important environmental contingencies. Similarly, established theories incorporate the experience of many preceding researchers and should not be given up quickly. With extreme flexibility, random factors, either mistakes in the linguistic input or fortuitous findings, would result in mistaken learning. As Braine (1971) argued, language learning, like all learning, should be buffered against the occasional mistakes overheard in the surrounding speech. The same can be said for scientific learning. When, however, scientific conservatism turns into dogma that is defended against heretics at all costs, then the laudable protective conservative tendencies become obstacles to progress. MBT performed a service in keeping the question of the effectiveness of corrections alive and attempting new approaches in settling it. Their and others' blindness to their own data suggests the dangers of a dogmatic approach. The near future will show whether the original nativistic anticorrection proposal is a scientific theory and therefore refutable through evidence, or a dogma extremely resistant to it.

Having focused in Chapters 3 to 5 on one training technique each and largely on one social stratum—English-speaking middle-class families—the horizon is greatly expanded in Chapters 6 and 7. Each of these chapters will include multiple training and learning phenomena, and the populations first include lower social-classes (Chapter 6), and then cross-cultural samples, encompassing (in principle) all languages and the entire world (Chapter 7). At the present state of the field, however, the empirical evidence still exhibits enormous gaps in the cross-cultural perspective, as is emphasized repeatedly.

6

Verbal Input and Verbal Learning as a Function of Lower SES Membership

Children should be seen not heard.
—Common saying

Most of the research surveyed in the previous chapters suffers from one handicap pertaining to cause–effect analyses. The evidence was mostly collected in Western middle-class homes so that the variations in input and outcome have to be assumed to be restricted. For causal analyses based on quantitative concomitant variation between presumed causes and effects, however, the wider the range of variation, the more significant the statistical inferences. The inclusion of populations from very diverse backgrounds can provide the larger ranges in variability to increase the confidence in causal explanations.

The two dimensions on which such diverse populations without organic handicaps are most commonly defined are social class and cultural membership. (Organic handicaps comprise a large set of extraneous factors that would be expected to distort normal input–learning relationships and they are therefore not included in this review.) The special population of the present chapter is the lower class, and especially lower-class minority groups, in the United States. A wide range of indigenous cultures, as described in the cross-cultural or anthropological literature, is surveyed in Chapter 7. Both the class and cultural dimensions entail multiple conceptual, methodological, and even political, complexities to be taken up below. The measurement variables that are subsumed in the title as "verbal" and are mostly referred to with the reifying and entifying term "language" will be more finely differentiated in accordance with the arguments of previous chapters. Potential cause–effect relationships will then be considered theoretically and factually explored.

Dimensions of Verbal Input and Interactions in Their Interrelationships With Nonverbal Aspects

A many-featured analytic approach is needed to specify verbal input, its effects, and the value of the learned skills for varying purposes. As to input differences, frequency of use, diverse functions (socioemotional versus complex referential-inferential ones, and selective emphasis on comprehension versus production), formal complexity (semantic as well as syntactic aspects), and degree of interdependence with nonverbal contexts (including gestural and situational information), have been discussed in many previous publications. They can therefore provide the independent variables for the present review. In the same manner as the input, the effects—the learned skills, should be finely analyzed in their differential adequacy for diverse communication tasks. Very often, the original studies do not provide these analyses and only report "average progress." A combination of the sparse reported evidence and critical analyses will therefore have to be substituted for such missing fine grained measurements.

Equivalences or Deficiencies in Verbal Skills

A problem in focusing upon differences between languages or dialects derives from the dogma of linguistic relativism, an overcompensation to the hubris of the Western 19th-century conception of an unilineal cultural evolution. In this evolution, Western culture and its languages were conceived of as the high point. Any specification of differences between Western middle-class language and those of other cultures or of minority groups is therefore often suspected, in reaction to the past hubris, as being ethnocentric or even racist. Researchers are consequently hesitant to admit—perhaps even to themselves—qualitative differences in input and performance. For example, Tizard and Hughes (1984) report concomitant differences in maternal input and child verbal achievements, yet on the same page (p. 158) they (almost) deny those differences. On the following page, they deny language deprivation but report that teachers, who had everyday experience with the language problems of the deprived children, did not accept their denial. Notwithstanding their own denial of language deprivation, Tizard and Hughes report clear effects of this deprivation: "Children from social class V are six times as likely to be poor readers at age seven as are those from social class I and 15 times as likely to be nonreaders" (p. 134). This documentation of effects combined with a refusal to acknowledge causes is analogous to a physician being called to a very sick child but refusing to make any causal diagnosis.

Yet, specifications of differences—in contrast to a simple judgmental rank-order—might be possible, and are needed to evaluate input and to develop remedies for language delay or deficiency. The originally enthusiastic response that Ong's (1982) differentiation of an oral and a literate style received indicates that differentiations are seen as necessary. The same conclusion can be drawn from the impact of Cummins' (1980) distinction between BICS (basic interpersonal communication skills) and CALP (cognitive academic language proficiency). The Prague functional school (e.g. Havarnek, 1964) has a long history of suggesting functional differences. In the same manner as equality before the law does not mean equal competence in all skills and fields of knowledge, so functionality of languages—for restricted purposes in specific ecological niches—does not mean their equal suitability in all settings and for all tasks. The well-known difficulties many developing nations have encountered in adapting their native tongues to techno-logical-bureaucratic-scientific communication tasks prove this point. Even a brief perusal of the *Language and Language Behavior Abstracts*, under the heading "Language Planning," amply substantiates this struggle for sufficiency.

The bipolar and historically sequential nature of Ong's distinction and especially a term like "savage" in one of Goody's (1977) titles (though intended ironically in this context) suggest, however, that special care is advisable when isolating diverse aspects of languages. An appreciation of their survival value in settings where they developed must be differentiated from their value as a tool for specific new purposes. Also, highly valued artistic features of a language could coexist with a lack of fit for modern purposes. To provide an example from a different domain: A sword or a dagger might be beautifully crafted, but a common and simple screwdriver or a wrench would be much more workable in taking apart a carburetor. In the language domain: As artistically marvelous as the Homeric epos is, its language would be of little use for describing even a simple chemical reaction. While the complexity of exploring distinctions between language styles, as for example, elaborated by the contributors to Weeks and Hoogestraat (1998), is fully recognized, in order to foster educational and occupational success for children and youth, the following general conclusion appears nevertheless possible: Functional sufficiency in modern contexts has to be the criterion against which general language skills in Western and Westernizing societies are measured if the educational and occupational success of the learners is of concern. While scientists and scholars have the luxury to be nonjudgmental about language styles, teachers and employers have to and will be very discriminating as to this sufficiency or the lack thereof.

Qualitative-Functional Differentiations

Several differentiations have been substantiated in the functional domain for diverse samples. They have often been defined as a contrast between socioemotional functions on the one hand and the referential function on the other (Blake, 1994; Bloom, Lightbown, & Hood, 1975). Functional differences entail at least in part formal differences and consequently differences in learning tasks. The interpersonal and expressive function will entail predominantly main-verb sentences, conveying who did what to whom, or who should do what, whereas the referential function entails many Copula sentences and a much larger range of vocabulary. Interpersonal and expressive functions can rely largely on formulaic phrases (e. g., *How are you?*) and on simple S–V–O or even V–O frames (mostly as directives) with substitutions of a quite narrow range of fillers. To describe complex relations in the object world, a large variety of linguistic devices is required and commonly employed.

Directive Functions

It would probably be fruitful to conceptualize a subset of directive speech as a language of constraint whose message function lies equally or more in the emotional tone of constraint than in specifying the exact nature of the constraint. For example: an angry *Shut up*, or *Stop this* entails little semantic content or linguistic information. The message is mainly conveyed through paralinguistic aspects, and an angry growl would almost equally fulfill the purpose. Yet, harried mothers might find little time for explanations or descriptions and direct most of their verbal interactions simply toward constraining their children. Such constraining messages appear to be the most restricted linguistically and consequently the least productive for language progress for children. Ward (1971) provides detailed descriptions of these phenomena from lower-class homes. The children might be advanced in acquiring the formulas they hear so often, but delayed in other aspects.

Although obvious in principle, it needs emphasizing that, in contrast to *simple* constraining or directive messages, directives *can* be more complex (Akhtar, Dunham & Dunham, 1991). A hierarchy of complexity exists in directive messages from, for example, a simple constraint (*Quiet*), to a simple command (*Turn on the T.V.*), to directions for how to proceed in an unfamiliar environment, and to directions that are delivered with complex toys to be assembled by the buyer or that explain the rules for how to play a game.

The complexity of directives seems to be related to cultural change. Delgado-Gaitan (1994) has observed how first-generation (American-born) Mexican-American families employ language quite extensively to instruct children in performing household tasks, in contrast to recent immigrants who rely on constraints and children's quiet observation, that is, on nonverbal learning. This suggests that acculturation is accompanied by increasingly sophisticated directive speech. The more this prescriptive speech also specifies diverse environmental relations, the more complex it will be referentially and syntactically. Those common sense facts have been neglected in some recent discussions of directive speech and are briefly discussed again in this chapter.

Vocal Communion

Malinowski (1923) emphasized "vocal communion," that is, language being employed mainly to establish and maintain affective bonds, as a very basic function that is even simpler than directive speech. Here too, referential aspects are quite unimportant. Examples of such verbal communion are found in prelinguistic baby talk, often in talk between lovers, and partly in agonistic verbal play (jiving, shucking) encountered in Black youth groups. Much social talk entails this function in part. Tannen (1990), when discussing "gendered speech," distinguishes such "rapport talk" from "report talk," the former focusing on communion and the latter focusing on the objective environment. Distinct class differences in reliance on these styles are substantiated below. It has to be expected that the learning of vocabulary and morphosyntctic features would be very different if the communion function remained predominant in some dyads or groups after the prelinguistic stage. Melodic, emotional, and formulaic aspects might flourish, while referential skills might be increasingly delayed.

Comprehension Versus Production

Another important functional differentiation pertains to whether a culture or subculture mainly intends to train comprehension or productive skills. As surveyed below, it has been consistently reported that some cultures and some nonliterate social classes maintain a value system wherein the child should be seen not heard, and where language is employed predominantly to direct or constrain the child's physical activities. (The term "nonliterate" is here differentiated from "illiterate." The former refers to a value system that does not esteem literary products but not to a lack of reading or writing skills, as does the term illiterate. Literate cultures are also often referred to as "book cultures.") If language is seen mainly as an instrument of constraint, children are not full communication partners and their verbal productions generally are largely unwelcome or even punished because constraints are unidirectional, being directed by the parent to the child. If little sophisticated production is desired in an environment, frequent hearing of a few formulas would suffice to understand them without analyzing them syntactically or even semantically. Such global and undifferentiated comprehension of formulas would result in minimal versatility—but also possibly high fluency in production. Examples of unanalyzed productive competence have repeatedly been reported from research on early stages of naturalistic second language acquisition (e. g., Wong-Fillmore, 1976).

Referential Functions

In the referential-inferential domain many subdivisions will probably have to be made that necessarily have strong implications for the formal, that is, semantic and syntactic, complexity of speech acts. This is especially the case if inferential aspects (logical analyses) are included in this domain. Yet even for purely descriptive messages, vocabulary size, as well as length and complexity of sentences, are factors that affect the efficiency of information transmission whenever the information is complex.

A preliminary subdivision of the referential function could be made into (a) prescriptive, (b) narrative, (c) expository-relational styles, which should be differentiated from (d) inferential, and (e) dialectic discourse. Prescriptive discourse, while predominantly having an interpersonal function (as discussed above under directive function), is often also somewhat referential. It could, for example, consist of a series of complex directions for how to put together a toy or how to get from one place to another in an unfamiliar landscape, therefore involving many references to objects, their features, and relations.

Narrative discourse relies mainly on subject–verb–object constructions with substitutions of well-known vocabulary items in the various slots. It tells who did what to whom, when, and where. Often it has achieved high artistic levels, as in historic ballads and the epic genre generally.

Expository-relational discourse, while still based on concrete content, requires innovative morphosyntactic constructions to reflect external relations in detail. Multiple prepositional phrases and nonfinite clauses are added to both full-verb and Copula sentences. Some subordination would be expected. The methods and result sections of research reports exemplify this type of discourse.

Inferential and Dialectic Discourse

Inferential discourse, leading from concrete phenomena to abstract conclusions requires complex multiclause sentences and careful differentiations of semantic fields of often intangible referents. Counterfactuals are one of the more sophisticated examples of this genre that prove difficult even in some literary cultures, such as the Chinese (Bloom, 1981). Sigel's (Sigel, 1986; Sigel & McGillicudy-Delisi, 1984) research on the "distancing function" focuses on a similar contrast on a lower level of complexity. The need for special (ideally mathematical) language aspects for future projections supports such a categorization. The conclusion section of research reports reflects this discourse.

Finally dialectic discourse is suggested as a term for the weighing and critical evaluation of contrasting theories, as these are differentially supported by evidence. Theoretical analyses employ this style predominantly.

Whereas these or similar differentiations (cf. Cassirer, 1955) still need to be explored more extensively as to their nature and their form–function relations, they indicate how many aspects are conflated in an undifferentiated discussion of "language competence" and its antecedents.

Quantitative Aspects of Input and Interactions

Quantitative aspects should optimally be differentiated into (a) straightforward input provided by adults, (b) production of utterances by the children, and (c) feedback provided by adults to mistakes or omissions in the children's utterances.

The latter might be most important for rapid progress, as several preceding chapters indicated. In actual studies, the distinction between input and feedback is mostly not maintained so that only the extent of adult speech addressed to children is generally described. Feedback is particularly focused on in the present discussion, whenever possible, on the basis of the primary literature.

In addition to general input and production frequencies, massing versus spacing—the patterning of exercises, should be important, as research on skill-learning has generally shown. This topic is almost never focused on in primary research and at best indirect indications can be found, as, for example, when discussions during mealtimes are described. Mealtimes are relatively brief, and extensive verbal productions therefore indicate close spacing of these utterances. Similar principles apply to extensive book reading and other specially planned opportunities for verbal interactions. Yet, much more careful empirical research is needed in this area.

Overall frequency in input differences between social classes were impressively documented in a recent publication of Hart and Risley (1995). Similar differences which entail relative input deprivation of lower SES children have been confirmed whenever input across social classes was given special attention. More specific dimensions of input deprivation are also commonly reported in cross-cultural research—albeit often combined with extensive input in simple interpersonal speech. These dimensions are documented below whenever relevant. Such frequency differences imply differences in rehearsal opportunities, subsequently in ease of recall, and in processing demands depending on whether or not processing has become almost automatic.

Causal Implications of the Differentiations

Certainly in a situation of multiple causes, that is, multiple forms of input, and multiple effects (the various subskills of language) causative conclusions need to be continuously reevaluated in order not to preempt further research through premature closure. The present survey is intended as one step in this cumulative exploration of empirical reports and scientific inferences.

Multiple implications of the suggested differentiations for cause–effect inferences exist. If differences in (sub)cultural language styles are accepted, this implies differences in the habitual input children experience and differences in the latter's language learning opportunities. For example, the directive subset of the interpersonal function in input has often been described (Nelson, 1973; Pine, 1992) as having negative consequences for language development. Extensive referential input results in skills for referential encoding.

At present, many of the arguments against cause–effect inferences suffer from a lack of specification of both the causes and the effects. Also, reasonably refined differentiations of the input are sometimes contrasted with the assertion that all children, whatever the input variations, acquired normal language competence. This is, of course, like computing a correlation when no variance is ascertained for one variable. The outcome statements are almost meaningless if no specification is provided for whom, how, and on which, subset of skills normality was ascertained. If a specific culture relies mainly on socio-emotional discourse, the learning tasks and their outcomes, the averages, will probably be very different from those in technological-bureaucratic societies. A very restricted input could then result in average development for the former culture, even if these averages would be considered greatly deficient as compared to the latter culture that provides enriched input.

Form-Function Relationships

Only a few restricted aspects of this enormous topic can be focused on. First, it needs to be considered whether language is the exclusive carrier of messages or whether the verbal channel is supported by nonverbal contexts. Then the question is briefly addressed what types of messages are transmitted. This is done be summarizing the orality-literacy contrast. Third, the controversy is reviewed whether a language or specific verbal skills can be justifiably called deficient. Finally, one narrow aspect, that of text comprehension as an instance of language deficiency, is considered for one aspect of cognitive performance—information uptake from written material.

Interdependence with Nonverbal Contexts

A fascinating contrast between diverse cultures—and arguably a causal explanation for the differences in language styles encountered—is hinted at by repeated reports of a differential association of verbal messages with nonverbal circumstances, the here-and-now or better, the here-and-habitual. The latter formula is preferable because habitual sequences of behavior can produce shared understanding as easily as does shared visual perception. Piaget (1936) has shown that even young infants learn to anticipate habitual actions of their mothers.

One of the few things seemingly agreed upon for early language acquisition in Western cultures (e.g. Bloom, 1973, 1993) is that children need to have conceptualized the referent before they can learn a label for it. Bloom, especially in her recent work, emphasizes the principle of relevance, that is, that the child has to have the referent in mind in order to learn a label for it from the input. The emphasis on joint visual attention on objects as a prerequisite for word learning (e.g., Snow, 1989; Tomasello & Farrar, 1986) derives from this principle. Whereas little controversy exists as to this need for co-occurrence of concept/percept and label, considerable leeway nevertheless appears to exist as to when this co-occurrence is established in diverse cultures. Vocabulary items or brief phrases could be learned before any specific meaning is attached to them. This will be shown from reports of cross-cultural studies.

Considering communicational demands on competent interaction partners, broader contextual influences are critical. In pretechnical, traditional cultures which comprise relatively few people, topics of discussion are restricted to subsistence and interpersonal concerns, almost exclusively in face-to-face interactions. The verbal messages are therefore consistently accompanied by information in nonverbal channels so that much of what is conveyed verbally could be anticipated from the knowledge of the context and from habitual patterns of behavior (the here-and-habitual). Most learning in apprenticeship situations also combines modeled nonverbal behavior with verbal descriptions and explanations of this behavior. In specialized occupations, such as for farmers and fishermen, extensive experience with soil types or with features of fish, respectively, have led to a large specialized vocabulary that is rote-learned in familiar environments and produced in habitual conversational contexts. For both comprehension and production, such contextualized speech can therefore be relatively simple and elliptic, as much of the information is conveyed through nonverbal channels and known from extensive experience. Consequently, the normal language competence of those social groups that rely almost exclusively on contextualized communication can remain on a less complex level than that of other groups (that is, book cultures) who employ extensively decontextualized speech.

In contrast to small pretechnical societies, in technological-bureaucratic societies the number of potential verbal interactants (including authors of written messages) is large and the range of potential topics is almost unlimited. Many of these topics refer to the there-and-then and are presented to an audience that often shares minimal presuppositions. These factors entail that the messages are highly unpredictable. Decontextualized speech and writing therefore require complete and unambiguous verbal encoding of all the information necessary for a stranger to understand the message. As all information needs to be conveyed linguistically, decontextualized language is both semantically and syntactically complex. Because these messages can take an almost infinite number of specific forms and convey equally varied contents, verbal skills have to be acquired that are complex enough to fulfill these requirements. The average level of language skills of children at specific ages would therefore have to be a good deal more complex than in the previously described pretechnical societies. Specific developmental delays seen in some cross-cultural studies of traditional societies support this assumption.

Interdependence of Message Form and Content

The above contrast between contextualized and decontextualized speech is related to the differentiation between orality and literacy of Ong (1982), Scribner and Cole (1981), or Goody (1977). Contextualized speech might generally be a subset of oral communication and would share some features of orality. Yet, orality is broader and need not be simple in either vocabulary or artistic achievement, as analyses of oral epic traditions (Lord, 1960; Parry, 1971) prove. However even this epic genre, a sophisticated subset of the narrative style, focuses mainly upon human actions and their results on objects. Animate subjects, action verbs, and concrete nouns are generally predominant. If a student coming from an oral culture expects descriptions of human actions when reading high school and college textbooks, her predominantly oral skills might prepare her only minimally for the new task. In contrast, the student's earlier learning might even produce negative transfer, as the latter genre mainly involves Copula sentences and compressed syntax with participles and gerunds of abstract verbs, which convey a great deal of inferential information but describe almost no human actions. Even problems with vocabulary can arise: For example, in one study of the writer, a text referred to the "discipline" (of psychology or geography, and so forth), while high school students interpreted it as the "discipline" required in sport competitions.

A Proposed Resolution of the Difference-Deficiency Controversy

A lack of finer differentiations, as indicated above, is often encountered in the notorious difference-deficiency controversy (Blank, 1975; Feagans & Farran, 1982; McLoyd, 1990). On the one hand, even children with a very deprived input will become functional in highly familiar contexts wherein they can rely on multiple rehearsed routines and supportive contexts. For those purposes they are not deficient. Children with much social-emotional input will probably be highly proficient in that genre. Yet, high levels of skills in jiving, rapping, shucking, or playing the dozens, that is, verbal bantering, would be of rather little use and possibly even be counterproductive in studying college science texts.

Language deficiency exists if a person has not been trained sufficiently so that needed language skills could be employed with minimal effort (requiring only a low amount of processing capacity) for a specific task. Deficiency is therefore in principle task-related and not person-related or social-class related. Accomplished scientists are often deficient in presenting their research in a foreign language. It might be an interesting question whether scientists, who are often awkward and uncomfortable when engaging in small-talk, might have learned to focus too exclusively on referential speech, becoming deficient in socioemotional language skills. As different social groups seem to train their children for different anticipated tasks, as cross-cultural research has shown so clearly (e.g., LeVine, Miller & West, 1988), their children will be both *pro*ficient in the tasks for which they are trained and *de*ficient in those not trained and mastered.

A Subset of Cognitive Implications of Language Skills

One reason the difference-deficiency question is so controversial is because it is seen as having strong implications for the Sapir-Whorf linguistic relativity hypothesis, that is, that language skills affect thinking skills. Language deficiency has consequently often been interpreted as cognitive deficiency, an interpretation understandably unwelcome to those defined as deficient. This complex topic is still unresolved and will not be focused on here in its original Whorfian sense. For the present purposes, a simpler relation can be considered that should be much less controversial: Language skills certainly do affect the comprehension of school discourse, such as lectures, and of scientific texts. If lectures and texts are not understood, or understood only with great difficulty, due to the need to focus on language form as well as content, the learning of new materials will be more difficult if not impossible. Lack of fluent skills in these task will also make it more difficult to productively express certain complex trains of thought-—as every scientist has noted who begins to present his research in a foreign language. Without drawing conclusions about the more central and complex aspects of the Sapir-Whorf hypothesis, a strong influence of language on learning and cognition in educational settings can be asserted with considerable confidence.

When considering language as a tool for comprehension, degrees of fluency or of automatic processing are especially important. It follows that it might not be the mastery per se of a structure but the ease of its usage that is decisive. This principle has often been overlooked in arguments emphasizing that lower-class students *can* produce specific constructions, even if it is admitted that they do it very infrequently (cf. Tough, 1977). Any researcher who reads scientific texts in a language of which he has acquired only imperfect mastery can attest to the principle that effortful verbal processing interferes with the efficient uptake and storage of large sets of information. This is the case even if the researcher can understand every sentence in principle, given enough time and resources for processing.

In summary, if language skills are seen as tools, well-mastered or not, fit for a specific task or not, then many of the old controversies need to be rethought and reformulated. The present analysis explores how diverse features of input might prepare children—or leave them unprepared—for the types of mastery that are required in technological-bureaucratic societies. These, or more complex, considerations should be employed in the evaluation of research reports and theoretical controversies about input–learning relationships. A three-element sequence needs to be considered simultaneously entailing input, acquisition, and task relevance of the acquired skills. Ideally, input and its intended results should be structured in respect to the communication tasks envisaged in the learner's future. This is done increasingly in second-language training when LSP (languages for specific purposes) courses are designed, for example, to teach "scientific-technical language" (e.g. Hutchinson & Waters, 1987). Other courses focus predominantly on the needs of the casual tourist or the businessperson. Middle-class families employ increasingly literate speech conventions both in public and in the home (Tannen, 1982, 1989). They have a great deal of experience with verbal educational tasks and can therefore fit their input to future educational requirements. Uneducated parents without this experience might find it almost impossible to accomplish this—despite their best intentions. They could not teach what they do not know. This applies a fortiori to input from only slightly older children, who are in many cultures and social classes the predominant interaction partners of young children.

SOCIAL CLASS DIFFERENCES
IN VERBAL MOTHER-CHILD INTERACTIONS
AND FILIAL LANGUAGE ACQUISITION

The conceptual challenge is great and the social urgency even greater to understand the well-documented social-class differences in those language skills that are needed for educational success. It is therefore astonishing how incomplete the information is about diverse forms of input and their differential effects in populations that differ from Western middle-class families. This is the case while millions of children enter school with deficient language skills and subsequently suffer educational failures. More emphasis has been devoted to deny the learnability of language (e.g., Wexler & Culicover, 1980) than to explore training and learning processes in lower-class families. Once learnability is denied, teachability (Rice & Schiefelbusch, 1989) becomes an object of challenge too, and language deficiencies are denied instead of being remedied.

In contrast to this invitation to pessimism, it is the goal of this chapter to search for specific causes in input features that could account for gaps in language skills. Specifically tailored input to fill these gaps can then be developed, based on the contrast between the input provided for lower-SES and middle-SES children.

Because social class differences are largely confounded with cultural differences and with bilinguality in the United States, more isolated non-Western cultures need to be focused on when trying to ascertain cultural differences per se. Differences reported on samples in the United States will be discussed according to social class membership, if no clear evidence exists that culture was the major causative factor. This is, however, an oversimplification due to a frequent conflation of the two major antecedent variables, social class and cultural background. Heath (1983) reported considerable differences between Black and White lower-class families, although their income levels were equivalent. Similar or more extreme input differences can be expected in recently immigrated families when compared to native speakers from the same social background.

On the other hand, there are arguments that multigenerational poverty produces a culture of poverty (Leeds, 1971; Lewis, 1959), so that class differences (differential degrees of education with the related deficits in vocabulary and syntax, and so forth) are seen as cultural differences in disguise. If "lower-class" predominantly implies lack of advanced education, then rural cultures in, for example, New Guinea or Africa, share this aspect of the lower-class. The central question is which types of language skills are emphasized in diverse ecological niches. Subsistence cultures seem to emphasize more personal interdependencies and the (language) skills needed for them. Both extremely poor lower-class modern groups, as well as traditional pastoral-agricultural societies, would consequently share the emphases that subsistence cultures put on socioemotional language skills. In contrast, technological cultures, fostering middle-class wealth, seem to focus more on object relations as expressed in abstract-scientific language. Support for this contrast is provided below, although its full elaboration requires an extensive separate study.

The paucity of evidence about demonstrable relations between input and acquisition does not imply a paucity of studies that focused on the outcome aspects of deficient input. The latter are even quite abundant, so that an exhaustive survey cannot be the goal of this review. Also, excellent reviews exist for the older literature (Cazden, 1966; Edwards, 1976; Edwards, 1979; Feagans & Farran, 1982; Hoff-Ginsberg & Shatz, 1982). Relevant evidence can also be found in even earlier reviews by McCarthy (1930, 1954). The present discussion presupposes these older findings and builds upon them.

Deficits in Linguistic Attainments

The following sections focus on input variables. However, the review begins with of the overwhelming evidence of linguistic attainments or lack of them. The early reports of McCarthy (1930, 1954), Davis (1937), Beckey (1942), Irwin (1948), and Templin (1957) consistently specified social class differences in articulation and language development generally. Templin emphasized that it takes lower-class children a year longer to reach mature articulation. Irwin (1948) indicated that these social class differences become especially noticeable at 18 months, an age for which other studies found that lower-SES mothers begin to spend much less time with their toddlers. As a logical consequence of this change in maternal attention, Pasamanick (1946) pointed out that, at the end of two years, the infants' language development, though not retarded, was significantly lower than were other domains of development. For more extreme variations of input and outcome, Raph (1965) provides a brief review of older orphanage studies that documented the almost complete absence of verbal interactions and enormous delays in language development.

The effects of input deprivation seem to appear most strongly in syntactic development and later in school success, according to several studies. Holzman (1983) summarized from Landau's (1970) master's thesis that lower-SES children were inferior, especially as far as the number of complex sentences were concerned. Williams and Naremore (1969) recorded syntactic deficits for African-American lower-SES children. These children employed a considerably smaller number of subordinate clauses, relative clauses, and complements. For white lower-SES children the trends were in the same direction but not as pronounced. Race plus lower class seemed to represent a double jeopardy. Blank (1975) reported that poor children even at five years of age had not yet mastered *why* and *when* questions correctly. For elementary schools, Tizard & Hughes (1984) recount that (British) children from social class V (lowest class) are six times as likely to be poor readers at age seven as are those from social class I and 15 times as likely to be non-readers" (p. 134). Berenson (1992) attests to the unchanged nature of these deficits during the adolescent period: "Nearly 50 percent of those who enter high school in the ninth grade fail to graduate, and of the graduates only twenty percent go on to four-year colleges" (p. 58). High school drop-out rates in poor areas of Chicago are very high—close to 60 percent of the students fail to graduate. Students beginning their education in the poorest elementary schools have high school drop-out rates in the range of 80 percent, varying little across schools. Of course, even high school graduation does not guarantee competence in those linguistic aspects that are required for college success.

It is certainly true that many variables, many of them motivational, intervene between preschool mother–child interaction and dropping out of high school. However, as many studies indicate, consistently lower verbal skills from preschool, to elementary school (six/seven year-olds), to high school, are an important factors. These studies are supported by the experience of almost every teacher who worked with children from lower-class backgrounds.

Cause–Effect Relations Between Input and Linguistic Attainment

In addition to the differences in language skills attained, indications for cause–effect relationships have been reported for half a century or longer. Most studies are, however, based on correlational designs and therefore open to multiple interpretations. Inferences need, consequently, to rely on the convergence of the evidence and have to integrate evidence from remedial interventions (an A-B design). Only such multiple convergence can increase the verisimilitude of the conclusions.

Milner (1951) studied first-grade Black children who were either high or low in language tests. Child language status and socioeconomic status correlated in her study in the range between .70 and .86. Specifically, the probable causal factors were: High-scorers had more breakfasts and dinners with families (implying more opportunities for adult–child conversation), parents used verbal methods of discipline, children received more praise and affection from their parents, more books were available, and parents read to them more frequently. Hilliard (1957) reported that children with rich information backgrounds were better equipped for reading. McCarthy (1961) found a relationship between verbal skills and parental availability. Nisbet (1961) reported that a large family is a handicap to verbal development, very probably due to diminished interaction between adults and each child, as Zajonc and Bargh (1980) argued so persuasively in their "confluence model." These latter findings also suggest negative effects of too much reliance on older siblings for child raising, as is so common in diverse cultures. This consideration will be important when evidence is discussed below pertaining to the extensive reliance on siblings for caregiving functions.

In explaining language delay and deficiency, Bernstein (1961) emphasized arbitrary authority and categorical demands, which imply that few or no reasons are given for demands in lower-class families. His distinction between elaborate and restrictive codes is generally known. Hess and Shipman (1965) explored Bernstein's proposals with an American sample and confirmed them impressively.

Walters, Connor and Zunich (1964) found a comparable lack of communication between mothers and children in an experimental study of lower-class mothers guiding their preschool children. On the more macroscopic level, support for cause–effect relations has therefore been available for decades. The following sections surveys more recent studies that explore differentiated features of these cause–effect relations.

Causes of Group Differences in Input

When focusing on input differences, their causes need to be briefly considered too. At least three basic principles can be differentiated that can produce differences in verbal interactions: The first is ecological-functional: In social groups that rely predominantly on face-to-face interactions about readily visible objects, complex verbal messages are needed less and will probably not be habitually employed. Commands given in such situations mainly specify which well-known act needs to be performed. The "when" of the performance is indicated by the timing of the command. If the desired response is not forthcoming, the command is repeated more loudly, with further increased emphasis at the third repetition; followed by physical punishment, if not yet successful. This has been described vividly by Ward (1971).

A further principle underlying input deficits is one of competence: If speakers do not know or do not habitually employ advanced linguistic constructions, they cannot or will not model them with any frequency for young language-learning children (Alexander & Entwistle, 1988). This applies for uneducated parents and even a fortiori for siblings who are only a few years older than the recipients of the language input. Because these older children themselves have never been trained in advanced language skills, the result is an *incapability* of employing and teaching higher language skills, and not just a lack of frequent input.

The third principle pertains to cultural attitudes: It has often been reported (see also below) that uneducated mothers do not treat their young children as communication partners. Ward (1971) confirmed this for her sample of Black parents: "The years from one or two to six, the most crucial for language learning, are the period of least adult contacts and stimulation for these children" (p. 88). "The oldest child present is the teacher" (p. 53). Delgado-Gaitan (1994) reports similarly for recent immigrants from Mexico to the United States that adults did not talk much with their children. The same was related almost verbatim for Kaluli parents in the tropical rain forest of Papua New Guinea (Ochs & Schieffelin, 1983), as is seen in Chapter 7. This principle is obviously widespread and does not need to be substantiated by many additional references. Such cultural tendencies imply not only that the children's utterances will not be expanded upon nor corrected through maternal replies, but often also that spontaneous speech of young children is unwelcome. Ward (1971) substantiates this most impressively through a quote from one of the mothers who complained of her son asking too many questions: *That boy talks so much. Oh! I be whip him all the time all the time* (p. 53). Ward concludes from this and multiple other observations that "speaking is often equated with the quality 'bad'" (p. 29). "His [the child's] experience in interacting with adults has taught him the value of silence or withdrawal" (p. 88). Tizard & Hughes (1984) also report that some working-class mothers admitted they disliked answering questions, a finding confirmed by cross-cultural studies, as summarized by Heath (1989). For example, Kulick (1986) reports from a village in Papua New Guinea that "adults expect children to be passive listeners. Good manners require that children answer talk directed to them but that they not initiate social conversations with their elders" (quoted in Heath, 1989, p. 343). Again from a very different culture and on the other side of the globe, Mexican-American families interpret children's spontaneous verbal participation in adult conversations as "falta de respeto" (Delgado-Gaitan, 1994, p. 65), missing respect, which is considered rather improper. More of this evidence is summarized below when frequencies are focused on.

If children are not considered communication partners, are even punished for speaking instead of being rewarded and guided, and are labeled *bad/horrible* (*Them children, they horrible*, as quoted by Ward, 1971, p. 28) when they begin to speak after the age of two, these values certainly will not be conducive to their learning advanced productive-language skills from adults. As lower-SES adults or those from nonliterate cultural backgrounds mainly require that their children understand their commands and follow them, low levels of skills—basically the understanding of formulas in familiar contexts—suffice. Later, productions of these same formulas can be based on relatively simple cognitive processes, such as rote learning and simple pattern abstraction. As the commands recur frequently, that is, the input is often rehearsed, such learning appears to occur naturally and no special training seems required. These common observations reinforce then the cultural laissez-faire attitudes toward language transmission.

Having specified the general principles, detailed findings are considered under the above discussed categorizations: frequency, function, morphosyntactic complexity, and relations to the nonverbal context. As language acquisition per se is of central interest, phenomena occurring during the preverbal period are not included in this limited survey and only the preschool years will be focused on.

Frequency Aspects

As indicated, several aspects of frequency need to be differentiated. First, whether it pertains to speech input or the child's production of utterances. Furthermore, frequent adult feedback, providing expansions, corrections, confirmations, and challenges might be the most important feature for learning. Some of these feedback aspects, when reported in the literature, are subsumed below under the diverse categories of input, though it has to be recalled that most studies have neglected feedback. Therefore lack of established evidence does not mean the behaviors are nonexistent.

Receptive Frequencies

Pertaining to frequency generally, Hart and Risley (1995) have recently presented extremely impressive results. A few summary data reflect the enormous differences in input between the three social classes these authors studied: welfare, working class, and professional families. The cumulative number of words addressed to the children from 12 to 37 months was approximately 10 million, 20 million, and 35 million for the three social classes, in the order mentioned above. Different nouns and modifiers addressed per hour to the children ranged from about 10 to 50 for the welfare families, from 50 to 150 for the working-class families, and between 100 and close to 200 for the professional families. Total words per hour addressed to the children ranged from about 500 for the welfare families to about 1,200 for the working-class families, and slightly above 2,000 for the professional families. As evident from these numbers, the ratio between input of welfare and professional families is generally one to four, with the working-class families lying between these two extremes.

These findings are well supported by other researchers. Alvarez (1986) studied verbal interactions in Mexican-origin homes during those times that parents themselves said they involved children in daily routines. He found that in 15 hours of such home recordings over 5 months, one child and her parents spent only 12 percent of the recording sessions engaged in conversation, the other a mere 23 percent. Much of the talk was "controlling in nature and characterized by the use of directives and requests for action" (p. 309). Compared to well-known middle-class samples, the above percentages are extremely low.

Heath (1983) provides verbatim evidence of the attitude of lower-class mothers that results in such input deprivation: The mother of Annie Mae argued: "Ain't no use me tellin' 'im: 'Learn dis, learn dat, what's dis? what's dat?' He just gotta learn, gotta know, " (p. 105). And a grandmother admitted: "We don't talk to our chil'rn like you folks do. We don't ask 'em 'bout colors, names'n things" (p. 109). Rondal (1985) has surveyed further studies and reported a convergence of findings about social class differences in amount of verbal input to children.

Interactional Frequencies

Mealtimes could obviously be fruitful times for verbal interaction. Often this is not the case in lower-class homes, either because there is little constructive speech or there are few shared mealtimes. Tizard and Hughes (1984) recorded that working-class children had fewer tête-à-tête lunches and therefore missed educational opportunities. Similarly Ward (1971) vividly describes how food was prepared in a big pot and children were ladled out a portion whenever any of them wanted food, without common mealtimes being observed. If mealtimes are shared, lower-SES children are still deprived of valuable input. Bossard (1954) observed mealtime conversations of 35 families and found SES differences in vocabulary, use of imagery, times children were interrupted, and child versus adult-directed speech, with lower-class children faring worse on all these variables. There are therefore not only fewer mealtimes but there is also less well-structured talk during mealtimes.

Those input deprivations have consequences. Milner (1951) reports that high-scorers on language skill tests had more breakfasts and dinners with families. Heath (1983) reported not only that children from working-class Black backgrounds received the lowest amount of input but also that they had difficulties in school in participating in conversations and in exchanging factual information. They also had difficulty thinking about information and concepts when they were abstracted from the people and situations in which they were first relevant. These are compelling indications for the impact of input deficiencies on a range of school performances and cognitive skills. Young (1970), as well as Ward (1971) added age-graded differentiations: During the first year (the prelinguistic period) the baby was held quite frequently and received considerable verbal input. However, from one to two years, the baby received much less attention from the mother, from two until schooling he was mostly monitored by an older child. That means that during a very important period for preschool language-learning adult input and feedback is extremely infrequent. Heath (1989) confirms this finding from Papua New Guinea: "adults engage very little with their young children [who] interact verbally primarily with other children" (p. 343). Minimal adult–child interaction, as reported by Young (1970), Ward (1971), and Heath (1989) means, of course, little chance for instructive conversations.

Besides casual conversation, joint reading has been shown to be an important form of verbal interaction. Frequency of reading should therefore be a decisive causal factor in the acquisition of higher language skills. A quote from Heath (1982) regarding a working-class, all-Black community shall stand for many further reports: "Adults did not read to children, and there were few pieces of writing produced especially for children. There were no bedtime stories, children's books, special times for reading, or routine sets of questions from adults to children in connection with reading" (p. 95). Lower-class Hispanic students of the writer confirmed this absence of books and the lack of maternal reading from personal experience. These findings become especially critical, when Hoff-Ginsberg's (1991) differentiations are taken into account. While she found considerable frequency differences between working class and upper-middle class mothers in the numbers of utterances during mealtime and dressing, reading was the only activity where there was absolutely no difference between the classes. Yet this is an activity in which Black lower-class mothers did not engage in with their children. The finding of Hoff-Ginsberg (1991) of no differences during reading, however, needs to be taken with caution because Ninio (1980b) ascertained that low-SES mothers talked less and provided less varied labels for actions and attributes even in book reading situations. Finer analyses might therefore find differences even in these instructionally supportive activities. Certainly Whitehurst and associates (e.g., Whitehurst et al. 1988) have demonstrated that maternal reading styles can be improved with very positive results for filial language learning. Yet, if children are almost never read to, they will miss whatever degree of enrichment their reading mothers could have provided.

Production Frequencies

As to opportunities for children to train productively their language skills, Heath (1986) summarizes: "Young children are almost never alone with only one adult...Good manners require that children answer talk directed to them but that they not initiate social conversations with their elders. Adults rarely ask children to answers questions for which adults know the answer except in teasing exchanges. Similarly parents rarely ask children to tell narratives about events in which parents themselves have participated" (Heath, 1986 p. 344). Also, the reports of surveys show fewer shared mealtimes entail not only lowered input, but also lowered chances to produce speech which can be responded to and improved upon by the parents.

The relative absence of expansions, corrections, and other more sophisticated forms of input and feedback, as they arise in verbal interactions between an expert and an apprentice, are discussed below in the context of morphosyntactic complexity. Their low frequency logically follows however, from the low level of verbal production that is permitted for preschool children just reviewed. Children therefore experience multiple deprivations: not only is input much less frequent, and not only are they given few chances for verbal production in the presence of adults, but this lack of productivity deprives them of feedback also. Specific interactional aspects are clarified in the following sections.

Functional Aspects

Language fulfills multiple functions, as has been recognized for millenia. Only two dimensions have, however, been focused on in most SES and cultural comparisons: the dimensions of comprehension (including that of directions) versus production, and a second dimension whose poles are mostly conceived as socioemotional versus referential speech. On the pole of socioemotional functions, a subset, directive speech, that is, a predominance of commands, has been quite consistently reported on. These categorizations in the literature are employed below.

A Predominance of Commands

There is broad agreement on two facts: First that lower-class or, more generally, uneducated mothers in many (but not all) cultures employ language largely to control the behavior of their children. Second, that this simple directive speech is associated with delayed language development. The emphasis is here on the word "simple" because, as argued above, directive speech can also be complex, if it guides the child in solving a problem. Schneiderman (1983) and Pine (1992) have more finely analyzed the varying levels of complexity in action-directed speech and the varying contexts and functions of "prescriptive speech," respectively, as they change with the age of the child. Syntactic complexity, however, appears almost nonexistent when lower-SES mothers direct their children to perform or desist from performing simple behaviors. Pine (1992) impressively substantiated the high negative correlations between various forms of directiveness and forms of responsiveness plus tutorial prompts, that is, the more complex forms of verbal input. Only a few pertinent reports are surveyed to indicate the breadth of the support across researchers, families, and study designs for these conclusions.

Bee and associates (1969) reported many verbally controlling interventions and also that lower-class mothers intrude physically in the child's problem solving. The predominance of directive speech was already included in Bernstein's definition of a restricted code, it was confirmed by Hess and Shipman (1965), again by Snow and associates (1976), by Hoff-Ginsberg (1992), and most recently by Hart and Risley (1995). The preponderance of directives in lower-class homes is well established by research spanning the last 40 years. In addition to being constraining and linguistically simple, directives also entail more expressions of disapproval about what the child had been doing, conveying therefore a negative motivational aspect. In accordance with the convergent reports in the surveyed literature, Cook-Gumperz (1973) concludes that, "imperative control involves a very low degree of linguistic mediation" (p. 175), so that little can be learned by children even from the verbal messages they attend to.

What Heath (1983) labeled "fussing," in accordance with the vernacular usage, is in principle quite similar to constraints and demands, but produced by children. It deals with children's statements about what they or others should or should not do, denials that they have done it, and similar assertions: all, at best, simple full verb sentences with simple pronominal subjects, as the few examples given by Heath illustrate. The emphasis is again on directing and constraining behaviors and not on linguistic skills.

Interestingly, Pellegrini, Brody, and Sigel (1985) report increased directiveness in parents of children with language impairments also. They indicate that preschool children with language disorders elicited a greater number of low-demand strategies, and these were *positively* correlated with the children's verbal performance. They argue that more directive communicative strategies of parents may be appropriate and effective adjustments to the children's low communicative skills. This points to a probable vicious feedback circle also in families where no physical impairment interferes with language development: First, directive speech in lower-class children might lead to delayed and deficient language development, and then this same delayed development might necessitate low-demand strategies, such as contextually supported directives, in order to communicate efficiently with these children.

Additionally, as found in many reports (e.g. Blake, 1994), these same children become astonishingly unresponsive to directives when uttered without special emphasis. They respond predominantly only after the third or a later repetition when it is produced in a loud and threatening tone. At this stage, it might be unreasonable to expect sophisticated linguistic constructions. In contrast to middle-class children who have been shown to learn the vocal turn-taking game even before they learn language, lower-class children seem to learn interaction patterns of disregarding verbal input. This tendency would prove detrimental to language acquisition whether at home or at school. This is a topic that deserves further detailed exploration. Directives result in school-related deficiencies, as indicated by Reger (1990) for a widely different sample. She found not only large SES differences in the use of imperatives in her Hungarian families, but also negative correlations in the range of $-.39$ to $-.77$ between the mothers' use of imperatives and subsequent filial language performance on a variety of measures.

The Socioemotional Function

Conceived more broadly than mere directives, Blake (1994) and other authors (Heath, 1983; Tough, 1982) have focused on a socioemotional function. Blake (1994) emphasizes for her African-American families that "a considerable amount of language use was committed to the management of interpersonal involvement" (p. 186) and that "it appears that a socioemotional orientation was imposed on the setting, and opportunities to use the requisite language functions were created through mother–child interactions" (p. 187). When comparing social groups, Blake found "a greater use of social expression and stereotype by A-A [African-American] children than be E-A [European-American] children matched for social class" (p. 175) and that "an interpersonal function was the most frequent" (p. 175). That is, she found a combination of class and cultural factors. An "objective" function was employed only in about 15 percent by all three A-A children, all remaining 85 percent were basically social. In the mothers' language only slightly more references to objective givens were found. During the first observation (about 21, 22 months), an average of 20 percent objective comments were made by mothers, and for the last observation (about 26 months) only 25 percent objective comments were recorded for two mothers. Those numbers are extremely low when compared to middle-class white mothers. Blake provides many verbatim examples of maternal directives and shows that the children's frequent use of *want* reflects the mothers's frequent use of *want*. The similarity in maternal and filial speech styles supports a conclusion of cause–effect relationships.

Blake's evidence and conclusions agree closely with those of Tough (1982) who argued that differences in language use (that is, greater use by poor children of language to talk about needs and wants) reflect an orientation shaped by "differences in children's experiences of the purposes for which language is used." Tough suggested that this orientation toward language use in poor children is the cause of poor school performance, as "their expectations about language do not support learning" (p. 13).

In accordance with this restricted input, Blake's (1994) figures demonstrate that the language development of her African-American participants is much slower than Roger Brown's Adam and Eve, whom Blake chose as comparison participants. Blake stresses accordingly a discontinuity between African-American homes and

European-American school requirements, that is, a deficiency of African-American children in the specific skills that are required in school. The same children master speech forms such as signifying, rapping, shucking, jiving, and playing the dozens, that is, verbal bantering. However, teasing, and emphatic self-reporting, is of little use for higher educational tasks in the school setting. Heath's (1983) descriptions of playsongs and of "fussing" indicate some of the roots of these interpersonal verbal skills. She also observes, however, that "the topics, or major content repetitions, in playsongs performed in Trackton differ markedly from those used at school" (p. 100). Here the discontinuity between home and school is again encountered, as it is in most reports on lower-class familial verbal interactions.

Extensive additional references to similar findings are found in a recent study by Hoff-Ginsberg (1991). The evidence can therefore be considered convergent. It needs, however, reemphasizing that the lower-social class is not a monolithic group. As Heath (1983) recorded in detail, the Black lower class is quite different from the White lower class in many aspects of their verbal interactions, even if both earn the same income. Hart and Risley's (1995) working-class families would also be categorized lower class, but they differ greatly from the welfare families. Parental education, as demonstrated by Delgado-Gaitano (1994) and many others, as well as parental mobility aspirations seem to be an even more important factor than class by itself.

Comprehension Versus Production

The consistent emphasis in lower-class families on production avoidance has been surveyed briefly above. Heath (1983) provides vivid evidence of the almost systematic neglect by adults of filial productions, even when the children begin imitating sections of the overheard adult conversations. Most of the adult conversations continue as if the child were not present and had not uttered a word. As Heath describes it, girls even have to resort to conversations with themselves in front of a mirror to create a conversation partner, their mirror image. The one exception when adults urge some productivity is the rare case when politeness formulas are requested: "What do you say?" - "Thank you." Yet, the predominance of such simple formulas does in no way result in productive flexibility, as the adult input is directive also in these cases and therefore contains little *linguistic* information.

What elicited productivity exists in the playsongs largely entails nonsense word plays (Heath, 1983). These teach the melody and prosody of language but not rare vocabulary and complex syntax, items emphasized in school. That is, even where production is accepted and supported, it is not the type that would provide the bases for school success. The same applies to the bantering in the peer group, as argued above.

Morphosyntactic Complexity

Linguistic complexity can be described in multiple ways. These have not been systematically explored in regard to SES differences in input. The field is therefore not yet ripe for a definitive summary, and the present survey can mainly provide indications and implications from the sparse evidence available about broader interactional phenomena. These phenomena are again subdivided as to vocabulary, syntactic simplicity as found in directives, feedback in expansions and corrections, degree of book reading and the involved complexity of literacy input, followed by preliminary conclusions. First a general consideration is suggested.

Complex input, if provided without support, could and would overwhelm the young language-learner. Bases have to be built by adults incrementally for the infant to master more complex input. One of them is a gradual build-up from simpler to more complex forms in the course of an interaction sequence. In middle-class families it has often been observed (e.g., Clark, 1974; Moerk 1983b) that themes are extended over many turns and that the adult and child gradually build up the complexity of phrases and clauses by rehearsing items and incorporating rehearsed items into subsequently more complex constructions. Clark (1974) expressed this aspect concisely in the title of one of her papers: "Performing without Competence."

Regarding these preconditions for the build-up of complexity, Alvarez' (1986) observation in lower-SES families is relevant. Interactions of less than one minute duration accounted for 95 percent of the adult–child interactions in his study of lower-SES Mexican-American families. Verbatim reports of lower-class verbal interactions demonstrate the same observation: themes are maintained only very briefly, often for only one brief utterance per dyadic partner. In interactions lasting less than one minute, little or no build-up of complexity is possible. Lack of extended conversation, that is, lack of building blocks in short-term memory that could be employed for the construction of more complex utterances is also implied in the frequently encountered reports that adults do not treat children as communication partners. These pragmatic aspects almost necessarily preclude verbal complexity in interactions of lower-class mothers with their very young children.

Vocabulary Training

Snow and associates (1976) found that lower-class mothers employed less substantive deixis, that is, they referred less to objects and their features by means of labels. They also provided much fewer exact repetitions, which could have functioned as confirmations as well as rehearsals, and might have provided improvements in phonetic aspects. Heath (1982) reported that "Trackton children do not learn to talk by being introduced to labels for either everyday objects or pictures and words in books" (p. 111). Ninio's (1980b) finding that even in arranged settings of picture book reading lower-class mothers provide less sophisticated input supports this comparative deprivation. The low-SES mothers talked less and provided fewer varied labels for actions and attributes than the higher-SES mothers. For later ages, Brophy (1970) confirms the same principles even in an experimental setting where parents might be more motivated to perform for the experimenter: She found very significant SES differences in preresponse labeling and focusing of attention in block sorting tasks. (With labeling she means "a specific label referring to the attributes [e.g. 'tall,' 'same mark')"; focusing is "drawing the child's attention to the relevant attributes" (p. 84). In accordance with the lack of parental guidance, lower-SES children on the average only attained a third to a half of the scores of middle-SES children in Brophy's study. These findings regarding restricted vocabulary have been well established for decades. Reports to support them need therefore not be massed.

Directives and the Entailed Simplicity of the Input

The fact that "imperative control involves a very low degree of linguistic mediation" (Cook-Gumperz, 1973, p. 175) has been discussed above together with its simplicity and negative effects on language skills and school success. Directives, as conveyed in lower-class homes, are not only syntactically very simple. They also almost exclusively employ only the verb stem without any ending, as polite circumlocutions in question form are uncommon. No training in complex verb phrases therefore occurs. As the addressee of the directive is the child, subject–noun phrases are absent too. Finally, with nonverbal contextual support, the object can mostly be referred to pronominally (*it*) or as *the thing*, a restricted code (Bernstein, 1961, 1964), indeed. Indirect support for these analyses derives from Baumrind's (1971) distinction between authoritarian and authoritative child raising, the former relying on brief directives and the latter providing extensive explanations of the reasons for commands and prohibitions. As these two styles are associated with lower and middle-SES, respectively, and as explanations involve more complex linguistic structures, it follows the latter are predominantly provided for middle-SES children.

Linguistic Expansions and Corrective Feedback

In contrast to widespread myths that disregard extensive empirical evidence on expansions as a subset of corrections, and corrections generally, both occur frequently in middle-class maternal input. They have been shown to be effective language-teaching tools, as argued in Chapter 5. It can therefore be expected that their differential occurrence in various social classes would influence grammatical aspects of language acquisition.

As to social class differences, convergent reports indicate that lower-SES children mainly receive corrective feedback for their nonverbal performances, whereas middle-SES children receive them extensively for verbal performances. For example, Bee and associates (1969) report that the use of directive speech implies a focus on the nonverbal outcomes of activities and not on the form of speech for lower-SES families. Heath (1989) supports Bee and associates by confirming that "accounts of black working-class children portray socio-cultural contexts in which bodily kinesthetic competence and interpersonal nonverbal signaling take early precedence over linguistic performance" (p. 343). Equally, studies of Mexican families indicate that "adults respond to children with evaluations of the [nonverbal] performance when they carry out directives (Uribe et al., 1994). In summary, as long as the nonverbal performance is considered satisfactory, no feedback is given to the verbal products of the children. Opportunities for learning from a "difference-by-comparison analysis (Simon, 1978) are therefore not provided. The complete disregard of children trying to break into adult conversations, as mentioned above, also entails a lack of linguistic corrections.

Ward (1971) provides numerical evidence that expansions accounted for less than five percent in her sample of Black Louisiana families, whereas Brown and Bellugi (1964) reported about 30 percent in middle-class families. Snow and associates (1976) found also that academic and middle-class mothers provided many more expansions than lower-class families. Miller (1982) was impressed by the extremely small number of corrections provided to her working-class, white south Baltimore children. That "expansions are virtually nonexistent" is emphasized by Ochs (1982) for her Samoan participants. This lack of focus on grammatical form might therefore occur in many or most uneducated social groups; a conclusion that becomes plausible when considering that corrections and expansions imply a metaperspective on relatively abstract principles of language, what linguists label rule conforming.

Both corrections and expansions involve contingent and relatively fine tuned responsiveness to the child's utterances. Whether it is the unresponsiveness documented here or Ninio's (1980) finding of differential fine tuning, both have implications for feedback. In Ninio's low -SES group only the proportion of maternal *what* questions was correlated with the infant's level, whereas *where* questions and labeling statements were not adjusted to the infant's level. Similarly, Blake (1994), who provides lengthy transcripts of mother–child interactions, documents an almost complete lack of tuning. The mother does not correct, she does not reward or expand, and her input is repeatedly far above the child's (one-word) level. It does therefore not stand in an optimum level of discrepancy to the child's level and is not in the zone of proximal development. This lack of tuning entails a lack of effective teaching by the mother. It results in unresponsiveness of the child even when the mother tries to elicit verbalizations.

Book Reading and the Entailed Complexity of Literary Styles

It is generally recognized that written texts are more complex, both in the range of their vocabularies and in their morphosyntactic aspects. Book reading entails a transition from the oral style of the early nursery to the literary style that will be needed in school.

Book reading by parents for their children would therefore be very conducive in establishing continuity between home and school. Extensive research (e.g., Dickinson, 1994) exists on the positive effects of book reading that has been surveyed most recently by Moerk (1996). Only some major points that are specific to SES differences are selected therefore for emphasis. Heath's (1982) impressive report from the Trackton community about the absence of reading is quoted above. This lack of reading implies a lack of narrative, of the distancing function common in reading, when future and past aspects or foreign locations are referred to. It also implies a lack of experience in translating from the visual (the pictures in picture books) into the verbal symbol system.

The last section of Heath's report stresses the rather complete deprivation: "There were no bedtime stories, children's books, special times for reading, or routine sets of questions from adults to children in connection with reading" Heath, 1982, p. 95). Teale (1986), too, reports for 24 low-income children in San Diego, Anglos as well as Blacks and Mexican-Americans, that they found little evidence of parent–child reading. The three exceptional cases who enjoyed considerable reading were also the most highly developed in emergent literary skills (p. 196). Also, as mentioned above, several samples of Mexican-American students from lower-class backgrounds have consistently affirmed to the writer that they were not read to. Even when some reading exists, it is sometimes less sophisticated in lower-SES families, as Ninio (1980b) found in Israel.

It has been proven for the last two decades (e.g., Moerk & Moerk, 1979) that picture books introduce in their captions not only a high percentage of new vocabulary items but also comparatives, superlatives, subjunctives, and past plus future tenses, therefore the morphosyntactic deprivations are encompassing when no books are read to children. From a complementary perspective, Speidel (1993) and Whitehurst and associates (1988) have shown, that provision of such experiences in remedial programs can substantially and quickly increase language and literacy skills. Concomitant variation between picture book training and acquisition of advanced language skills has therefore even been experimentally demonstrated.

PRELIMINARY CONCLUSIONS

Can conclusions be drawn from the evidence of social-class differences surveyed so far? Certainly, the evidence is not complete nor perfect; but equally certainly, it is impressive in its convergence. Linguistic delays have been consistently supported by research into children's competence, going back for about 65 years. They are also only too obvious to every teacher of lower-class children. On the input side, the evidence is somewhat more recent and much less extensive, but barely less consistent. The same phenomena are reported across studies and samples and these phenomena are theoretically consistent with the delay and deficit reported in the children's competence. The studies comparing social classes in both input quality and speed of language acquisition confirm consistent concomitant variations between these two sets of variables. The prerequisites for cause–effect interpretations appear therefore given even if they still need to be confirmed by contingency based (Bloom, 1993; Moerk, 1983b, 1985a) and multivariate time-series analyses.

Methodologically, one might object that in many cases input and competence phenomena were established partly with different samples and that the data can therefore not be related to each other. Although this objection is correct for some of the studies, it does not appear critical. When the consistency of the findings across samples is considered, it becomes evident that these samples are drawn from the same population. Conceptually, the input data from any sample of this rather homogeneous low-SES population can then be related to the output data from the same population. Therefore the evidence for concomitant variation can be considered across samples.

From the above evidence and the conclusions suggested, it appears that Bernstein (1961, 1964) was correct in principle in his differentiation of an elaborated and restricted code. Additionally, his assertion that a restricted code in the home is harmful for the acquisition of those aspects of language that are fundamental in an industrial-bureaucratic society and that are required to succeed in its educational system, is upheld only too strongly through the educational failures of many lower-class children. News media report that 3,000 teenagers drop out of high school daily. What happened to Bernstein is that the bearer of bad tidings was attacked and not the causes of the bad tidings. Killing a messenger never undid a lost battle, and not recognizing an illness will not cure a patient. The surveyed evidence therefore deserves to be taken seriously; and even more, the children who suffer from such deficient input need to be taken seriously and remedies need to be developed.

The above survey could provide multiple vantage points from which to initiate such remedies. It has shown a relatively complex causal network, not only from multiple antecedents to language delay, but even more, how the antecedents themselves are interrelated. Cultural attitudes derived from nonliterary backgrounds suggest that language teaching is not necessary; and uneducated parents might also be aware that they would be unable to provide such teaching. As no instructional activities are intended, extensive interactions of parents with children appear not needed, especially as soon as older siblings can take care of their younger ones. Even simple occasions for conversations, such as mealtimes or playing with toys, are missed or underutilized. All these aspects can, in principle, be remedied in relatively cost-effective ways. Specific remedial interventions would also provide valuable experimental data for future causal analyses. There exists, however, a potentially serious objection against the above conclusions: Reports from cross-cultural studies of input and language development often assert normal development despite input that might seem very different and deficient and that is, as already indicated above, quite similar to that found in lower-SES homes. These cross-cultural studies are therefore be focused on with great care in Chapter 7 in order to evaluate whether rich input might not be required after all, at least for advanced language mastery in non-Western cultures.

7

Cultural Differences in Verbal Mother–Child Interactions and Filial Language Acquisition

> Among the Indians, the topics of conversation are but few, limited for the most part to the deeds of the day, the number of animals they have killed and of those which escaped, and other incidents of the chase.
> —Alexander Henry (1809).

Before even beginning a review of cross-cultural research on language acquisition several serious constraints have to be acknowledged: First, when interpreting reports from exotic countries and linguistic communities, a reviewer has to rely mainly on English glosses of the interactions that were recorded in the native tongues. Information might easily be lost in this translation and reinterpretation. As far as prosodic aspects are concerned, such loses are certain. Second, any independent evaluation of verbal interactions in any language depends, of course, on the wealth of information provided by the original investigators. As is so obvious from studies of English-speaking dyads, tens and hundreds of hours of careful recordings could not yet induce diverse investigators to agree on training and learning phenomena. Unambiguous interpretations will be much more difficult for relatively brief cross-cultural samples and examples. With brief samples the question also arises whether they were representative and whether they exhaustively covered all language training and learning situations. The answers to these two concerns are almost certainly negative. The absence of specific input phenomena in the published reports from exotic linguistic communities might therefore be equally, or more, due to a lack of full recording and to possible bias in what was selected for publication as to a real lack of linguistic information in the input. It appears from these considerations that a great deal of caution is required in interpreting any brief reports about unknown and little explored languages. This applies especially to assertions about the nonexistence of certain types of linguistic information or about deficiencies in instructional support of any kind.

An even more serious obstacle arises in the evaluation of the outcome phenomena. Any tests designed for Western samples would probably have to be considered invalid due to the wide range of differences in the languages and the samples of speakers. Yet, if children are reported to develop "normally" (as is often asserted in the literature), the nature and the establishment of the norms would need to be specified carefully. What if language development in the entire culture that is reported on would be one to two years slower than Western middle-class language development? The children who develop "normally" as far as the local comparison group is concerned would nevertheless be far behind those in Western cultures. For example, Pye (1992) reports that Mayan parents do not become concerned about language delays until children are three or four years old. He provides an example from a child, aged 25 months, who is in the one-word stage. Yet, the father of the child and Pye, the investigator, seem to consider this extremely slow development "normal," although it represents a delay (compared to Western middle-class children) of about 15 months. In other words, it took this child about two and a half times as long as Western middle-class children to get to this level of language skill. Additionally, the vocabulary produced by the child was restricted to *chick*, *daddy*, and *there*; certainly far from the 50 words reported for Western children much earlier. Similarly, Ochs and Schieffelin (1984) provide data (example 6, p. 297), showing that Persio, aged 27 months, would be considered extremely language-delayed phonetically, semantically, and morphosyntactically in comparison with Western children. Schieffelin (1979, pp. 132–135) provides an equally impressive example of Wanu (26 months and 3 days) who is extremely unproductive in verbal interactions with his mother. He also seems stuck in a primitive phase of the one-word stage, producing only utterances such as *mine*, *where*, *eat*, and as a maximum *Mama eat* even in prodded imitations.

In the face of this relaxed attitude of many preeducational cultures toward language development, it is impressive that diverse authors in Slobin's (1985–1997) series on *The Crosslinguistic Study of Language Acquisition* report folk remedies against language delay in several of these cultures. This means that even with these relaxed norms an unspecified number of their children do not acquire language normally. Lack of informative input could certainly be an important factor if one considers the rudimentary character of this input, as described below. An assertion such as "one implication of such work (Ochs, 1982; Schieffelin, 1979) was that the American style was not necessary for normal language acquisition to occur" (Shatz, 1991, p. 141) is therefore premature and misleading. Certainly, Shatz admits immediately after this sentence that "direct cross-cultural comparisons of cultures and languages as different as Samoan and American are difficult indeed" (p. 141). Yet, while admitting this, strong conclusions should not be drawn from such shaky comparisons.

Even more complex is the question of what is developed. If there is any validity behind either Ong's (1982) differentiation between orality and literacy, or Cummins' (1980) contrast between BICS and CALP, then multiple criteria of output complexity would need to be defined in order to make comparisons between cultures. For example, in some preliterate cultures rote learning of standing formulas or of simple frames with well-known fillers, might suffice for most everyday communication. If such unanalyzed routines were learned early and employed almost exclusively, then any complexity measures, and especially MLU, could be very misleading in ascertaining levels of language skills. A fit example might be the Kaluli culture, reported on by Schieffelin (1990), a small nonliterate population of approximately 1,200 people, with sixty to ninety individuals comprising a village, and engaging in gardening, hunting, and fishing, as their forebears did. How many new and unexpected constructions could be expected in input and how much fewer would be needed in everyday output to communicate successfully—by means of utterances mostly supported by nonverbal and very familiar behavioral contexts?

In technological-bureaucratic cultures with hundreds of millions of members from very widely differing backgrounds, analytic and abstracting skills are absolutely necessary to abstract meaning from widely varying input. In order to convey messages about all the widely varying contents one might have to talk about, equally complex synthetic skills are needed (cf. Hymes, 1961). Only if these contrasting demands on a successful communicator, that is, the culturally required outcome variables, had been carefully differentiated, could it be established whether the children in diverse cultures acquire the same complex and abstract linguistic skills at comparable ages. As has been surveyed in preceding chapters, only children from families who provide enriched input prove generally well-prepared for educational tasks that increase in complexity from elementary school to the university. From this outcome perspective, the school problems of minority children from rather illiterate backgrounds prove that serious deficits exist in the required linguistic skills. Across widely differing cultures, the gaps would be expected to be even more extreme.

In respect to the complexity of the problems, it is greatly astonishing to find that the published literature is generally very miserly regarding verbatim transcripts, whether in the original languages or in English glosses. For example, the publication of Ochs and Schieffelin (1984), which is so commonly referred to when emphasizing normal language acquisition despite input differences between cultures, provides altogether six utterances of Kaluli mothers and five utterances of a Samoan mother addressed to children in the verbal stage. Even entire books on language socialization (e.g., Schieffelin, 1990) contain by far too little and too restricted (the *elema* pattern) verbatim information of the input for evaluating the claims of the authors. As Harris (1992) correctly criticized, quantification of the amount and variety of language input is not even attempted. The same studies contain almost no specification of how normal development was defined or measured. Nevertheless, based on the extremely slight verbal evidence, a great deal of potential misinterpretation has been spread across much of the literature. Also, it will be resistant to extinction since it cannot be independently evaluated—and conforms nicely to the predominant nativist ideology. (It might require a Derek Freeman correcting juvenile interpretations of Margaret Mead to rectify this state of afairs.) Any inferences about cause-effect principles, or their absence, drawn from such sparse reports have to be considered as absolutely premature. A lack of obvious concomitant variation could be due to a lack of recording, a lack of reporting, or misconceived matches between presumptive causes and effects.

Again only a selective evaluation of better known studies will be presented together with evidence from the often extremely brief remarks which are found in several chapters of Slobin's (1985–1997) edited volumes. Anthropological linguists still need to provide more extensive and representative samples of all the forms of verbal interaction. They also need to present short-term longitudinal and long-term recordings to provide the opportunity for independently evaluating extended training and learning processes in those cultures and languages.

The present survey of the available evidence is structured in the same manner as that pertaining to social-class differences: Frequency aspects are followed by functional aspects, by evaluations of morphosyntactic complexity (as far as evidence exists), and finally by a consideration of the potential impact of narratives as language training devices.

Frequency Aspects in Verbal Interactions

Several types of frequency phenomena can be differentiated on the basis of research reports, although the types of phenomena are not fully mutually exclusive. For all aspects only general categorical impressions are provided in the literature without detailed numerical data. The following survey has therefore also to be rather categorical and cannot provide correlational evidence.

Amount of Interactions with Adults Versus with Children

This subcategory entails at least implicitly differences in input complexity because young children cannot be expected to provide complex input. This fact will not be emphasized but needs to be kept in mind as a criterion for evaluating the data. Pye (1992) puts strong emphasis on minimal adult input. He reports "even at the toddler state, K'icje' parents did not talk very often with their children. They certainly lacked any concept of talking with their children for the sake of their language development and were not conscious of their children's particular stage of linguistic development" (p. 244). Heath (1989) confirms from a village in Papua New Guinea that young children are given over to the care of older siblings who engage them in considerable language play and specifies: "However adults engage very little with their young ... and the young interact verbally primarily with other children" (p. 343). Rabain-Jamin (1994), who compared French mothers with African immigrants to France reported that African mothers do not usually talk to their children during child care or diapering. Harkness and Super (1977) affirm that "in contrast (to United States middle-class), the Kipsigis mothers of Kokwet take a much less active role in teaching their children to talk...the majority of the mothers judged that children learn to talk primarily from other children...the total amount of mothers' speech to their children was small: only 67 utterances, on the average, during a two-hour recording." (p. 327). This number has to be compared with the input provided by Western parents. For example, the parents of Adam and Eve, the famous observational participants of Roger Brown and his research group at Harvard, produced about 300 to 600 and even up to 900 utterances per two hours of interaction, that is about ten times as many as Harkness and Super report for Kipsigis families.

These findings, while clearly convergent, have to be complemented by aspects of educational-aspirational differences between families. In a Maya Indian community in highland Guatemala, Rogoff (1990) found that mothers with more education as well as mothers with more modern practices used verbalizations more and demonstration less. These reports reflect the contrast between book cultures and nonbook cultures as well as the transition between these two cultures in some families, with the mother being the most important person helping the child progress toward the more advanced culture. Uribe, LeVine, & LeVine (1994) report from rural Mexican mestizo families a correlation of .50 between maternal schooling and the amount of verbal behavior directed toward the infant, with SES held constant. The same principle was observed by Delgado-Gaitan (1994). These congruent findings from diverse cultural groups indicate that it is an educational culture and not SES per se that is the important variable. Accordingly and in contrast to the above non-book cultures, Erbaugh (1992) reports from Chinese families, who belong to an ancient book-culture, consistent questioning and emphasis on correct talk, that is, very active language teaching by parents, independent of SES.

Rehearsal Phenomena

The above brief survey should, however, not be taken to imply that nonbook cultures are not at all responsive to the infant's input requirements. Various forms of adaptation to these requirements have been reported. The simplest is repetition. Bavin (1992) shows that Walpiri adults exhibit repetition both within and across their own utterances, giving the child multiple chances to analyze the input perceptually and to decode it. Additionally, Kulik (1986), as reported in Heath (1989), remarks that adults repeat key words, when they simplify their utterances by abbreviating them. Both these forms of repetition involve massed training within brief time intervals.

There is also the seeming exception to sparse input in the training procedures of Kaluli mothers, as reported by Schieffelin (1979). These mothers elicit imitation extensively (the *elema* pattern) and insist that their children learn socially functional phrases. Here closely spaced repetition is again encountered, and this repetition evidently occurs frequently enough to insure retention. As the topics trained are eminently useful for everyday social interaction, rehearsals of the same or very similar phrases can be expected over the weeks and months of the learning process for any specific phrase. In this manner, spaced rehearsals are assured. Schieffelin has therefore shown that, when considered necessary for specific purposes, mothers engage in quite active teaching and rehearsal, combining massed and spaced rehearsals. However, they teach a very restricted set of formulaic phrases.

When it was emphasized in the preceding sections that infants and toddlers interact primarily with older siblings, this too implicitly entails considerable rehearsals besides the simplifications mentioned earlier. Same-age or slightly older children will not have the highly varied vocabulary or the ability to speak in complex sentences. With such conversation partners, constrained in topics and language skills, repetition of standing formulas are almost inevitable. These interactions, as well as language play, therefore also entail massed and spaced rehearsals.

These remarks on massing and spacing provide the occasion to raise the question of overall patterning of training in nonindustrial cultures and Western lower-class adult–child communication. It is commonly reported that these "caregivers do not engage in 'conversations' with infants over several exchanges" (e.g., Ochs & Schieffelin, 1984, p. 296). Such a statement would imply that relatively massed rehearsals, as found in Western middle-class imitations and repetitions, might be absent and learning might be harder. Yet, the *elema* pattern suggests that a great deal of immediate rehearsal might occur and massed initial training might be the norm for some training contents. Quite immediate rehearsals are also encountered in examples of child–child interactions, provided by the same authors, wherein communication partners imitated (and slightly altered) each other's utterances. Although further original data are needed to explore the question of rehearsal density more fully, it appears that such density is assured for a narrow range of items despite differences in interactional styles. It is a simple mathematical principle that the smaller the number of types, the larger the proportional frequency of tokens of each type in a fixed amount of input. Certainly the speed of learning should be influenced by massing and spacing phenomena as well as by the diversity of items to be learned.

Watson-Gegeo and Gegeo (1986), too, report from the Kwara'ae, a Melanesian culture in the Solomon islands, that the adults employ a repetition eliciting impera-tive *'uri*, meaning "thus," urging the child to repeat what came after this imperative. The modeling-imitation patterns reported by these two authors are apparently intentional language-teaching devices. These same authors emphasized also that "getting a child to repeat starts very early" (p. 25) and "by the time they [children] are able to speak, the habit of trying to repeat has been established, the intonation contours for ...basic repeating are familiar" (p. 25). In psychological terms, the parents have established a habit of generalized imitation (Gewirtz & Stingle, 1968; Rheingold, Gewirtz, & Ross, 1959) already before the children are able to speak. Later, training interventions can build on this habit. It will be documented below that the Kwara'ae employ additional language-training exercises that are quite comparable to those in Western cultures.

When considering such a wealth of training, it seems that assertions by some authors of minimally supported learning in remote cultures might be due more to minimal observation or minimal sensitivity of researchers to the aspects of training than to actual lack of training. Also, as emphasized repeatedly in this book, forms of training need to be related to fine-grained descriptions of the items trained and the overall end product that is aimed at and acquired in diverse societies or social groups. Yet, if such training is absent or rare, then the effects are readily visible as, for example, Harkness and Super (1977) concluded: "The trends in language socialization that we have described relate negatively, in general, to the rate of acquisition of syntax and vocabulary" (p. 328). Therefore such cause–effect relations between input deprivation and developmental delay or deficit exist across classes and cultures. They indicate that teaching and learning principles are central, indeed.

Functional Aspects

Several aspects of the functional dimension are again differentiated, as they were in Chapter 6 when SES differences were discussed. In the domain of the social-communicative function directiveness has been broadly focused on and is surveyed first. Additional aspects are then summarized, followed by contrasting comprehension with production in their instructional aspects.

The Directive Function or a Predominance of Commands
As already indicated when SES differences in functional uses of language were discussed, there is scarcely a field in naturalistic language research where findings are as congruent. It appears that in most pretechnological cultures studied to date early utterances directed toward children are *primarily* commands. This might be directives given directly to the child or they might be directives taught to children in order for them to be used in asserting themselves against other children. It seems, Austin's (1962) emphasis on *How to Do Things with Words* is adopted most closely by uneducated parents of young children.

Yet, despite this congruence in reports, differentiations have to be made: While for some low-educational groups the word *primarily* could mean almost exclusively, in other cultures *primarily* appears mainly to describe temporal priority. In these cultures, directive use is followed by more advanced forms of use, often of the narrative-dialogic sort. With dialogic uses, these cultures approximate the well-known mother–infant dialogues in Western cultures. The aspects of language taught might, however, be quite different even if diverse cultures employ narrative styles. One might select the oral style that is action-oriented and the other might focus more on objects and their relations. The latter would probably involve a larger vocabulary and more complex syntax. Such a contrast is seen repeatedly in the factual reports summarized below.

Only a few cross-cultural reports are cited to substantiate the general findings of directiveness of speech. Kulik (1986) as summarized in Heath (1989) reported that adults mainly direct commands to their young children. Pye (1992) reports for a Mayan mother that her speech to the child is "in the form of commands or just his name" (p. 243). She ignores his verbalization directed to her. Heath (1989) summarizes from a village in Papua New Guinea: "Adults talk to their children primarily in offering commands" (p. 343) and Harkness and Super (1977) report that the Kokwet mothers' most frequently mentioned language-teaching technique (mentioned by 55 percent of the mothers) was giving commands, such as "Bring the kettle." In the mothers' recorded speech to their children, imperatives were the most common form of utterances (47 percent). Greenfield and Lave (1982) suggest a very plausible ecological explanation for this predominance of directive speech in rural cultures with minimal formal education: "Commands seem to be important in informal education in pastoral and agricultural societies where children perform important economic tasks at a young age" (p. 187).

In terms of language skills, obeying commands requires the development of comprehension rather than production skills. Comprehension is not only easier than production, requiring only recognition in primed (Tulving & Thomson, 1973) contexts, it can also predominantly rely on global, diffuse intake and rarely requires articulated analysis. Also, the range of the commands, and as a consequence, the verbal constructions modeled, will naturally be restricted in the case of young children, which results in simple and therefore restricted (in Bernstein's sense) input.

Additional Aspects of the Social-Communicative Function

A second formulation often found in the literature refers more generally to social communicative functions of language. While the exact meaning of this term is not fully clear in many sources—because almost all language use is social-communicative—the term's use as contrasted to a referential function suggest that this category is conceived as influencing other persons and includes—at least as a subset—directives. It might sometimes even be largely overlapping with this subset. Mundy-Castle (1974) elaborates a contrast between socioaffective socialization and technological intelligence but indicates that the former's domain can be broader than just directiveness, including the expression of feelings, self-assertion, onomatopoeic sound-plays, and other aspects. As most investigators provide only minimal verbatim interactional evidence and almost no quantitative data, the exact relationships between the concepts of directive speech and social-communicative speech, as employed in diverse sources, have to remain uncertain. Yet, it is clear that both directive and the social-communicative utterances focus on interpersonal aspects as contrasted with object relations.

The sociocommunicative function, including rudimentary directives, is already found in higher animal communication as threatening noises, wooing songs, cries of pain, and so forth. In contrast, no untrained animal has been reported to describe the objective environment for a cospecies member (predator-specific warning cries being a borderline exception). It can therefore be inferred that the sociocommunicative function is more primordial, utilizing less complex, even if often more pleasing, forms of language. The repeatedly encountered reports of partially coded vocalizations and onomatopeia support this hypothesis.

Bakeman and associates (1990) report, for example, that in the !Kung culture (Botswana) children are not encouraged to take an interest in objects through comments or stimulation from the people around them. Yet, caregivers consistently respond when the children engage in social communicative acts. Rabain-Jamin (1994) confirmed a similar contrast: Wolof mothers, who immigrated recently to Paris, emphasized social exchanges in highly consistent settings. They made proportionally more direct requests for action than did French mothers who emphasized the "logical pole" more whereas the African mothers emphasized the "social pole" (Rabain-Jamin's terms) of speech. Rabain (1979) showed for children in Senegal that vocal and verbal exchanges between mother and infant take place chiefly via onomatopoeia, partially coded vocalizations, and short rhythmic phrases associated with chanting. Blake (1994) and Ochs (1982) also emphasize the predominance of this social-communicative function over the referential one. All this implies considerable linguistic simplicity in input and use.

Comprehension Versus Production

A closely related report that applies almost universally for nonbook cultures is that comprehension is by far the dominant goal set for children during the early years and that production is often actively discouraged. Production especially in the form of questioning, is seen as having negative implications, showing lack of respect to adults or simply being a bother to adults.

Thompson (1983) reports from the Yintjingga, an Australian aboriginal group, that children's learning proceeds in relative silence and that even questions of adults directed to young children need not be answered. Heath (1989) stresses from Samoa that no emphasis is placed on eliciting replies from children. Adults expect children to be passive listeners. Ochs and Schieffelin (1984) report that Kaluli mothers do not treat their children as communication partners. It will be remembered that this is almost verbatim what Ward (1971) substantiated for her black-American families. Harkness and Super (1977) state that "it is clear that young children in Kokwet learn a great deal about *not* talking" (p. 328). They also concur that "the relative absence of language teaching by the Kipsigis mothers is somewhat reminiscent of reports on class differences in speech in young children." Finally they emphasize "the traditional emphasis on language comprehension rather than production fits within the larger cultural values of obedience and respect as they are realized in many African societies." That is, not only is the input much more sparse, as shown above, there is an active discouragement of the more demanding process of language production.

John-Steiner and Osterreich (1975) report that Pueblo children have to listen *quietly* to long stories but are not allowed to ask questions or verbally reflect on what they hear. The same is recounted by Phillips (1983) for Warm Springs Indian children. As mentioned above under SES differences, this pattern has also been found by Delgado-Gatain (1994) for Mexican families recently immigrated to the United States. In this case, the cultural values were probably more influential than social-class membership.

The emphasis on comprehension must be joined by some production at some stage of development. This developmental sequence is difficult to follow in most reports, as they refer in their interpretative comments mainly to children, without giving specific ages. Also, cultures vary as to when they introduce the more complex aspect of production. Three or more differentiations of production skills will have to be made once more cross-cultural data are available: (a) Rote repetition without any, or with little, comprehension. (b) Production of rote formulas with only a vague and contextual grasp of their meaning. Finally, (c) innovative constructions of utterances. Degrees of novelty or generativity can vary continuously for utterances, as Bolinger (1976) has demonstrated so forcefully.

In the case of the *elema* pattern (Schieffelin, 1979a) or the *uri* pattern (Watson-Gegeo & Gegeo, 1986), the imitated utterances could be produced without being even partially understood. Good vocal imitation skills would be sufficient. Later, even if formulas are produced with some understanding, they might not have been within the children's productive competence if the latter had been required to construct them without adult scaffolding. This is the extreme pole of rote production.

In quite some cultures adults speak through children: A request directed to another adult present will be spoken to the child, who then transmits the message and receives the response for subsequent retransmission. This interaction pattern certainly could not be the case for the two-year-olds referred to above that were still in the one-word stage even in imitation, and the literature is silent on its gradual introduction. Yet, this performance too requires no spontaneous construction and little semantic analysis even in older children. Ochs (1982) also reports that "the caregiver prompts the child in the production of socially appropriate conversational contributions" (p. 98), such as greetings, calling out to others, learning the names of siblings and friends, and so forth. Praise and other rewards are provided when the child produces the desired verbal behavior; and corrections help children to approximate the desired forms. Also in this case of quite intensive training of sociocommunicative skills little or no generativity is involved.

At a later stage, when children begin to produce narratives of their own activities, they will most commonly employ the common full-verb sentence frame, a structure overheard thousands of time in the input. It remains to be cross-culturally explored how closely these productions resemble common models in the input in their lexemes and their semantic structures. When Moerk (Moerk & Moerk, 1979; Moerk & Vilaseca, 1987) explored this question for American middle-class families, close resemblances were found. Considering the common habits of modeling-prompting-imitation, as reflected in the *elema* and *uri* patterns, direct input-influences are highly probable.

The above considerations suggest that even more advanced productions by children are often only reproductions and entail little novelty and even less linguistic generativity. If such novelty is not needed, the training and learning processes can differ from those in complex technological societies, where the variety of topics to be conveyed linguistically can be almost unlimited and some produced sentences might be genuinely new in both meaning and form. (Though, how often has the reader heard genuinely new linguistic forms—outside of modern poetry?)

Morphosyntactic and Psychological Complexity in Training and Learning

Before the relatively sparse evidence on morphosyntactic complexity in input is surveyed, a few general methodological and theoretical considerations are in order. The argument in the preceding paragraphs suggests that psychological exploration of language training and learning should focus more on processing complexity and less on the complexity of surface structures. Although exact measurements of processing complexity do not yet exist, some overall estimates are possible and defensible. For example, comprehension is generally easier than production even in its demands on memory: the former relying on rather global recognition whereas the latter requires spontaneous recall. Similarly, few would doubt that immediate imitation is easier than spontaneous production without any model or other support. Equally, rote-based production is seen as easier than rule-based production of the same complexity. As infants the world over prove, the learning of contentive vocabulary is easier than the acquisition of functors—and once items have been learned and overlearned they can be produced almost automatically without a trace of analysis of their elements. Linguistic complexity can then be handled by means of psychologically simple processes. Considering training and learning, *psychological* simplicity and complexity are the variables of greatest interest.

These considerations are directly relevant for cross-cultural comparisons: Often astonishing numbers of vocabulary items for closely related concepts are reported for some languages, suggesting a complex linguistic system. For example, Löfgren (1981) reports that Swedish farmers could name 75 different types of soil, and fishermen had 25 different terms for "herring." When they wanted to convey the message that a specific soil had specific characteristics they could do this with one well-known vocabulary item and did not need to compose a syntactically complex message. *System complexity* resulted therefore in *psychological simplicity*. Similarly, Long (1996) reports for the Dena'ina in Alaska that they have an entire lexicon for streams. "It makes a difference if a stream is a river, a tributary, the outlet of a lake, a straight stretch of water, a place of fast or slow current, covered with slush ice or overflow ice" (p. 409). The multiplicity of labels for "snow" in the Eskimo language and that for "sand"' in Arabic is commonplace knowledge too. Here again simple word-concept associations replace the more complex processes that would be required for encoding all the differentiating features in lengthy morphosyntactic constructions. In these cases, the languages might appear complex from a linguistic point of view, but they simplify processing from a psychological perspective by relying predominantly on rote memory and straightforward associations of a percept/concept with a label when training and using the labels.

Having indicated some needed precautions in any evaluation of complexity in language training, some factual reports can be surveyed and preliminarily evaluated. Yet, null-reports—especially those asserting the absence of features—have to be treated with great caution, as lack of recording cannot be distinguished from lack of existence in the generally restricted samples. Yet, as null-reports suggest at least that the occurrence is infrequent, they can be related to the often encountered evidence of quite slow language development in the cultures from which these null-reports derive. If such concomitant variation is confirmed in the future, then the importance for effective language-acquisition of specific training procedures that are missing would be confirmed too. This is logically the *modus tollens* procedure, as contrasted to the more common *modus ponens* procedure, comparable to the two *A*-phases in an *A-B-A* design.

Initial Simplifications of the Input

It appears from the sparse verbatim examples provided in cross-cultural studies that it is common for adults to simplify their language input to young children on many occasions. Even more, their modal language productions directed to young children might be so simple, that is, simple commands of two or three words, and repeated so frequently that special simplification is not needed. Heath (1989) reports for a small village in Papua New Guinea that, in speaking to their children, parents "sometimes simplify their language, abbreviating their syntax and repeating key words" (p. 343). Bavin (1992) reports for Walpiri that adults employ stylized speech to children up to about age of five. At first they use uninflected verb stems when talking to children; generic terms are used and semantic oppositions are reduced in baby talk in "an attempt to simplify the system" (p. 323). These examples, in addition to the famous studies of Ferguson (e.g., 1964) on baby talk suggest that a graduated approach to providing language input is quite common. Logically, it is barely conceivable, considering the low proficiency of young children, that adults would not be forced to simplify their input if they want to get a message across. Additionally, whether adults simplify their input greatly or partially, the form of input received from older siblings and from peers needs to be considered also as a source of simplified input.

Expansions, Corrections, and Other Explicit Training Techniques

As already repeatedly indicated, corrections and the corrective function of many expansions have often been denied due to the dominant nativistic ideology, even though the empirical evidence for their occurrence is overwhelming (cf. Moerk,

1992, 1994, 1996, and Chapter 5 in this volume). When the linguistic data are sparse, as in cross-cultural studies, and when these denials of corrections and expansions cannot independently be evaluated, the denials need therefore to be taken with extreme skepticism. Corrections and expansions depend also on the verbal context. If a child predominantly repeats the simple phrases the mother modeled, as in the *elema* pattern, neither expansions nor corrections should predominate. With these precautionary considerations, the somewhat sparse evidence can be surveyed.

Ochs (1982) reports that Samoan caregivers do not expand children's utterances. Yet in the few examples Ochs provides, caregivers mainly commanded their one-word-stage infants to call out a name. There is little to expand here, although the mother rewarded and corrected the child. One wonders, however, about the total context: When the child is in the one or two-word stage and adults provide contingent verbal responses, even if to other siblings as Ochs reports, they would have to invest extreme attention to consistently avoid expanding the child's preceding utterance. Och's null-statement appears therefore even logically implausible and needs to be carefully evaluated. Lieven (1984) summarizes from Ochs and Schieffelin that Kaluli and Samoan "adults initiate such conversation whenever the child shows an interest in a person or an object ....The child obtains a great deal of externalized support for speaking" (p. 20). Lieven (1994) also stresses the emphasis on "correct" talk in Kaluli and Samoan comunities. As Schieffelin describes the Samoan cultural distinction between "soft" and "hard language, "soft" being the baby's attempts and "hard" the correct adult forms, such a distinction would also imply adult corrections in order to move the child from the "soft" to the "hard" stage.

Yet, much more instructional work seems to be performed by Kaluli parents, as the following example suggests. Ochs and Schieffelin (1984, pp. 292–293) report in Example 5 the following sequence of maternal models. (The often repeated request *elema* is omitted in the following summary.)

Kaluli text		Translation
Abe nowo		Whose is it?
Ge nowo		Is it yours?
Ge oba		Who are you?
Gi	suwo	Did you pick?
Ni nuwe	suke!	My grandmother picked!
We ni nuwe	suke!	This my grandmother picked!

(Some utterances that are single words in the original are separated above by a space to indicate more clearly the repetition of identical or similar elements; also the epsilon in some words is replaced by an "e". The maternal models above are generally followed by the request *elema*, *Say this*, and they are generally repeated by the child.)

Both the original text and the English translation show that considerable substitution training is added to the modeling and massed rehearsal in this interaction. This one brief example (and it is the only one provided by Ochs and Schieffelin (1984) of a Kaluli mother speaking to a child who can respond verbally!) suggests that more explicit scaffolding occurs in this nonliterate society than was analyzed by the original authors. Slobin (1975) described input in (literate) Estonian that strikingly supports these conclusions. He reported for himself and his students, who were completely unfamiliar with Estonian, that "repetitions with slight alteration sometimes made it possible for us to identify new words, and occasionally we could discriminate the meaning of such words from watching what was going on between mother and child" (p. 285). This was possible on the basis of an one-time observation of a two-year-old girl interacting with her mother, that is, at a time when the interactions were already quite complex. Therefore, input provided for young children appears both syntactically and semantically quite informative, regardless of the culture.

A striking contrast to some of the often-quoted statements by Ochs and Schieffelin, who downplay input, is found in the work of Watson-Gegeo and Gegeo (1986) about the Kwara'ae of the Solomon Islands. These two authors provide many verbatim examples wherein they show that the caregivers engage in nearly all the language-training activities encountered in Western cultures: Much correction of phonology, morphology, syntax, and word choice is reported and substantiated. Additionally, the authors describe multiple correcting routines (pp. 24ff). Families are concerned when children progress slowly in their language skills, frames are repeated with variation and substitution, and expansions are common. The authors find close similarities in their data to those of Peters (1983) and Bruner (1978), the latter emphasizing the adult language assistance support system and scaffolding.

Demuth (1992), too, reported that in Sesotho, a Bantu language, parents make "extensive use of question and prompt routines" and provide "an optimal environment." She stresses "the rich verbal environment of Sesotho children" (all quotes p. 629).

It is not possible for this writer to even guess at the source of the differences in the reports of Ochs/Schieffelin versus Watson-Gegeo and associates and Demuth. Was it the authors' different paradigms, and their differential anticipation, recording, and attention? Or was it really such a profound difference in those non-Western groups? As the Kwara'ae employed Western loan-words even in the relatively few examples given, it might be Western contact that produced real differences. Perhaps it was only a differential focus on age groups, as Watson- Gegeo and Gegeo's child-interaction partners were generally more advanced. Certainly language training has to be adapted to the child's level to be meaningful and effective. Careful on-site evaluations as well as methodological and ideological analyses are needed before any strong conclusions about non-Western cultures are drawn.

Even if great precautions are needed concerning the generalized deprecation of language teaching, differential training intensities, especially regarding more complex forms, appear plausible. Rabain-Jamin (1994) reports that, unlike French mothers, African mothers were much less responsive to their children's utterances. This implies almost necessarily a lower degree of expansions and corrections which have been proven so informative (Moerk, 1992; Nelson, 1977) in Western mother–child interactions. Rabain-Jamin also emphasizes that metalanguage was more frequent among the French mothers (about 4 times as high) as compared to African mothers. As many as 81 percent of the French mothers' metalinguistic utterances referred to their infants' utterances as contrasted with 47 percent of African mothers' metalinguistic utterances. These differences should have an impact on the learning processes. The same author observed that "African cultures do not endow words with the educational function of planning, as an organizer of ongoing activity" (p. 156), an important cognitive aspect of language use. One is reminded of Sigel's (1986) research on "the distancing function," which is also less developed in American lower-class children.

Narratives as Language Training Devices

In addition to the emphasized homologies, great cultural differences in early language training might also be found. This is exemplified nicely in the narrative styles of Hungarian Romani, as reported by Reger and Gleason (1991). Reger and Gleason describe how the Gypsy culture relies much more than Western cultures on narratives, that is, story telling, and thereby introduces rather complex language quite early. Caregivers surround even the preverbal infant with stories and include him and his potential future exploits in the plot, employing his name for one of the characters, thereby probably attracting and maintaining the child's attention. How the parents help the child to analyze the stream of the narrative is not fully shown by the authors. Yet parents often employ testing questions to which their young children respond with one- and two-word utterances. Clearly, analytical interactions are hereby added to the wholistic text presentation. One would need long-term studies over the entire childhood period to discover changes in such patterns of training. Reports from many Native American tribes also show that narratives fulfill an important function in language and cultural training (Tharp, 1994).

The Romani and some other cultures might proceed from global comprehension to differentiating and analytic procedures, whereas Western middle-class cultures initiate the instruction with greater early emphasis on elements—vocabulary—followed by syntheses. The widely explored contrast between expressive and referential styles (Nelson, 1981) even in dyads from Western cultures comes to mind as a close parallel.

Indicating another contrast, Heath (1989) summarizes from some cross-cultural studies that special ties between labels and their referents—either by attention-focusing deictic gestures or bodily or visual contact—are established relatively infrequently in some societies. When Australian aborigine fathers teach their sons the names of animals, places, and clans, their referents are not physically present at the time of the teaching. Blake (1994) reported in a similar manner that small

African children in Paris are often told about their relatives who live in Africa and whom the children have never met.

As seen from the reports of Australian aborigines and African mothers in Paris, verbal forms can be acquired before comprehension, almost as empty molds. (This fact accounts, of course, for the need for dictionaries in literate societies.) Children's predilections for sound play, and students' use of terms they do not (fully) comprehend are other examples of the learning rather empty forms. Once the forms are well mastered, even a single contextual demonstration of their meaning (meeting a talked-about relative; looking up a word in a dictionary) might lead to full mastery. Otherwise, children, like second-language learners, might gradually demarcate semantic fields of words and phrases based on verbal as well as nonverbal contexts. Such approximations to meaningful use stand in stark contrast to the conviction abstracted from research with Western dyads that children have to have a concept in mind before they can learn a label for it. Extensive differential analyses will be required to understand these diverse courses of language training and learning.

Whereas such encounters with language through narratives might be extensive, it has nowhere been shown whether children learn to understand these narratives quickly or not. Much repetition is implied in most reports. These repetitions would make very slow learning feasible. As these narratives were often about the not-here-and-now, in the case of Romani caregivers even of imagined future activities of the child (told to the neonate), understanding and linguistic analysis might be only a quite remote goal. Also, production, that is *story telling* by children, as contrasted to mere listening, occurs much later and often requires special training. The latter was well described for the training of Yugoslav bards (Lord, 1960). The competence resulting from merely listening to stories might therefore be rather narrow and quite different (wholistic and more passive) from that attained with Western training methods—despite the fact that both competencies develop normally.

With narratives and their comprehension, the discussion has arrived at relatively complex language products and language skills. It remains to be explored whether degree of *psychological* complexity of language training and everyday language use (not degree of complexity of the full linguistic system) is related to other aspects of complexity or modernity of cultures. As Hymes (1961) has persuasively argued, there is an "embarrassing contradiction between an evolutionary view of culture and a non-evolutionary view of culture's part, language" (p. 80). Language is, of course, employed to communicate about those evolutionary aspects of culture. How could it remain unchanged when a culture increases in complexity (Hymes, 1964)? Also, relationships with maternal education, substantiated previously, support an hypothesis of increasing complexity in language training and learning with cultural change within and across families. The question follows logically from this of whether higher degrees of complexity in early training, if found, prepare children to cope more easily and rapidly with Western cultural demands of schooling. The differential success in the American educational system of children from book cultures compared to those from relatively nonliterate backgrounds suggest such a differential readiness based on the home environment. Normal development within a subculture does therefore not indicate that language skills attained are equivalent to those attained in other cultures. According to the present evidence and arguments, it could indicate a considerable deficit in regard to those language skills required in technological-bureaucratic cultures.

CONCLUSIONS

The evidence surveyed and interpreted here suggests conclusions that might be unwelcome to some: Quite extensive differences seem to exist in language skills between social classes and cultures. After decades of linguistic relativism, hard reality in the form of failing students should oblige researchers to accept this fact. Such differences in educational success indicate at least differential suitability for the demands of technological-bureaucratic societies. This can be attested by every school teacher who instructs pupils from poverty backgrounds. It is also attested indirectly on a worldwide scale in the struggles of many nations to adapt their languages for modern, technological use—or in their adopting English or French for technological and scientific discourse. Accepting differences does, however, not necessarily mean a rigid rank-ordering as to quality or value, whatever such a label might mean. This insight might make the conclusions just drawn less odious. Although Homer's or Vergil's language might be largely unfit to convey messages common in Western technological-bureaucratic contexts (the Vatican needs continuously to update its Latin), nobody would argue that ancient Greek or classical Latin were low-level languages. Comparisons have to be related to specific tasks. The function communication is put to in complex modern cultures is that of comprehending and producing unexpected, culture-neutral, messages over a large array of contents. Only if this form of functionalism is fully integrated into research on language transmission and acquisition, can evaluations be function-specific and interventions adequate to their goals.

On a more basic level, this refined theoretical conception can be related to well-established principles: It is a question how much uncertainty, in the information-theoretic sense of, for example, Wiener (1950), has to be handled by a language community predominantly in the verbal channel. The emphasis is on language community and not on an entified language. As argued in Chapter 1, nobody ever learned or mastered a language in its entirety. In very small oral cultures with only a few thousand members, some persons might come close to the full mastery of their language. For a world-spanning language like English that deals with all fields of science and the humanities, encompassing multiple local and specialized idioms, only very partial mastery can be achieved by individuals. Each language community teaches its children what it *believes* are the probably necessary skills and it can only teach what it has *mastered* itself.

This last assertion might require some explication: A rather isolated black community with little higher education, such as the one studied by Ward (1971) in Louisiana, cannot be conversant with many aspects of the literary English their children will need in school and in future occupations. Their estimates of what the children might need depend on their own past and present experience, which mostly derives from nonmainstream settings. This argument applies a fortiori to an isolated traditional agricultural language group that only recently came into contact with Western cultures. Even more important than the belief system of parents and relatives is their knowledge base. If parents have acquired minimal versatility in those educational skills that are based on language, they *could not* teach those skills to their children even if they had the desire and motivation to do so. This is probably the main reason why child language-levels are so highly correlated with maternal education, as attested consistently in the literature. Other cognitive aspects should, however, not be overlooked. For good teaching, mothers would need both to be able to decenter (to notice the changing learning needs of their children). For optimal teaching, they also would need to anticipate the latter's future needs (in school, and so forth), habitually employing a sophisticated future-time frame. Lower-class, harried mothers might not be focused enough most of the time to accomplish either task. If they did not learn to employ the distancing function of language habitually, they might not be able to do it despite their best intentions.

Having clarified some background factors, the factor of informational uncertainty can be analyzed further. Uncertainty can be lowered through the here-and-habitual, that is the nonverbal context. If people communicate almost exclusively with familiar people in familiar settings, not much novelty is involved and well-learned routines generally suffice: Consider an old married couple living on an isolated farm that is cut off from all sources of external information. How much novel communication will they engage in? In agricultural societies that deal almost exclusively with the exigencies of plowing, sowing, and harvesting, the range of meanings will be very limited, and communication can rely on a few frames with a restricted number of elements that are substituted in the slots of the frames. Uncertainty is increased by the number of people one interacts with and especially by the number of strangers one needs to interact with; strangers who might employ different linguistic styles and talk about unfamiliar topics. This implies that language has to handle much more uncertainty in large societies and open cultures than in traditional small and closed groups. To accomplish this, users cannot rely on standing formulas, neither for comprehension and even less for production.

This challenge of modernity implies not only a much larger vocabulary, but even more importantly, a rather abstract, analytic, and synthetic approach to the new messages that are received and conveyed. Especially in more technical/scientific communication, it is not sufficient to *approximately* comprehend or convey the meaning of an entire phrase. (Consider vaguely understanding how to handle a dangerous instrument!) In contrast, for everyday communication, Wong-Fillmore (1976) described so well for second-language learning children how approximate understanding suffices on the playground. Habits of only partial analysis generalize, and even college students often seem not have read test questions carefully before they answer them. Yet, in such educational contexts each individual element of a phrase might carry diacritical information that requires careful analysis. For the latter type of tasks, CALP (cognitive academic language proficiency) needs to be particularly trained (Cummins, 1980).

The acquisition of such higher level skills builds upon bases established in the home (cf. Moerk, 1985a) and continues until the college years, utilizing new input and feedback to refine and expand the skills. If children from lower-SES homes or traditional cultures are not prepared for these skills, they probably will have difficulty becoming readers (cf. Tizard & Hughes, 1984). Not reading much, they will not be able to learn the more advanced language forms (literacy skills) employed in written materials and they will experience the cumulative deficit that contributes to 3,000 teenagers dropping out of high school per day.

The same principles apply on the international level: Migration brings members of diverse cultures into intimate contact with the requirements of Western functioning. And the world-wide spread of technology and of bureaucratic systems leaves few niches that do not require language skills that are adapted to them. It is therefore of great practical importance that levels of language and the diverse training and learning methods needed to establish these levels, including technological-bureaucratic literacy skills, are taken seriously by child-language researchers. Trying to find teaching and learning principles that help children catch up when deficient in linguistic competence and to master the increasing tasks of education presents further theoretical challenges. Combined with other domains of skill training and learning, such investigations might even produce insights into new forms of learning. On the other hand, simply asserting that an unanalyzed end-product emerges miraculously, without sufficiently analyzing its potential determinants, will result only in mystification and will leave nations and individual without the guidance they need.

8

Evaluative Retrospect and Prospect

> To know requires exertion, it is intellectually easiest to shirk effort altogether by
> accepting phrases which cloak the unknown in the undefinable.
> —Pearson, 1899

The extensive evidence on input features and their effects on L1 acquisition has been surveyed in Chapters 3 to 5. Findings on relative deprivation causing delays and deficits in language acquisition, as presented in Chapters 6 and 7, complement the *modus ponens* argument of the preceding chapters. This impressive evidence has been established despite some serious drawbacks in methodologies, as discussed in Chapter 2. It can therefore be concluded that the evidence relating to input and acquisition could only be even more securely established if improved methodologies were employed.

Just because of these achievements of the field, the critical reader might, however, have been left with considerable puzzlement: How could a field that is between 100 and 200 years old, whose data are so abundantly and so readily at hand, and which has produced impressive evidence for the wealth of input and its effects, be at present still in a state where almost everything is controversial and where misleading conclusions are so predominant? While year in and year out about two billion young people acquire the various levels of widely differing, and therefore learned, mother tongues, learnability of language has been seriously questioned and rejected in some quarters. While the educational systems of all industrial countries spend large amounts of resources in teaching children the more advanced aspects of their mother tongue, with considerable success in most cases, the teachability of language has been rejected by some. Instead of exploring teaching and learning processes, the predominant theories have fallen back on an outdated faculty psychology, or on modularity (a technical and more persuasive label) which Fodor (1983) borrowed, or even on the hoary concept of instinct (Pinker, 1994). Instinct is a vague label that can explain everything and therefore explains nothing and which consequently had been eliminated from scientific discourse as demonstrably empty.

Considering this discrepancy between rich evidence and theoretical confusion the question arises as to the causative factors.

RETROSPECT ON SOME IMPEDIMENTS TO EMPIRICAL PROGRESS

Certainly many factors contributed to this predicament: from concern for personal reputations once a theory has been associated with an individual and needs to be defended, to simple power relations, and to conceptual rigidity, as vividly described by Heisenberg (1970/1974) in the following quote:

> ...when new groups of phenomena compel changes in the pattern of thought...even the most eminent of physicists find immense difficulties. For the demand for change in the thought pattern may engender the feeling the ground is to be pulled from under one's feet...I believe that the difficulties at this point can hardly be overestimated. Once one has experienced the desperation with which clever and conciliatory men of science react to the demand for a change in the thought pattern, one can only be amazed that such revolutions in science have actually been possible at all (p. 162).

Yet, in addition to personal foibles and widespread cognitive limitations, major epistemological problems deserve attention. Some of them are briefly outlined in the following.

A Mismatch of Discipline and Endeavor

Whereas the brief survey of the repeated relapses from empiricism to romanticism sketched in Chapter 1 suggested a partial explanation for the recent reliance on empty speculations by those scientists who refused to attend to empirical evidence, more penetrating analyses seem required when considering the widespread neglect and even the denial of the established findings, as shown in the preceding chapters. One aspect that might explain the miscarriage of linguistic theories of L1 acquisition and their recourse to empty labeling seems to lie in the nature of the object of study as contrasted with the predominant approaches in linguistics.

Description of Production Data Only

The approach most readily suggesting itself to a linguistically trained observer is the description of filial productions at various developmental stages. This approach, for which the science of Linguistics appeared to have the necessary tools, was followed in the early studies of nursery speech. Parents, who were often linguists, relied therefore unquestioningly on it in their pioneering research. No causal factors were ascertained and no functional explanation was therefore possible.

Capturing Changes in Potential Determiners

Yet, equally important as descriptions of verbal performance in the output, are those of the accompanying changes in the input that precede and accompany the changing output. For this task, Linguistics seems much less appropriate. Sociology or Ethnomethodology (Garfinkel, 1967) might be better suited for the recording of such interdependencies. Some relatively neglected psychological endeavors, such as the ecological psychology of Barker and Wright (1955) and Barker (1968), would also provide some tools to explore temporally extended interaction processes. Systems Theory, as explored since the 1950s, seems best fit to capture the feedback processes (Chapters 4 and 5) observable in mother–child or, more generally, expert–apprentice interactions. These fields, however, do not provide the tools to specify language training and learning processes or even to describe linguistic productions in detail.

Explaining Language Learning

For explanatory purposes, that is, to understand the *acquisition* of language skills, learning concepts inevitably need to be added. In addition to the rather elementary motor learning that can be observed during the early years of language acquisition, resulting in the correct enunciation of words, a wide array of perceptual-cognitive learning phenomena would seem to be relevant for any approach aiming at the *explanation* of language acquisition. Extensive psychological knowledge about the diverse fields of learning, about perception, and about cognition would therefore seem to be a prerequisite for anybody attempting this task. Three disciplinary competencies need to be combined to establish explanatory sufficiency: Linguistics for the specification of input and output; Systems Theory for capturing the dynamic feedback processes in the expert–apprentice dyad; and Perceptual/Learning Psychology for the intake and learning processes.

An analogy from a familiar field of natural science might clarify the above distinctions: In astronomy, a good telescope alone in a dark backyard can already make possible rich descriptions of the constellations in the night sky. This is the observational approach previously discussed. If, however, not only static constellations but the dynamic relations between stars and their planets are of interest, long-term observations, data storage, and comparisons are required. Such observations could result in Keppler's description of planetary motion. This is the dynamic conception previously discussed in "Capturing Changes." Yet neither of these two approaches would provide any insights into the dynamics of star formation or the cause of the movement of planets around stars. Newton's law of gravity was required to explain the latter, and more complex principles of physics and chemistry had to be borrowed to foster an understanding of the formation and disintegration of stars. These are equivalent to the explanatory approaches discussed in "Explaining Language Learning"; they require the integration of diverse domains of science.

With this differentiation of approaches to language acquisition one central problem of the field becomes evident. While causal explanations require encompassing knowledge of diverse fields of psychological research in perception, cognition, and learning in addition to the extended recording of input and contingent filial performance, the most influential explanations were formulated by linguists whose command of these fields might vary widely and might have been generally incomplete. This discrepancy between the task and the conceptual tools to accomplish it almost necessarily had to lead to failures and consequently to relapses into simplistic explanations that could be easily imagined. Neither did it help that the attention of the field was directed by Chomsky (1959) to the one-sided tool-set in Skinner's (1957) *Verbal Behavior*, a set which Chomsky passionately rejected. Chomsky seems to have conceived of Skinner's approach as the only learning approach psychology offered. Yet, while reinforcement and frequency phenomena are certainly important in L1 training and learning, as partly seen in the preceding chapters, a Skinnerian behaviorist approach does not seem to entail explanatory sufficiency. The association of innate, "emitted" responses of animals to new stimuli is categorically different from the learning of the completely new topographies of responses in language, responses that convey messages to cospecies members. An integration of diverse psychological approaches would have served the field better than Chomsky's violent rejection of one narrow learning approach.

A Mismatch of Conceptual Schemes and Data

Not only the *lack* of the necessary conceptual tools, but perhaps even more the *existence* of ill-fitting schemes produced impediments to scientific progress. It is well known that ingrained conceptual schemes can easily constrain and even suppress new viewpoints. Linguistics, deriving some of its main roots from ancient rhetoric and the post-Renaissance study of Greek and Latin, focused for most of its history exclusively on adult language productions and within that focus predominantly on the written word. Also, it was not just any adult language production, such as that of manual laborers engaged in shared activities or casual speech in the home, but formal, written language products that were mostly studied. Those were products of advanced competence in isolation from other channels of information transmission. This tradition had several consequences that engendered serious impediments for research on child language development.

The Core Unit

The central concept in linguistics is the *sentence*. Yet, in early child-language, a sentence is nowhere to be found. Single words, combinations of two or three words, irrespective of grammatical correctness, are the common phenomena. Careful study of early productions suggests strongly that they do not reflect any concept of *sentence*. The informed reader will remember proposals, such as reduction transformations, performance restrictions, and other salvage operations that were proffered to explain away the embarrassing fact that presumably preexisting knowledge was nowhere to be found in the behavior that should express it. As sentences could not be found, they had to be invented as deep structures.

As especially Bakhtin (e.g., 1986) emphasized, the essence of language is the utterance, as opposed to the sentence, and language is essentially dialogic, needing to be analyzed in relation to the actual event of the human interaction. The central unit of analysis has therefore to be the dialogic feedback cycle, as observed in mother–child interactions, and the analysis will focus on relations between utterances and not those between words in one sentence or between hypothesized elements of an elliptic sentence.

Such considerations have profound implications for dynamic explanations of performance: Contingencies between utterances and elements of these utterances, not rules for the construction of sentences will be the focus. As is well known, young children's performance is notoriously unpredictable and seems, for a considerable period, to be influenced minimally by prescriptive grammatical rules. On the other hand, it can be readily shown that imitations, corrections, and their impacts, and other inter-utterance relationships are determining variables.

Lack of Differentiation of the Object of Acquisition

Linguistics being focused on the very narrow segment of verbal products of authors could, without serious problems, presume that it was dealing with a unitary *language*. Such a unitary entity invited reification and necessarily resulted in the relative neglect of the varieties of performances found in each language community. Consequently, a conceptualization of different end products and different learning paths leading to them, such as in the training of "English for Special Purposes," was almost unthinkable. This led to many of the problems indicated in Chapters 6 and 7, of authors asserting that children had learned language despite greatly suboptimal input. It also resulted in perplexities when these children nevertheless failed in school language tasks. With the assumption of one language and one competence, conflicting evidence became invisible, unacceptable, or at best marginalized.

Focus on a Single Channel

Linguistics, as the name specifies, focuses exclusively on *language*. Yet infants' interactions with the physical and social environment are extensive for about one year before the first verbal productions appear. Thereafter, during the early stages of language acquisition, most elements of each message are conveyed nonverbally (Moerk, 1974), and for all of life human beings communicate by means of multiple channels in person-to-person situations. The infant's and child's increasing skills in information management, including the nonhuman context and paralinguistic channels, therefore needed to be explored to understand how subsequent verbal message-structures might build—and arguably can be shown to be built (Bruner, 1973, 1974; Moerk & Wong, 1976)—onto the preceding multichannel messages. This dependency can then explain the structure of verbal products. Linguists, due to their exclusive approach would have no way of following these developmental transformations and accounting empirically for the later occurring verbal structures.

Despite all the obstacles which the field of Linguistics faced, Chomsky, with his seemingly charismatic personality and due to his position at MIT, swayed a large number of psycholinguists. More than a generation of investigators has entered the field relying on Linguistics with its one-sided diet of easy labels that remained undefined and therefore vague. They formed schools (Barsky, 1997; Harris, 1993), and with the establishment of entrenched schools the dynamics of research changed from a search for the best tools for empirical research to the devoted defense of paradigms, as implied by the above quote of Heisenberg.

NEAR-TERM POTENTIALS
OF THE FIELD OF L1 ACQUISITION

The prospects of the field, like all prospects dealing with the future, remain shrouded in some uncertainty. On the one hand, we have the rich and still growing empirical evidence as surveyed partially in the preceding chapters. The actual empirical findings on first language acquisition are much broader, because only those studies most relevant for the present chapters were included in this review. There is much further potential evidence in the rich archives established in the CHILDES system that is accessible to every interested researcher. Remembering Max Planck's famous conclusion that a new generation of researchers is needed to welcome new ideas, the many new names appearing in the pertinent journals appear promising too. With increasing numbers of persons entering the research domain who are versed in learning principles, the range of conceptualizations has become wider in scope also.

From the wealth of detailed findings, broader principles have emerged that might provide the heuristic bases for accelerated advances and for the avoidance of blind alleys. Only a few major ones can be briefly considered.

Early and Simple Learning

First, the evidence for early and even prenatal perceptual learning is secure enough to prove a long history of perceptual learning before the appearance of the first approximations to language. Investigators appear also increasingly willing to accept the evidence of simple rote learning of formulas at least for the early stages, as contrasted to rule-based generativity. These findings of extensive early rote learning as the basis of early language performance accord well with what is known about the capacities of the infant and even the tendencies of adults. For adult chess players, the crucial contrast between expert and novice is that between prestored routines and on-line computation: the more expert, the more extensive the application of routines. Process explanations of observed performances become increasingly possible when these proven early learning tendencies are taken into account.

Structural Homologies in the Nonverbal Domain

With increased emphasis on the preverbal period, another conceptualization is being rediscovered: the conceptual, meaning-based antecedents of syntactic structures. Goldberg's (1995) emphasis on "constructions" and "a construction grammar," resurrects cognitive-semantic structures as basis for language acquisition. Such cognitive-semantic structures were originally conceptualized by Piaget as "schemas" (cf. Moerk, 1975b). They were expanded by Piaget's student Sinclair de Zwart (1973) and by Bruner (1973). Schlesinger (1974) made similar proposals, and Moerk and Wong (1976) empirically demonstrated how stable semantic frames were expressed in infant behavior and were observed thousands of times by infants when watching adults. An Agent–Action–(Object) frame and an Object–Features frame, homologous to the Subject–Verb–(Object) and the Subject–Complement sentence, are therefore securely established before any syntactic structures appear. Brown's (1973) famous ten semantic relations reflect similar cognitive structures related to temporal and spatial context. For the subsequent step in the learning process, Moerk (1992) documented in detail how the Agent–Action–Object structure was verbally modeled by Eve's mother in massed form and then gradually acquired by Eve herself. The continuum from preverbal structure to homologous verbal input structure and then the structure of verbal output has therefore been demonstrated. As these preverbal structures are experiential-cognitive, they are necessarily universal and would explain whatever is universal in linguistic universals.

Explaining Universals in Language

These cognitive universals are important for the explanation of language universals, which are sometimes (but not systematically) adduced to support nativistic arguments in addition to the poverty of the stimulus argument that was discussed in Chapter 1 (and factually refuted in Chapters 3 to 5). To evaluate this secondary argument, several subcategories of the postulated universals need to be differentiated and it needs to be examined whether they could derive from preverbal experiences. If they can be shown to derived from perceptual and cognitive processes, then the temptation to postulate innate bases should be resisted, and a blind alley can be avoided.

First, semantic universals—such as that every language has a term for the sun, or for eyes, and so forth—are obviously experiential universals and therewith based on perceptual-cognitive concepts. A specific assumption of a linguistic, as contrasted to a cognitive, basis is therefore unnecessary.

Second, so-called "substantive universals," such as that all languages have vowels and consonants, or form questions, are either analytic as part of the definition of oral language (natural sign-languages do not analyze words into vowels and consonants) or they are due to pragmatic requirements, respectively, such as the need to obtain information from a cospecies member.

As to the more controversial formal universals, Crystal's (1987) conclusion that "it is clear that 'absolute' (or exceptionless) universals do not exist" (p. 85) should give a first reason for caution. Furthermore, most of the claimed universals pertain to categories, such as agent, causation, patient, that are obviously elements of cognitive schemas which evolve from universal pre- and nonverbal experiences. They certainly do not appear de novo in language. Other relative universals (common but not exceptionless), such as that the subject precedes the object in most languages, might be pragmatically based, considering the importance (mostly human) agents have for the infant and for human beings generally. Attention is first focused on the most important aspect, the human agent or the potentially dangerous animal, and this object of attention would then be conveyed first in a message. On the other hand, if the subject is obvious from the context, it can be omitted in many languages. This suggest that it is not a linguistically fundamental element but contingent on communicational requirements.

Universals also depend on restriction in perceptual and cognitive processing. For example, a universal upper limit in the length of sentences in oral exchanges is due to an upper limit in length of attention span and short-term memory that are shared by all human beings. Acoustic/phonetic universals would probably fall into the same category. Explanatory sufficiency for any type of presumed universals can therefore be derived from a thorough knowledge of developmental processes. Chomsky's second argument for innateness, based on purely linguistic universals, must be considered as extremely weak or unsupported. Contrasted to the extremely rich evidence of the wealth of the stimulus, the theoretical choice between nativistic and learning paths should be almost self-evident.

A Skill Learning Perspective

Out of the many possible approaches to language learning, a skill training and learning conception appears to be most promising. Several domains of skill training, such as sports training or the acquisition of expertise in chess, have been extensively explored. Structural and functional homologies exist in the acquisition of diverse skills. These homologies could not only guide research but they also provide the promise that a consistent set of principles valid across subdomains could be established. In this manner, L1 research would follow the ideal procedure of science, progressing both cumulatively and integratively and not needing to develop disparate microtheories for each domain separately.

LONG-TERM PROSPECTS: THE EXPERT–APPRENTICE SYSTEM AND SKILL TRANSMISSION/ACQUISITION MODEL

As argued above, children's verbal performance proceeds in the context of the social and voluble environment. The process is therefore embedded in a system of reciprocal influences. This would be almost self-evident if it had not been so often neglected. Like all systems, the mother–child (expert–apprentice) system is goal-seeking with two sets of goals: the immediate one of getting a message across, and a second long-term goal of closing the gap between expert and apprentice performance.

Moerk (1986, 1989) has repeatedly sketched out such a expert–apprentice, skill-based approach to language learning by elaborating the benign guidance the expert provides for the rather incompetent apprentice. This was most clearly expressed when Moerk (1989b), argued that "the LAD was a lady," mostly the mother, who does the intellectual work for the infant of analyzing, synthesizing, and abstracting language structures (Moerk, 1985a). Further homologies have been suggested by Moerk (1986, 1989b), and they can also be found in the extended research on expertise (e.g., Glaser & Chi, 1988). A broad domain of explanatory potential opens up with these perspectives and the present sketch can be brief, relying on this extensive background.

Parallels in First and Second Language Skill Training

Four major settings for language transmission exist: First, that in the home in early childhood, then the school-based training in first-language skills extending up to the college years, finally the settings of second language transmission, which should be subdivided into informal or formal ones. While there are still some controversies about homologies between L1 and L2 acquisition, they certainly exist, and have been repeatedly elaborated as well as continuities between the early and later learning of one and the same language (e.g., Gathercole, 1988; Long, 1996; McLaughlin, 1981). A focus on later language learning has the advantage of emphasizing the training of differentiated verbal skills: BICS (basic interpersonal communication skills) versus CALP (cognitive academic language proficiency), as differentiated by Cummins (1980). In foreign language teaching, ESP (English for special purposes) has been increasingly adopted. These conceptions focus on the functionality of language and on the training of specific skills tailored to specific tasks. They therefore counteract the tendency to reify language and they relate differential training methods to differential outcomes.

Parallels in Language Skill-Training and Other Skill Training

In developmental psychology, several valuable explorations of skill learning can serve as analogues. Rogoff's (1990) work on "apprenticeship" as well as the studies of Greenfield (e.g., Childs & Greenfield, 1980) are examples largely from cross-cultural research. Bruner (1973, 1974) has emphasized skills for the earliest stages of development. Fischer (1980) as well as Paris and Lindauer (1982) have broadly applied a similar conception for later cognitive development.

The homologous phenomena in L1 acquisition that are also found in all fields of skill training have been surveyed extensively in Chapters 3, 4, and 5. All advanced skills need intensive and lengthy exercise (Chapter 3). In skill training, fine-tuning (Chapter 4) of the expert's demands to the changing skill levels of the apprentice is common. Finally, skills are learned most effectively when the learner receives rather immediate and detailed feedback as to minor flaws in her/his performance. This corrective feedback (Chapter 5), too, is carefully tuned to the processing potential of the learner, while much positive acknowledgment is added to these corrections so as not to discourage the learner.

A skills perspective can further contribute to the resolution of the controversy as to corrections discussed in Chapter 5. In the skills domain, two kinds of feedback are generally differentiated: Knowledge of results, the well-known trial-and-error/success, versus knowledge of performance. The original argument against corrections was directed against knowledge of results, asserting that children get their needs fulfilled despite linguistic mistakes and that they are not differentially rewarded for correct versus incorrect utterances. Knowledge of performance, in contrast, is exemplified by Brown's famous expansions, showing the child how to express a message more fully and correctly without making the pragmatic effect dependent on the correctness of the message.

Skills are decomposable (Simon, 1969) into subroutines, as seen in one and two-word sentences, and they can be compiled, as seen in the gradually established longer utterances. Bruner (1983) has focused extensively on both the subroutines and their later compilation in the field of L1 acquisition. With frequent repetitions, skills become automatized (Schmidt, 1975) and require minimal information processing capacity. The same obviously applies to language skills, as every advanced second-language learner has experienced. The conclusion of Chase and Simon (1973) that chess skill depends on "a vast, organized memory of specific information about chessboard patterns" (p. 279) is very closely relevant for L1 skills in that both require vast memories, stress patterns or structures, and rely on readily available perceptual-motor skills.

Goal-Directedness of Systems and of Skill Training

With all skill training and the corrections involved, goals are necessarily given and incrementally striven after. Often two goals are combined, a short-term and a long-term one. The short-term one of getting a message across depends much on immediate feedback loops to correct misunderstandings and confirm correct communication. The long-term goal, acquiring perfection in the skill, requires not only a great deal of information transmission, but also considerable emphasis on motivational and emotional aspects, that is rewards, in order to maintain the intensive involvement in the learning process.

The questions of motivation and emotion are seen as obviously relevant in L2 research but have been greatly neglected in L1 research. The evidence regarding motivational factors is, despite this neglect, quite clear, as exemplified in Table 4 of Chapter 2. "Reward" in the form of agreement or imitation is provided frequently. In research on picture book reading the pleasantness of the activity, a emotional-motivational feature, is often emphasized. This contrasts with evidence from children with language delay or disturbance, where often hostile and negative emotional surroundings interfere with free verbal communication. Such contrasts in goal attainment can serve to remind the research community that motivational and emotional aspects are also of great relevancy in L1 acquisition.

Because informative feedback is self-evident in language transmission, it is clear that cognitive-learning as well as behaviorist concepts are necessary for the understanding of the dynamics of these interactions. A combined effort of heretofore antagonistic psychological schools is therefore called for in the exploration of skill transmission, as was recommended in Chapter 1 and modeled throughout this book.

Temporal Aspects of Skill Training

Complex skills are acquired over prolonged periods of training, necessitating new methodologies of research and new conceptions as to incremental acquisition processes. While methodological aspects for L1 research were discussed in Chapter 2, the homologies in other well-explored domains of skill training provide supporting evidence for the need for such methods. Whether it is the training needed to become a piano virtuoso or an Olympic sports performer, decades of training are involved in both. A leap from early input to expert competence, what was called the projection problem in L1 research, would not make any sense under skill-learning assumptions. Similar conceptual pitfalls, such as neglecting the level of the learner when evaluating the effectiveness of specific corrections, can be avoided when the length of the multi-level process is kept in mind.

The complexities of lagged effects also stand out in long-term processes. In all cases of skill training, immediate feedback is important, while improvements might appear only after varying lags. This combination of short-term feedback loops and varying-interval lags before the desired performance is achieved is one of the most basic interactional phenomena in skill training/learning (Moerk, 1992), but still requires much conceptual and methodological analysis. Experience in other fields of skill training could guide these analyses.

CONCLUDING REMARKS

Whereas a prediction more than a decade ago of "an evolving paradigm shift" (Moerk, 1986, p. 19) away from empty nativist labeling to a skill-learning conception was overly optimistic, the hope is possibly more justified at present. As indicated in Chapter 2, several scientists at leading universities have rediscovered contingencies as an important principle in the training/learning process and therefore also for the research endeavor. A recent paper in *First Language* even carried the subtitle "A Sequential Analysis" (Tenenbaum & Leaper, 1998) even if the approach was still restricted to the three-term contingency patterns already analyzed by Moerk (1990). As discussed extensively in Chapter 5, Morgan and associates (1995) have even attempted time-series analyses. Improved methods, as recommended in Chapter 2, are therefore entering the field. Their importance can perhaps be indicated through an analogy. Contingency approaches are the microscope of language-acquisition research, demonstrating what happens within seconds of an input utterance, or of a filial (often imperfect) production. Temporally extended time-series analyses would be the telescope for the training approach, exploring long-term cause–effect dynamics. How far would some of the natural sciences have gotten without these two instruments?

Equally promising is the applied field, where Yoder and Warren (1998) have begun adapting intervention methods not only to the needs of the children but also to the response tendencies of individual mothers. This will be centrally important for interventions, as Moerk (1985b) has shown clear differences in the teaching styles of mothers, even when their children progressed satisfactorily in their language skills. Differentially adapted training methods will be even more important with intellectually handicapped children or with mothers who do not have the motivation and attention span of middle-class mothers (cf. Moerk, 1998). Such approaches suggest that finely tailored intervention methods should replace the one method fits all approach of *motherese*, which is equivalent to the past habit of bloodletting as the only medical intervention or the Freudian method as the exclusive psychotherapeutic method. The overwhelming evidence surveyed in Chapters 3 to 5, and also that from a *modus tollens* perspective in Chapters 6 and 7, suggest that a younger generation of researchers, less burdened with old ideologies and preconceptions, has returned to differential analyses of open questions.

However, old ideas and theories still reside in the power centers of the field. Even in empirical reports genuflections before the nativistic credo have become almost de rigueur before researchers dare to present their findings—which mostly contradict the nativistic credo. Mystification in the form of Chomsky's generativity or in arguments that young children are language makers are still common, while nobody would argue that young children are also culture makers, though there should be little argument that language is a subset of culture. If the young child who learns to use his mother tongue more or less efficiently is a language maker, than every teenager driving around in a beat-up Chevy joins Ford and GM as a car maker, and when he learns to conform to traffic laws, he is a lawmaker. What are all those children who grow up with serious language deficits? Makers of deficient languages?

Considering such ready reliance on slogans, it would be overly optimistic to assume that the romantic trend, described in Chapter 1, is ebbing quickly or that power bastions are abandoned willingly. Some nativists are highly skillful in rhetoric and have exploited these skills extensively in browbeating their opponents (Sampson, 1997, p. 161). Also, endearingly simple systems are apt to draw large crowds of adherents, as the Roman philosopher Seneca knew already. An innate language organ without substantiation is such an endearingly simple answer to a complex problem.

Even new problems threaten. Pinker (1994) has already laid the first foundation for the exploitation of nativism for more sinister purposes. He has suggested the explanation of individual differences in verbal performance on the basis of innate differences. This is only one step from the explanation of racial differences on the same basis. When Herrnstein and Murray (1994) reopened the controversy as to innate bases of racial IQ differences, they encountered a vivid social response. Exactly the same logical argument based on lower average performances of some groups could be applied to language skills. Accordingly, Pinker's (1994) *Language Instinct* drew a crowd of admiring adherents quickly. At a time of widening gaps between social classes and of an increasing tendency to blame the victims, such "scientific" explanations coming from Harvard and MIT can certainly be misapplied. Instead of establishing optimal remedial approaches that are also motivating for children and mothers from lower-class and oral backgrounds, scientists invite destructive implications based on a nativism that stresses innate individual and therewith group differences. These, consequently, disparage remedial and preventive intervention. Billions of children and of illiterate adults need help in acquiring the CALP (cognitive academic language performance) skills required for success in the information age that affects almost every corner of the world. Yet, paradoxically, it is becoming fashionable to pronounce that children cannot be trained in the prerequisite language skills and even that parents are relatively unimportant for the development of their children (e.g., Lewis, 1997); while politicians cut Welfare Programs and force mothers to engage in menial work instead of spending instructional time with their children. If powerful instructional strategies require fine-tuned sensitivity to the unique response history of the learner (cf. Chapter 4), the recent cultural trends of disparaging the influence of parents have to be judged extremely counterproductive as contrasted with the valid—and effective—attempts at parent-education (e.g., Gordon, 1970, 1972). Western culture seems caught again in a conflict between technological advance and postromantic escapism, as it was around 1900, when Nietzsche and Bergson became famous with their slogans entailing backward-looking romantic ideologies.

References

Akhtar, N., Dunham, F., & Dunham, P. J. (1991). Directive interactions and early vocabulary development: The role of joint attentional focus. *Journal of Child Language, 18*, 41–49.

Alexander, K. L., & Entwistle, D. R. (1988). Achievement in the first 2 years of school: Patterns and processes. *Monographs of the Society for Research in Child Development, 52* (2, Serial No. 218).

Allen, R. E., & Oliver, J. M. (1982). The effects of child maltreatment on language development. *Child Abuse & Neglect. The International Journal, 6*, 299–305.

Alvarez, L. (1986). *Home and school contexts for language learning: A case study of two Mexican-American bilingual preschools.* Unpublished doctoral dissertation, Stanford University, Stanford, CA.

Ament, W. (1899). *Die Entwicklung von Sprechen und Denken beim Kinde.* Leipzig: E. Wunderlich.

Andersen, E., Dunlea, A., & Kekelis, L. (1993). The impact of input. *First Language, 13*, 23–49.

Anderson, J. R. (1981). *Cognitive skills and their acquisition.* Hillsdale, NJ: Erlbaum.

Anderson, J. R. (1982). Acquisition of cognitive skills. *Psychological Review, 89*, 369–406.

Anderson, J. R. (1987). Skill acquisition: Compilation of weak-method problem solutions. *Psychological Review, 94*, 192–210.

Andrick, G. R., & Tager-Flusberg, H. (1986). The acquisition of color terms. *Journal of Child Language, 13*, 119–1354.

Anglin, J. M. (1977). *Word, object, and conceptual development.* New York: Norton.

Arbib, M. A., Conklin, E. J., & Hill, J. C. (1987). *From schema theory to language.* Oxford: Oxford University Press.

Atkinson, M. (1986). Learnability. In P. Fletcher & M. Garman (Eds.), *Language acquisition* (pp. 90–108). New York: Cambridge University Press.

Atkinson, M. (1987). Mechanisms for language acquisition: Learning, parameter-setting and triggering. *First Language, 7*, 3–30.

Atkinson, M. (1992). *Children's syntax.* Oxford: Blackwell.

Atkinson, R. C. (1972). *Ingredients for a theory of instruction.* (Technical Report 187). Institute for Mathematical Studies in Social Science, Stanford University.

Austin, J. L. (1962). *How to do things with words.* London: Oxford University Press.

Baer, D. M. (1970). An age-irrelevant concept of development. *Merrill-Palmer Quarterly, 16*, 238–245.

Baer, D. M., & Deguchi, H. (1985). Generalized imitation from a radical-behavioral viewpoint. In S. Reiss & E. Bootzin (Eds.), *Theoretical issues in behavior therapy* (pp. 179–217). New York: Academic Press.

Bakan, D. (1967). The test of significance in psychological research. In D. Bakan (Ed.), *On method* (pp. 1–29). San Francisco: Jossey-Bass.

Bakeman, R. (1978). Untangling streams of behavior. Sequential analysis of observational data. In G. P. Sackett (Ed.), *Observing behavior. Vol. 2: Data collection and analysis methods.* Baltimore: University Park Press.

Bakeman, R., Adamson, L. B., Konner, M., & Barr, R. G. (1990). !Kung infancy: The social context of object exploration. *Child Development, 61*, 794–801.

Bakeman, R., & Gottman, J. M. (1986). *Observing interaction. An introduction to sequential analysis.* New York: Cambridge University Press.

Baker, C. L. (1979). Syntactic theory and the projection problem. *Linguistic Inquiry, 10*, 533–581.

Baker, G. P., & Hacker, P. M. S. (1984). *Language sense and nonsense.* Oxford: Basil Blackwell.

Baker, L., & Cantwell, D. P. (1982). Psychiatric disorders in children with different types of communication disorders. *Journal of Communication, 15*, 113–126.

Baker, N., & Nelson, K. E. (1984). Recasting and related conversational techniques for triggering syntactic advances by young children. *First Language, 5*, 3–22.

Bakhtin, M. M. (1986). *Speech genres and other late essays.* (Translated by Vern W. McGee.) Austin: Texas University Press.

Bard, E. G., & Anderson, A. H. (1994). The unintelligibility of speech to children: Effects of referent availability. *Journal of Child Language, 21*, 623–648.

Barker, R. G. (1968). *Ecological psychology.* Stanford, CA: Stanford University Press.

Barker, R. G., & Wright, H. F. (1955). *Midwest and its children.* New York: Harper & Row.

Barnes, S., Gutfreund, M., Satterly, D., & Wells, G. (1983). Characteristics of adult speech which predict children's language development. *Journal of Child Language, 10*, 65–84.

Barsky, R. (1997). *Noam Chomsky. A Life of Dissent.* Cambridge, MA: MIT Press.

Bates, E., Bretherton, I., Beeghly-Smith, M., & McNew, S. (1982). Social bases of language development: A reassessment. In H. W. Reese & L. P. Lipsitt (Eds.), *Advances in Child Development and Behavior* (Vol. 16, pp. 8–75). New York: Academic Press.

Bates, E., & Carnevale, G. F. (1993). New directions in research on language development. *Developmental Review, 13*, 436–470.

Bates, E., & MacWhinney, B. (1987). Competition, variation, and language learning. In B. MacWhinney (Ed.), *Mechanisms of language acquisition* (pp. 157–193). Hillsdale, NJ: Erlbaum.

Baumrind, D. (1971a). Harmonious parents and their preschool children. *Developmental Psychology, 4*, 63–72.

Baumrind, D. (1971b). Current patterns of parental authority. *Developmental Psychology Monographs, 1*, 1–103.

Baumrind, D. (1980). New directions in socialization research. *American Psychologist, 35*, 639–652.

Bavin, E. L. (1992). The acquisition of Walpiri. In D. I. Slobin (Ed.), *The crosslinguistic study of language acquisition* (Vol. 3, pp. 309–371). Hillsdale, NJ: Erlbaum.

Becker, A. L. (1984). Toward a poststructuralist view of language learning: A short essay. In A. Z. Guiora (Ed.), *An epistemology for the language sciences* (pp. 217–220). Detroit: University of Michigan Press.

Becker, J. A. (1988). The success of parents' indirect techniques for teaching their pre-schoolers pragmatic skills. *First Language, 8,* 173–182.

Becker, J. A. (1991). Pragmatic skills and the acquisition of linguistic competence. In R. R. Hoffman & D. S. Palermo (Eds.), *Cognition and the symbolic processes. Applied and ecological perspectives* (pp. 327–334). Hillsdale, NJ: Erlbaum.

Beckey, R. E. (1942). A study of certain factors related to retardation of speech. *Journal of Speech Disorders, 7,* 223–249.

Bee, H. J., van Egeren, L. F., Streissguth, A. P., Nyman, B. A., & Leckie, M. S. (1969). Social class differences in maternal teaching strategies and speech patterns. *Developmental Psychology, 1,* 726–734.

Behrend, D. A. (1988). Overextensions in early language comprehension: evidence from a signal detection approach. *Journal of Child Language, 15,* 63–75.

Bell, S. (1903). The significance of activity in child life. *Independent, 55,* 911–914.

Bellinger, D. (1980). Consistency in the pattern of change in mothers' speech: Some discriminant analyses. *Journal of Child Language, 7,* 469–487.

Benedict, H. (1979). Early lexical development. Comprehension and production. *Journal of Child Language, 6,* 183–200.

Bereiter, C., & Engleman, S. (1966). *Teaching disadvantaged children in the preschool.* Englewood Cliffs, NJ: Prentice-Hall.

Berenson, E. (1992). Beyond multiculturalism: Race, class, and American schools. *Contention, 2,* 51–67.

Berko, J. (1958). The child's learning of English morphology. *Word, 14,* 150–177.

Berman, R. A. (1981). Language development and language knowledge: Evidence from the development of Hebrew morphophonology. *Journal of Child Language, 8,* 609–626.

Bernstein, B. (1961). Social class, linguistic codes, and grammatical elements. *Language and Speech, 5,* 221–240.

Bernstein, B. (1964). Elaborated and restricted codes: Their social origins and some consequences. *American Anthropologist, 66* (2), 55–69.

Bernstein, B., & Henderson, D. (1969). Social class differences in the relevance of language to socialization. *Sociology, 3,* 1–20.

Blake, I. L. (1994). Language development and socialization in young African-American children. In P. M. Greenfield & R. R. Cocking (Eds.), *Cross-cultural roots of minority child development* (pp. 167–195). Hillsdale, NJ: Erlbaum.

Blake, J. (1989). *Family size and achievement.* Berkeley: University of California Press.

Blalock, H. M. (1963). Correlated independent variables: The problem of multicollinearity. *Social Forces, 42,* 233–237.

Blank, M. (1975). Mastering the intangible through language. In D. Aaronson & R. W. Rieber (Eds.), Developmental psycholinguistics and communication disorders. *Annals of the New York Academy of Sciences, 263* (pp. 44–58). New York: New York Academy of Sciences.

Bloom, A. (1981). *The linguistic shaping of thought. A study in the impact of language on thinking in China and the West.* Hillsdale, NJ: Erlbaum.

Bloom, L. (1973). *One word at a time: The use of single-word utterances before syntax.* Mouton: The Hague.

Bloom, L. (1993). *The transition from infancy to language: Acquiring the power of expression.* Cambridge: Cambridge University Press.

Bloom, L. M., Lightbown, P., & Hood, L. (1975). Structure and variation in child language. *Monographs of the Society for Research in Child Development, 40* (Serial No. 160).

Bloom, L., Margulis, C., Tinker, F., & Fujita, N. (1996). Early conversations and word learning: contributions from child and adult. *Child Development. 67,* 3154–3175.

Blount, B. G., & Padgug, E. J. (1977). Prosodic, paralinguistic, and interactional features in parent-child speech: English and Spanish. *Journal of Child Language, 4,* 67–86.

Boesche, R. (1996), *Theories of tyranny. From Plato to Arendt.* University Park: Pennsylvania State University Press.

Bohannon, J. N., MacWhinney, B., & Snow, C. (1990). No negative evidence revisited: Beyond learnability or who has to prove what to whom. *Developmental Psychology, 26,* 221–226.

Bohannon, N. N., & Marquis, A. L. (1977). Children's control of adult speech. *Child Development, 48,* 1002–1008.

Bohannon, J. N., III, Padgett, R. J., Nelson, K. E., & Mark, M. (1996). Useful evidence on negative evidence. *Developmental Psychology, 32,* 551–555.

Bohannon, J., & Stanowicz, L. (1988). Adult response to children's language errors: The issue of negative evidence. *Developmental Psychology, 24,* 684–689.

Bohannon, J., & Stanowicz, L. (1989). Bidirectional effects of imitation and repetition in conversation: A synthesis within a cognitive model. In G. E. Speidel & K. E. Nelson (Eds.), *The many faces of imitation in language learning* (pp. 121–145). New York: Springer-Verlag.

Bolinger, D. (1976). Meaning and memory. *Forum Linguisticum, 1,* 1–14.

Bonvillian, J. D., Raeburn, V. P., & Horan, E. A. (1979). Talking to children. The effects of rate, intonation, and length on children's sentence imitation. *Journal of Child Language, 6,* 459–467.

Boring, E. G. (1957). *A history of experimental psychology.* (2nd ed.). New York: Appleton-Century-Crofts.

Bossard, J. H. S. (1954). *The sociology of child development.* (2nd ed.). New York: Harper.

Bower, T. G. R. (1972). Object perception in infants. *Perception, 1,* 15–30.

Bower, T. G. R. (1974). *Development in infancy.* San Francisco: W. H. Freeman.

Bowerman, M. (1976). Semantic factors in the acquisition of rules for word use and sentence construction. In D. Morehead & A. Morehead (Eds.), *Normal and deficient child language* (pp. 99–179). Baltimore, MD: University Park Press.

Bowerman, M. (1987). Commentary: Mechanisms of language acquisition. In B. MacWhinney (Ed.), *Mechanisms of language acquisition* (pp. 443–466). Hillsdale, NJ: Erlbaum.

Braine, M. D. S. (1963). The ontogeny of English phrase structure. The first phase. *Language, 39,* 1–13.

Braine, M. D. S. (1971). On two models of the internalization of grammar. In D. I. Slobin (Ed.), *The ontogenesis of grammar* (pp. 153–186). New York: Academic Press.

Braine, M. D. S. (1988). Modeling the acquisition of linguistic structure. In Y. Levy, I. M. Schlesinger, & M. D. S. Braine (Eds.), *Categories and processes in language acquisition* (pp. 217–259). Hillsdale, NJ: Erlbaum.

Brandenburg, G. C., & Brandenburg, J. (1919). Language development during the fourth year: the conversation. *Pedagogical Seminary, 26,* 27–40.

Broen, P. A. (1972). The verbal environment of the language-learning child. *ASHA Monograph, 17.*

Brophy, J. E. (1970). Mothers as teachers of their own preschool children: The influence of socioecnonomic status and task structure on teaching specificity. *Child Development, 41,* 79–94.

Brown, A. L. (1975). The development of memory: Knowing, knowing about knowing, and knowing how to know. In H. W. Reese (Ed.), *Advances in child development and behavior* (Vol. 10, pp. 103–152). New York: Academic Press.

Brown, R. (1958). *Words and things.* New York: Free Press.

Brown, R. (1968). The development of wh-questions in child speech. *Journal of Verbal Learning and Verbal Behavior, 7,* 279–290.

Brown, R. (1973). *A first language: The early stages.* Cambridge, MA: Harvard University Press.

Brown, R., & Bellugi, U. (1964). Three processes in the child's acquisition of syntax. *Harvard Educational Review, 34,* 133–151.

Brown, R., Cazden, C., & Bellugi, U. (1969). The child's grammar from I to III. In J. P. Hill (Ed.), *Minnesota symposia on child psychology* (Vol II, pp. 28–73). Minneapolis: University of Minnesota Press.

Brown, R., & Fraser, C. (1963). The acquisition of syntax. In C. N. Cofer & B. S. Musgrave (Eds.), *Verbal behavior and learning: Problems and processes* (pp. 158–201). New York: McGraw-Hill.

Brown, R., & Hanlon, C. (1970). Derivational complexity and order of acquisition in child speech. In J. R. Hayes (Ed.), *Cognition and the development of language* (pp. 11–53). New York: John Wiley & Sons.

Brumark, A. (1989). *Blindness and the context of language acquisition.* Stockholm: Institutionen för Nordiska Sprak.

Bruner, J. S. (1973). Organization of early skilled action. *Child Development, 44,* 1–11.

Bruner, J. S. (1974). The organization of early skilled action. In M. P. M. Richards (Ed.), *The integration of the child into a social world* (pp. 167–184). London: Cambridge University Press.

Bruner, J. S. (1975). The ontogenesis of speech acts. *Journal of Child Language, 2,* 1–19.

Bruner, J. (1978). On prelinguistic prerequisites of speech. In R. N. Campbell & P. T. Smith (Eds.), *Recent advances in the psychology of language* (pp. 199–214). New York: Plenum Press.

Bruner, J. (1983). *Child's talk. Learning to use language.* New York: W. W. Norton & Co.

Buium, N., Rynders, J., & Turnure, J. (1974). Early maternal linguistic environment of normal and Down's syndrome language-learning children. *American Journal of Mental Deficiency, 79,* 52–58.

Burton, R. R., Brown, J. S., & Fischer, G. (1984). Skiing as a model of instruction. In B. Rogoff & J. Lave (Eds.), *Everyday cognition: Its development in social context* (pp. 139–150). Cambridge, MA: Harvard University Press.

Bybee, J. L., & Slobin, D. I. (1982). Rules and schemas in the development and use of the English past tense. *Language, 58,* 265–289.

Campbell, B. A., & Jaynes, J. (1966). Reinstatement. *Psychological Review, 73,* 478–480.

Campbell, B. A., & Spear, N. E. (1972). Ontogeny of memory. *Psychological Review, 79*, 215–236.

Caplan, D., & Chomsky, N. (1980). Linguistic perspectives on language development. In D. Caplan (Ed.), *Biological studies of mental processes* (pp. 97–108). Cambridge, MA: MIT Press.

Carey, S. (1978). The child as word learner. In M. Halle., J. Bresnan, & G. A. Miller (Eds.), *Linguistic theory and psychological reality* (pp. 264–295). Cambridge, MA: MIT Press.

Carey, S. (1982). Semantic development: The state of the art. In E. Wanner & L. R. Gleitman (Eds.), *Language acquisition: The state of the art* (pp. 347–389). Cambridge: Cambridge University Press.

Cassirer, E. (1955). *The philosophy of symbolic forms: Language.* New Haven: Yale University Press.

Catania, A. C. (1972). Chomsky's formal analysis of natural languages. A behavioral translation. *Behaviorism, 1*, 1–15.

Catania, A. C. (1992). *Learning* (2nd ed.). Englewood Cliffs, NJ: Prentice Hall.

Catania, A. C. (1998). *Learning* (3rd ed.). Upper Saddle River, NJ: Prentice Hall.

Caudill, W. A., & Frost, L. (1973). A comparison of maternal care and infant behavior in Japanese-American, American, and Japanese families. In W. P. Lebra (Ed.), *Mental health research in Asia and the Pacific: Vol. 3. Youth, socialization, and mental health* (pp. 3–15). Honolulu: The University of Hawaii Press.

Cazden, C. B. (1966). Subcultural differences in child language: An interdisciplinary review. *Merrill-Palmer Quarterly, 12*, 185–219.

Cazden, C. B. (1972). *Child language and education.* Chicago: Holt, Rinehart and Winston.

Cazden, C. (1979). Peekaboo as an instructional model: Discourse development at home and at school. *Papers and Reports on Child Language Development, 17.*

Cazden, C. B. (1983). Peekaboo as an instructional model: Discourse development at home and at school. In B. Bain (Ed.), *The sociogenesis of language and human conduct* (pp. 33–58). New York: Plenum.

Chapman, R. S. (1979). Mother–child interaction in the second year of life. Its role in language development. In R. L. Schiefelbusch & D. D. Bricker (Eds.), *Early language: Acquisition and intervention.* Baltimore, MD: University Park Press.

Chapman, R. S., Leonard, L. B., & Mervis, C. B. (1986). The effect of feedback on children's inappropriate word usage. *Journal of Child Language, 13*, 1010–1117.

Chase, W. G., & Simon, H. A. (1973). Perception in chess. *Cognitive Psychology, 4*, 55–81.

Chess, T. A., & Birch, H. G. (1970). The origin of personality. *Scientific American, 223*, 102–109.

Chi, M. T. H., Glaser, R., & Farr, M. J. (Eds.). (1988). *The nature of expertise.* Hillsdale, NJ: Erlbaum.

Childs, C. P., & Greenfield, P. M. (1980). Informal modes of learning and teaching: The case of Zinacanteco weaving. In N. Warren (Ed.), *Studies in cross-cultural psychology* (Vol. 2, pp. 269–316). London: Academic Press.

Chomsky, C. S. (1969). *The acquisition of language in children from 5 to 10.* Cambridge, MA: MIT Press.

Chomsky, N. (1959). Review of B. F. Skinner. *Verbal Behavior Language, 35*, 26–58.

Chomsky, N. (1965). *Aspects of the theory of syntax.* Cambridge, MA: MIT Press.

Chomsky, N. (1980a). *Rules and representations*. New York: Columbia University Press.

Chomsky, N. (1980b). On cognitive structures and their development: A reply to Piaget. In M. Piatelli-Palmerini (Ed.), *Language and learning: The debate between Jean Piaget and Noam Chomsky* (pp. 35–52). Cambridge, MA: Harvard University Press.

Chomsky, N. (1981). *Lectures on government and binding*. Dordrecht: Foris.

Christopoulos, C., Bonvillian, J. D., & Crittenden, P. M. (1988). Maternal language and child maltreatment. *Infant Mental Health Journal, 9*, 272–286.

Chukovsky, K. (1963). *From two to five*. Berkeley: University of California Press.

Clark, E. V. (1977). First language acquisition. In J. Morton & J. C. Marshall (Eds.), *Psychologinguistic series. Developmental and pathological* (pp. 1–72). London: Elek Science.

Clark, E. V. (1982a). The young word maker: A case study of innovation in the child's lexicon. In E. Wanner & L. R. Gleitman (Eds.), *Language acquisition: The state of the art* (pp. 83–103). Cambridge, MA: Cambridge University Press.

Clark, E. V. (1982b). Language change during language acquisition. In M. E. Lambs & A. L. Brown (Eds.), *Advances in developmental psychology* (Vol. 2, pp. 171–195). Hillsdale, NJ: Erlbaum.

Clark, R. (1974). Performing without competence. *Journal of Child Language, 1*, 1–10.

Clark, R. (1977). What's the use of imitation? *Journal of Child Language, 4*, 341–358.

Cohen, L. B. (1979). Our developing knowledge of infant perception and cognition. *American Psychologist, 34*, 894–899.

Cohen, M. (1930). Observation sur les dernieres persistances du langage enfantin. *Journal de Psychology, 27*, 390–399.

Colombo, J. (1986). Recent studies in early auditory development. In G. J. Whitehurst (Ed.), *Annals of child development* (Vol. 5, pp. 53–98). Greenwich, CT: JAI Press.

Cook-Gumperz, J. (1973). *Social control and socialization. A study of class differences in the language of maternal control*. London: Routledge & Kegan Paul.

Cornell, E. H. (1984). Developmental continuity of memory mechanisms: Suggestive phenomena. In R. Kail & N. Spear (Eds). *Comparative perspectives on the development of memory* (pp. 287–316). Hillsdale, NJ: Erlbaum.

Cross, T. (1975). Some relationships between motherese and linguistic level in accelerated children. *Papers and Reports on Child Language Development, 10*. Stanford University, Stanford, CA.

Cross, T. (1977). Mothers' speech adjustments: The contributions of selected child listener variables. In C. E. Snow & C. A. Ferguson (Eds.), *Talking to children: Language input and acquisition*. (pp. 151–188). Cambridge: Cambridge University Press.

Cross, T. G. (1978). Mothers' speech adjustments and child language learning. Some methodological considerations. *Language Sciences, 1*, 3–25.

Cross, T. G., & Morris, J. E. (1980). Linguistic feedback and maternal speech: Comparisons of mothers addressing infants, one-year-olds, and two-year-olds. *First langauge, 1*, 98–121.

Cross, T. G., Nienhuys, T. G., & Kirkman, M. (1985). Parent–child interaction with receptively disabled children: Some determinants of maternal speech style. In K.E. Nelson (Ed.), *Children's language* (Vol. 5, pp. 247–290). New York: Gardner Press.

Cruttenden, A. (1994). Phonetic and prosodic aspects of baby talk. In C. Gallaway & B. J. Richards (Eds.), *Input and interaction in language acquisition* (pp. 135–152). New York: Cambridge University Press.

Crystal, D. (1987). *The Cambridge encyclopedia of language.* New York: Cambridge University Press.

Culp, R. E., Watkins, R. V., Lawrence, H., Letts, D., Kelly, D. J., & Rice, M. L. (1991). Maltreated children's language and speech development: Abused, neglected, and abused and neglected. *First Language, 11,* 377–389.

Cummins, J. (1980). The cross-lingual dimensions of language proficiency: Implications for bilingual education and the optimal age issue. *TESOL-Quarterly, 14,* 175–188.

Darwin, C. (1966). *The origin of species.* Harvard: Harvard University Press. (Original work published 1859)

Davis, E. A. (1937). The development of linguistic skills in twins, singletons with siblings and only children from age five to ten years. *Institute of Child Welfare Monograph Series No. 14,* Minneapolis: University of Minnesota Press.

Dawe, H. C. (1942). A study of the effect of an educational program upon language development and related mental functions in young children. *Journal of Experimental Education, 11,* 200–209.

de Houwer, A. (1987). Nouns and their companions. In A. de Houwer & S. Gillis (Eds.), *Perspectives on child language* (pp. 55–73). Brussels: Editions de l'Universite de Bruxelles.

Delacroix, H. (1934). *Le langage et la pensee.* Paris: Alcan.

Delgado-Gaitan, C. (1994). Socializing young children in Mexican-American families: An intergenerational perspective. In P. M. Greenfield & R. R. Cocking (Eds.), *Cross-cultural roots of minority child development* (pp. 55–86). Hillsdale, NJ: Erlbaum.

DeLoache, J. S., & DeMendoza, O. A. P. (1987). Joint picture book interactions of mothers and 1-year-old children. *British Journal of Developmental Psychology, 5,* 111–123.

Demetras, M. J., Post, K. N., & Snow, C. E. (1986). Feedback to first language learners: The role of repetitions and clarification questions. *Journal of Child Language, 13,* 275–292.

Demuth, K. (1992). The acquisition of Sesotho. In D. I. Slobin (Ed.), *The crosslinguistic study of language acquisition* (Vol. 3, pp. 587–638). Hillsdale, NJ: Erlbaum.

Dennis, W. (1960). Causes of retardation of institutional children: Iran. *Journal of Genetic Psychology, 96,* 47–59.

dePaulo, B., & Coleman, L. M. (1986). Talking to children, foreigners, and retarded adults. *Journal of Personality and Social Psychology, 51,* 945–959.

de Villiers, J. G. (1985). Learning how to use verbs: Lexical coding and the influence of the input. *Journal of Child Language, 12,* 587–595.

de Villiers, J. G., & de Villiers, P. A. (1985). The acquisition of English. In D. I. Slobin (Ed.), *The crosslinguistic study of language acquisition* (Vol. 1, pp. 27–139). Hillsdale, NJ: Erlbaum.

de Villiers, J. G., Tager-Flusberg, H., & Hakuta, K. (1977). Deciding among theories of the development of coordination in child speech. *Papers and Report on Child Language Development, 13,* 118–125.

Dickinson, D. K. (Ed.). (1994). *Bridges to literacy.* Oxford: Blackwell.

Dollaghan, C. (1985). Child meets word: "Fast mapping" in preschool children. *Journal of Speech and Hearing Research, 28*, 449–454.

Dunn, J., & Wodding, C. (1977). Play at home and its implication for learning. In B. Tizzard & D. Harvey (Eds.), *The biology of play* (pp. 45–58). London: Heinemann.

du Preez, P. (1974). Units of information in the acquisition of language. *Language and Speech, 17*, 369–376.

Durkin, K. (1978). Minds and language: Social cognition, social interaction and the acquisition of language. *Mind and Language, 2*, 105–140.

Edwards, A. D. (1976). *Language in culture and class.* London: Heinemann.

Edwards, J. (1979). *Language disadvantage.* London: Edward Arnold.

Elias, N. (1991). *The symbol theory.* London: Newbury Park.

Ellis, R., & Wells, C. G. (1980). Enabling factors in adult–child discourse. *First Language, 1*, 46–62.

Ely, R., & McCabe, A. (1994). The language play of kindergarten children. *First Language, 14*, 19–35.

Erbaugh, M. S. (1992). The acquisition of Mandarin. In D. I. Slobin (Ed.), *The crosslinguistic study of language acquisition* (Vol. 3, pp. 373–455). Hillsdale, NJ: Erlbaum.

Ernst, C., & Angst, J. (1983). *Birth order: Its influence on personality.* New York: Springer.

Estes, W. K. (1978). On the organization and core concepts of learning theory and cognitive psychology. In W. K. Estes (Ed.), *Linguistic functions in cognitive theory: Handbook of learning and cognitive processes.* (Vol. 6, pp. 235–292). Hillsdale, NJ: Erlbaum.

Faerch, C. (1985). Metatalk in foreign language classroom discourse. *Studies in Second Language Acquisition, 7*, 184–199.

Farrar, M. J. (1990). Discourse and the acquisition of grammatical morphemes. *Journal of Child Language, 17*, 607–624.

Farrar, M. J. (1992). Negative evidence and grammatical morpheme acquisition. *Developmental Psychology, 28*, 90–98.

Feagans, L., & Farran, D. C. (Eds.). (1982). *The language of children reared in poverty.* New York: Academic Press.

Feiring, C., & Lewis, M. (1981). Middle class differences in mother–child interaction and the child's cognitive development. In T. M. Field, A M. Sostek, P. Vietze, & P. H. Leiderman (Eds.), *Culture and early interactions* (pp. 63–91). Hillsdale, NJ: Erlbaum.

Ferguson, C. A. (1964). Baby talk in six languages. *American Anthropologist, 66*, 103–114.

Ferguson, C. A. (1977). Baby talk as a simplified register. In C. E. Snow & C.A. Ferguson (Eds.), *Talking to children. Language input and acquisition* (pp. 219–238). Cambridge: Cambridge University Press.

Fernald, A. (1984). The perceptual and affective salience of mothers' speech to infants. In L. Feagans, C. Garvey, & R. Golinkoff (Eds.), *The origins and growth of communication* (pp. 5–29). Norwood, NJ: Ablex.

Fernald, A., & Mazzie, C. (1991). Prosody and focus in speech to infants and adults. *Developmental Psychology, 27*, 209–221.

Fernald, A., & Simon, I. (1984). Expanded intonation contours in mothers' speech to newborns. *Developmental Psychology, 20*, 104–113.

Festinger, L. (1957). *A theory of cognitive dissonance.* Evanston, IL: Row & Peterson.

Feyerabend, P. (1975). *Against method.* London: New Left Books.

Fischer, K. W. (1980). A theory of cognitive development: The control and construction of hierarchies of skills. *Psychological Review, 87,* 477–531.

Fischer, K. W., & Corrigan, R. (1981). A skill approach to language development. In R. E. Stark (Ed.), *Language behavior in infancy and early childhood.* (pp. 245–273). Amsterdam: Elsevier/North Holland.

Fischer, K. W., Kenny, S. L., & Pipp, S. L. (1990). How cognitive processes and environmental conditions organize discontinuities in the development of abstractions. In C. N. Alexander & E. J. Langer (Eds.), *Higher stages of human development* (pp. 162–187). New York: Oxford University Press.

Fischer, K. W., & Pipp, S. L. (1984). Processes of cognitive development: Optimal level and skill acquisition. In R. J. Sternberg (Ed.), *Mechanisms of cognitive development* (pp. 45–80). San Francisco: W. H. Freeman.

Flavell, J. H. (1985). *Cognitive development.* Englewood Cliffs, NJ: Prentice-Hall.

Fodor, J. (1983) *Modularity of mind: an essay on faculty psychology.* Cambridge, MA: MIT Press.

Fodor, I. A., Bever, T. G., & Garrett, M. F. (1974). *The psychology of language. An introduction to psycholinguistics and generative grammar.* New York: McGraw-Hill.

Forner, M. (1979). The mother as LAD: Interaction between order and frequency of parental input and child production. In F. R. Eckman & A. J. Hastings (Eds.), *Studies in first and second language acquisition* (pp. 17–44). Rowley, MA: Newbury House.

Franco, F., & D'Odorico, L. (1985). The determinants of baby talk: Relationship to context. *Journal of Child Language, 12,* 567–586.

Fraser, C., & Roberts, N. (1975). Mothers' speech to children of four different ages. *Journal of Psycholinguistic Research, 4,* 9–16.

Freeman, N., & MacWhinney, B. (Ed.). (1989). Mechanisms of language acquisition. *Journal of Child Language, 16,* 470–475.

Friel-Patti, S., Finitzo-Hieber, T., Conti, G., & Clinton, K. (1982). Language delay in infants associated with middle ear disease and mild, fluctuating hearing impairment. *Pediatric Infectious Disease, 1,* 104–109.

Furrow, D., Baillie, C., McLaren, J., & Moore, C. (1993). Differential responding to two- and three-year-olds' utterances: The role of grammaticality and ambiguity. *Journal of Child Language, 20,* 363–375.

Furrow, D., Moore, C., Davidge, J., & Chiasson, L. (1992). Mental terms in mothers' and children's speech: Similarities and relationships. *Journal of Child Language, 19,* 617–631.

Furrow, D., Nelson, K., & Benedict, H. (1979). Mothers' speech to children and syntactic development: Some simple relationships. *Journal of Child Language, 6,* 423–442.

Gagne, R. M. (1962). The acquisition of knowledge. *Psychological Review, 59,* 355–365.

Gagne, R. M. (1968). Contributions of learning to human development. *Psychological Review, 75,* 177–191

Gallaway, C., Hostler, M. E., & Reeves, D. (1990). Speech addressed to hearing-impaired children by their mothers. *Clinical Linguistic Phonetics, 4,* 221–237.

Garcia, M. R. (1994). Influencie del habla materna en los inicios de la adquisicion del lenguaje: primeras palabras y primeros enunciados de mas de una palabra. *Revista de Logopedia, Foniatria y Audiologia, 14,* 148–155.

Garfinkel, H. (1967). *Studies in ethnomethodology.* Englewood Cliffs, NJ: Prentice-Hall.

Garnica, O. (1977). Some prosodic and paralinguistic features of speech to young children. In C. E. Snow & C. A. Ferguson (Eds.), *Talking to children. Language input and acquisition* (pp. 63–88). New York: Cambridge University Press.

Garvey, C. (1977a). Play with language and speech. In S. M. Ervin-Tripp & R. C. Mitchel-Keenan (Eds.), *Child discourse* (pp. 27–47). New York: Academic Press.

Garvey, C. (1977b). Play with language. In B. Tizard & D. Harvey (Eds.), *Biology of play* (pp. 74–99). Philadelphia: J. B. Lippincott.

Gass, S. M. (1997). *Input, interaction, and the second language learner*. Mahwah, NJ: Erlbaum.

Gass, S. M., & Madden C. G. (Eds.). (1985). *Input in second language acquisition*. Cambridge, MA: Newbury House.

Gathercole, V. C. (1986). The acquisition of the present perfect: Explaining differences in the speech of Scottish and American children. *Journal of Child Language, 13,* 537–560.

Gathercole, V. C. (1988). Some myths you may have heard about first language acquisition. *TESOL Quarterly, 22,* 407–435.

Geer, A. E., & Schick, B. (1988). Acquisition of spoken and signed English by hearing-impaired children of hearing impaired and hearing parents. *Journal of Speech and Hearing Disorders, 53,* 136–143.

Gergen, K. J. (1985). The social constructionist movement in modern psychology. *American Psychologist, 40,* 266–275.

Gerhardt, J. (1989). Monologue as a speech genre. In K. Nelson (Ed.), *Narratives from the crib* (pp. 171–230). Cambridge, MA: Harvard University Press.

Gesell, A. (1945). *The embryology of behavior.* New York: Harper.

Gewirtz, J. L., & Stingle, K. G. (1968). Learning of generalized imitations as the basis for identification. *Psychological Review, 75,* 374–397.

Gibson, E. J., (1969). *Principles of perceptual learning and development.* New York: Appleton-Century-Crofts.

Gibson, E. J. (1984). Perceptual development from the ecological approach. In M. E. Lamb, A. L. Brown, & B. Rogoff (Eds.), *Advances in developmental psychology.* (Vol. 3, pp. 243–286). Hillsdale, NJ: Erlbaum.

Gislason, G. (1984). In defense of small nations. *Daedalus, 113* (1), 199–211.

Givon, T. (1985). Function, structure, and language acquisition. In D. I. Slobin (Ed.), *The crosslinguistic study of language acquisition. Vol. 2: Theoretical issues* (pp. 1005–1027). Hillsdale, NJ: Erlbaum.

Glaser, R. & Chi, M. T. H. (1988). Overview. In M. T. H. Chi, R. Glaser, & M. J. Farr (Eds.), *The nature of expertise* (pp. xv-xxviii). Hillsdale, NJ: Erlbaum.

Gleason, J. B. (1981). Phonological modifications in adult's speech to infants: Some implications for theories of language acquisition. In T. Megers, J. Larer, & J. Anderson (Eds.), *The cognitive representation of speech* (pp. 289–293). North-Holland Publishing.

Gleitman, L. R., & Warner, E. (1984). Current issues in language learning. In M. H. Bornstein & M. E. Lamb (Eds.), *Developmental psychology: An advanced textbook* (pp. 181–240). Hillsdale, NJ: Erlbaum.

Gold, E. M. (1967). Language identification in the limit. *Information and Control, 10,* 447–474.

Goldberg, A. E. (1995). *Constructions. A construction grammar approach to argument structure.* Chicago: University of Chicago Press.

Goldfield, B. A. (1987). The contribution of child and caregiver to referential and expressive language. *Applied Psycholinguistics, 8*, 267–280.

Goldstein, H. (1984). Effects of modeling and corrected practice on generative language learning of preschool children. *Journal of Speech and Hearing Disorders, 49*, 389–398.

Goodman, J. C., Lee, L., & de Groot, J. (1994). Developing theories of speech perception: Constraints from developmental data. In J. C. Goodman & H. C. Nusbaum (Eds.), *The development of speech perception: The transition from speech sounds to spoken words* (pp. 3–33). Cambridge, MA: MIT Press.

Goodsitt, J., Raitan, J. G., & Perlmutter, M. (1988). Interactions between mothers and preschool children when reading a novel and familiar book. *International Journal of Behavioral Development, 11*, 489–505.

Goody, J. (1977). *The domestication of the savage mind.* New York: Cambridge University Press.

Gordon, I. J. (1970). Parent participation in compensatory education. Urbana: University of Illinois Press.

Gordon, I. J. (1972). What do we know about parents as teachers? *Theory into Practice, 11*, 146–149.

Gordon, P. (1990). Learnability and feedback. *Developmental Psychology, 26*, 217–220.

Gordon, R. A. (1968). Issues in multiple regression. *American Journal of Sociology, 73*, 592–616.

Gottman, J. M. (1979). Time-series analysis of continuous data in dyads. In M. E. Lamb, S. J. Soumi, & G. R. Stephenson (Eds.), *Social interaction analysis: Methodological issues.* Madison: University of Wisconsin Press.

Gottman, J. M. (1981). *Time-series analysis: A comprehensive introduction for social scientists.* New York: Cambridge University Press.

Gottman, J. M. (1990). *Sequential analysis. A guide for behavioral researchers.* New York: Cambridge University Press.

Gottman, J. M., & Bakeman, R. (1979). The sequential analysis of observational data. In M. E. Lamb, S. J. Suomi, & G. R. Stephenson (Eds.), *Social interaction analysis: Methodological issues* (pp. 185–206). Madison: University of Wisconsin Press.

Gottman, J. M., Markman, H., & Notarius, C. (1977). The topography of marital conflict: A sequential analysis of verbal and nonverbal behavior. *Journal of Marriage and the Family, 39*, 461–477.

Greenfield, P., & Lave, J. (1982). Cognitive aspects of informal education. In D. A. Wagner & H. W. Stevenson (Eds.), *Cultural perspectives on child development* (pp. 181–207). San Francisco: W. H. Freeman.

Grice, H. P. (1975). Logic and conversation. In P. Cole & J. Morgan (Eds.), *Syntax and semantics* (Vol. 3, pp. 41–58). New York: Seminar Press.

Grimshaw, J., & Pinker, S. (1989). Positive and negative evidence in language acquisition. *Behavioral and Brain Sciences, 12*, 341–342.

Gross, P. R., Levitt, N., & Lewis, M. W. (Eds.). (1996). *The flight from science and reason.* New York: The New York Academy of Sciences.

Guillaume, P. (1971). *Imitation in children.* Chicago, IL: University of Chicago Press. (Original work published 1926)

Halberstam, D. (1969). *The best and the brightest.* New York: Random House.

Hampson, J., & Nelson, K. (1993). The relation of maternal language to variation in rate and style of language acquisition. *Journal of Child Language, 20*, 313–342.

Harkness, S. (1976). Cultural variation of mothers' language. *Word, 28*, 495–498.

Harkness, S. (1977). Aspects of social environment and first language acquisition in rural Africa. In C. E. Snow & C. A. Ferguson (Eds.), *Talking to children. Languge input & acquisition* (pp. 309–316). New York: Cambridge University Press.

Harkness, S. (1988). The cultural construction of semantic contingency in mother-child speech. *Language Sciences, 10*, 53–67.

Harkness, S. (1990). A cultural model for the acquisition of language: Implications for the innateness debate. *Developmental Psychobiology, 23*, 727–740.

Harkness, S., & Super, C. M. (1977). Why African children are so hard to test. In L. L. Adler (Ed.), *Issues in cross-cultural research. Annals of the New York Academy of Sciences, 285*, 326–331.

Harlow, H. F. (1959). The development of learning in the rhesus monkey. *American Scientist, 47*, 459–479.

Harris, A. E. (1975). Social dialectics and language: Mother and child construct the discourse. *Human Development, 18*, 80–96.

Harris, D. B. (Ed.) (1957). *The concept of development*. Minneapolis: University of Minnesota Press.

Harris, M. (1992). *Language experience and early language development: From input to intake*. Hillsdale, NJ: Erlbaum.

Harris, M., Barrett, M., Jones, D., & Brookes, S. (1988). Linguistic input and early word meaning. *Journal of Child Language, 15*, 77–94.

Harris, M., Jones, D., Brookes, S., & Grant, J. (1986). Relations between the non-verbal context of maternal speech and rate of language development. *British Journal of Developmental Psychology, 4*, 261–268.

Harris, R. A. (1993). *The linguistics wars*. New York: Oxford University Press.

Hart, B. (1991). Input frequency and first words. *First Language, 11*, 289–300.

Hart, B., & Risley, T. R. (1995). *Meaningful differences in the everyday experience of young American children*. Baltimore: Paul Brookes.

Hatch, E. M. (1983). *Psycholinguistics: A second language perspective*. Rowley, MA: Newbury House.

Hatch, E. M., Peck, S., & Wagner-Gough, J. (1979). A look at process in child second-language acquisition. In E. Ochs & B. B. Schieffelin (Eds.), *Developmental pragmatics* (pp. 269–278). New York: Academic Press.

Havarnek, B. (1964). The functional differentiation of the standard language. In P. Garvin (Ed.), *A Prague school reader on esthetics, literary structure and style* (pp. 3–16). Washington, DC: Georgetown University Press.

Hayes, D. P., & Ahrens, M. G. (1988). Vocabulary simplification for children: A special case of 'motherese'? *Journal of Child Language, 15*, 395–410.

Heath, S. B. (1982). Protean shapes in literacy events: Ever-shifting oral and literate traditions. In D. Tannen (Ed.), *Spoken and written language: Exploring orality and literacy* (pp. 91–117). Norwood, NJ: Ablex.

Heath, S. B. (1983). *Ways with words: Language, life, and work in communities and classrooms*. Cambridge: Cambridge University Press.

Heath, S. B. (1986). Separating 'things of the imagination' from life: Learning to read and write. In W. H. Teale & E. Sulzby (Eds.), *Emergent literacy* (pp. 156–172). Norwood, NJ: Ablex.

Heath, S. B. (1989). The learner as cultural member. In M. L. Rice & R. L. Schiefelbusch (Eds.), *The teachability of language* (pp. 333–350). Baltimore: Paul Brookes.

Heckhausen, J. (1987). Balancing for weaknesses and challenging developmental potential: A longitudinal study of mother–infant dyads in apprenticeship interactions. *Developmental Psychology, 23,* 762–770.

Heisenberg, W. (1970/1974).(P. Heath, Trans.), *Across the frontiers.* New York: Harper & Row.

Henry, A. (1809/1985). Massacre at Michilimackinae. In F. Drimmer (Ed.), *Captured by the Indians. Fifteen firsthand accounts, 1750–1870.* New York: Dover.

Herrmann, T. (1995). *Allgemeine Sprachpsychologie. Grundlagen und Probleme.* (2nd ed.). Weinheim, Germany: Beltz.

Herrmann, T., & Graf, R. (1996). Konzeptuelles and semantisches Wissen aus psychologischer Sicht *Arbeiten der Forschungsgruppe Sprache und Kognition.* Mannheim: Universitaet Mannheim.

Herrnstein, R. J., & Murray, C. (1994). *The bell curve: intelligence and class structure in American life.* New York: Free Press.

Hess, R. D., & Shipman, V. C. (1965). Early experience and the socialization of cognitive models in children. *Child Development, 36,* 860–886.

Hickey, T. (1991). Mean length of utterance and the acquisition of Irish. *Journal of Child Language, 18,* 553–569.

Hilliard, G. H. (1957). Informational background as a factor in reading readiness and reading progress. *Elementary School Journal, 38,* 255–263.

Hirsh-Pasek, K., Kemler Nelson, D. G., Jusczyk, P. W., Cassidy, K. W., Druss, B., & Kennedy, L. (1987). Clauses are perceptual units for young children. *Cognition, 26,* 269–286.

Hirsh-Pasek, K., Treiman, R., & Schneiderman, M. (1984). Brown & Hanlon revisited: mothers' sensitivity to ungrammatical forms. *Journal of Child Language, 11,* 81–88.

Ho, D. Y. F. (1994). Cognitive socialization in Confucian heritage cultures. In P. M. Greenfield & R. R. Cocking (Eds.), *Cross-cultural roots of minority child development* (pp. 285–313). Hillsdale, NJ: Erlbaum.

Hoff-Ginsburg, E. (1986). Function and structure in maternal speech: Their relation to the child's development of syntax. *Developmental Psychology, 22,* 155–163.

Hoff-Ginsberg, E. (1990). *Social class, maternal speech, and child language development.* Paper presented at the Fifth International Congress for the Study of Child Language, Budapest, July 15–20.

Hoff-Ginsberg, E. (1991). Mother–child conversation in different social classes and communicative settings. *Child Development, 62,* 782–796.

Hoff-Ginsberg, E. (1992). How should frequency in input be measured? *First Language, 12,* 233–244.

Hoff-Ginsberg, E., & Shatz, M. (1982). Linguistic input and the child's acquisition of language. *Psychological Bulletin, 92,* 3–26.

Holding, D. E. (Ed.). (1981). *Human skills.* New York: John Wiley.

Holland, J. G., & Skinner, B. F. (1961). *The analysis of behavior.* New York: McGraw-Hill.

Holzman, M. (1983). *The language of children. Development in the home and school.* Englewood Cliffs: Prentice Hall.

Holzman, M. (1984a). The verbal environment provided by mothers for their very young children. *Merrill-Palmer Quarterly, 20* , 31–42.

Holzman, M. (1984b). Evidence for a reciprocal model of language development. *Journal of Psycholinguistic Research, 13*, 119–146.

Hood, L., & Bloom, L. (1979). What, when, and how about why: A longitudinal study of early expressions of causality. *Monographs of the Society for Research in Child Development, 44*, (6, Serial No. 181).

Howard, M. (1991). *The lessons of history.* New Haven, CT: Yale University Press.

Howe, C. J. (1981). *Acquiring language in a conversational context.* London: Academic Press.

Hunt, J. M. (1961). *Intelligence and experience.* New York: Ronald Press.

Hutchinson, T., & Waters, A. (1987). *English for specific purposes.* Cambridge: Cambridge University Press.

Huttenlocher, J., Haight, W., Bryk, A., Seltzer, M., & Lyons, T. (1991). Early vocabulary growth: Relation to language input and gender. *Developmental Psychology, 27*, 236–248.

Hymes, D. H. (1961). Functions of speech: An evolutionary approach. In F. C. Gruber (Ed.), *Anthropology and education* (pp. 55–83). Philadelphia: University of Pennsylvania Press.

Hymes D. H. (1964). Introduction to Part III. In H. D. Hymes (Ed.), *Language in culture and society* (pp. 115–220). New York: Harper & Row.

Ingram, D. (1975). If and when transformations are acquired by children. *Monograph Series on Language and Linguistics. Georgetown University, 27*, 99–127.

Inhelder, B., Sinclair, H., & Bovet, M. (1974). *Learning and the development of cognition.* Cambridge, MA: Harvard University Press.

Irwin, O. C. (1948). Infant speech: The effect of family occupational status and of age on use of sound types. *Journal of Speech and Hearing Disorders, 13*, 224–226.

Itkonen, E. (1996). Concerning the generative paradigm. *Journal of Pragmatics, 25*, 471–501.

Jakobson, R. (1960). Concluding statement: Linguistics and poetics. In T. A. Sebeok (Ed.), *Style in language* (pp. 350–377). Cambridge, MA: MIT Press.

Jencks, C., & Phillips, M. (1999). *The Black-White test score gap.* Washington, DC: Brookings Institution.

John-Steiner, V. P., & Osterreich, H. (1975). *Learning styles among Pueblo children: Final report to the National Institute of Education.* Albuquerque: University of New Mexico Press.

Kagan, J. (1970). The determinants of attention in the infant. *American Scientist, 58*, 298–306.

Kagan, J., & Tulkin, S. (1972). Mother–child interaction in the first year of life. *Child Development, 43*, 31–41.

Kahneman, D., & Tversky, A. (1972). Subjective probability: A judgment of representativeness. *Cognitive Psychology 3*, 430–454.

Kail, R. V., & Hagen, J. W. (1982). Memory in childhood. In B. Wolman (Ed.), *Handbook of developmental psychology* (pp. 350–366). Englewood Cliffs, NJ: Erlbaum.

Karzon, R G. (1985). Discrimination of polysyllabic sequences by one-to-four-month-old infants. *Journal of Experimental Child Psychology, 39*, 326–342.

Käsermann, M.-L., & Foppa, K. (1981). Some determinants of self correction: An interactional study of Swiss-German. In W. Deutsch (Ed.), *The child's construction of language* (pp. 77–104). New York: Academic Press.

Kasper, G. (1984). Repair in foreign language teaching. In G. Kasper (Ed.), *Learning, teaching and communication in the foreign language classroom* (pp. 213–241). Aarhus: Aarhus University Press.

Kavanaugh, R. D., & Jirkovsky, A. M. (1982). Parental speech to young children: A longitudinal analysis. *Merrill-Palmer Quarterly, 28*, 297–311.

Kaye, K. (1980). Why we don't talk 'baby talk' to babies. *Journal of Child Language, 7*, 489–507.

Kaye, K. (1982). *The mental and social life of babies*. Chicago: University of Chicago Press.

Keller, S. (1963). The social world of the urban slum child: Some early findings. *American Journal of Orthopsychiatry, 33*, 823–831.

Kelly, M. H., & Bock, J. K. (1988). Stress in time. *Journal of Experimental Psychology: Human Perception and Performance, 14*, 389–403.

Kemler-Nelson. D. G., Hirsh-Pasek, K., Jusczyk, P., & Wright Cassidy, K. (1989). How the prosodic cues in motherese might assist language learning. *Journal of Child Language, 16*, 55–68.

Kendler, H. H., & Kendler, T. S. (1962). Vertical and horizontal processes in problem solving. *Psychological Review, 69*, 1–16.

Kendler, T. S., & Kendler, H. H. (1959). Reversal and nonreversal shift in kindergarten children. *Journal of Experimental Psychology, 58*, 56–60.

Kenny, D. A. (1979). *Correlation and causality*. New York: John Wiley & Sons.

Klein, W. (1996). Essentially social: On the origin of linguistic knowledge in the individual. In P. B. Baltes & U. M. Staudinger (Eds.), *Interactive minds* (pp. 88–108). New York: Cambridge University Press.

Köhler, W. (1939). Simple structural functions in the chimpanzee and the chicken. In W. D. Ellis (Ed.), *A source book of gestalt psychology* (pp. 217–227). New York: Harcourt Brace.

Krashen, S. D. (1980). The input hypothesis. In J. E. Alatis (Ed.), *Current issues in bilingual education*. (pp. 168–180). Washington, DC: Georgetown University Press.

Krashen, S. D. (1985). *The input hypothesis: Issues and implications*. London: Longman.

Kuczaj, S. A. (1982a). On the nature of syntactic development. In S. A. Kuczaj (Ed.), *Language development. Vol. 1: Syntax and semantics*. (pp. 37–71). Hillsdale, NJ: Erlbaum.

Kuczaj, S. A. (1982b). Language play and language acquisition. In H. W. Reese (Ed.), *Advances in child development and behavior* (pp. 197–234). New York: Academic Press.

Kuczaj, S. A. (1983). *Crib speech and language play*. New York: Springer.

Kuhn, T. S. (1962). *The structure of scientific revolutions*. Illinois: University of Chicago Press.

Kulick, D. (1986). *Language shift and language socialization in Gapun: A report on fieldwork in progress*. Paper presented at the Second International Conference on Papua Languages, Port Moresby.

Küntay, A., & Slobin, D. I. (1996). Listening to a Turkish mother: Some puzzles for acquisition. In D. I. Slobin, J. Gerhardt, A. Kyratzis, & J. Guo (Eds.), *Social interaction, social context, and language: Essays in honor of Susan Ervin-Tripp* (pp. 265–286). Hillsdale, NJ: Erlbaum.

Lakatos, I. (1970). Falsification and the methodology of scientific research programmes. In I. Lakatos & A. Musgrave (Eds.), *Criticism and the growth of knowledge* (pp. 91–105). London: Cambridge University Press.

Lakatos, I. (1978). *The methodology of scientific research programmes: Philosophical papers* (Vol.1). New York: Cambridge University Press.

Lambert, W. E. (1975). Culture and language as factors in learning and education. In A. Wolfgang (Ed.), *Education in immigrant students* (pp. 55–83). Toronto: Ontario Institute for Studies in Education.

Landau, D. E. (1970). *A comparative study of the language of matched groups of lower-class and middle-class preschool children.* Unpublished master's thesis, Tufts University.

Landes, J. E. (1975). Speech addressed to children: Issues and characteristics of parental input. *Language Learning, 25*, 355–379.

Langley, P., & Simon, H. A. (1981). The central role of learning in cognition. In J. R. Anderson (Ed.), *Cognitive skills and their acquisition* (pp. 361–380). Hillsdale, NJ: Erlbaum.

Larsen-Freeman, D. (1976). An explanation for the morpheme acquisition order of second language learners. *Language Learning, 26*, 125–134.

Larsen-Freeman, D., & Long, M. R. (1991). *An introduction to second language research.* London/NY: Longman.

Leeds, A. (1971). The concept of the "culture of poverty": Conceptual, logical, and empirical problems. In E. B. Leacock (Ed.), *The culture of poverty: A critique* (pp. 226–284). New York: Simon & Schuster.

Lefebvre-Pinard, M., & Reid, L. (1980). A comparison of three methods of training communication skills: Social conflict, modeling, and conflict-modeling. *Child Development, 51*, 179–187.

Leonard, L. B. (1989). Language learnability and specific language impairment in children. *Applied Psycholinguistics, 10*, 179–202.

Leopold, W. F. (1939–1949). *Speech development of a bilingual child.* Evanston, IL: Northwestern University Press.

Leopold, W. F. (1971). The study of child language and infant bilingualism. In A. Bar-Adon & W. F. Leopold (Eds.), *Child language: A book of readings* (pp. 1–13). Englewood Cliffs, NJ: Prentice-Hall.

Levelt, W. J. M. (1974). *Formal grammars in linguistics and psycholinguistics.* The Hague: Mouton.

LeVine, R. A., Miller, P. M., & West, M. M.. (1988). Parental behavior in diverse societies. *New directions in child development, No. 40.* San Francisco, CA: Jossey-Bass.

Levy, Y., & Schlesinger, I. M (1988). The child's early categories: Approaches to language acquisition theory. In V. Levy, I. M. Schlesinger, & M. Braine (Eds.), *Categories and processes in language acquisition* (pp. 261–276). Hillsdale, NJ: Erlbaum.

Lewis, M. (1997). *Altering Fate. Why the past does not predict the future.* New York: Guilford Press.

Lewis, O. (1959). *Five families: Mexican case studies in the culture of poverty.* New York: Basic Books.

Lieven, E. V. M. (1978). Conversations between mothers and young children: Individual differences and their possible implication for the study of language learning. In N. Waterson & C. Snow (Eds.), *The development of communication.* (pp. 173–187). New York: Wiley & Sons.

Lieven, E. V. M. (1984). Interactional style and children's language learning. *Topics in Language Disorders, 4,* 15–23.

Lieven, E. V. M. (1994). Crosslinguistic and crosscultural aspects of language addressed to children. In C. Gallaway & B. J. Richards (Eds.), *Input and interaction in language acquisition* (pp. 56–73). New York: Cambridge University Press.

Löfgren, O. (1981). Människan i landskapet—landskapet i människan. In L. Honko & O. Löfgren (Eds.), *Tradition och miljö: Ett ekologist perspektiv* (pp. 1–153). Lundt, Sweden: Liber Läromedel.

Long, M. (1996). The role of the linguistic environment in second language acquisition. In W. C. Ritchie & T. K. Bhatia (Eds.), *Handbook of second language acquisition* (pp. 413–468). San Diego: Academic Press.

Lord, A. B. (1960). *The singer of tales.* Cambridge, MA: Harvard University Press.

Lord, C. (1975). *Is talking to baby more than baby talk? A longitudinal study of the modifications of linguistic input to young children.* Paper presented at the Meeting of the Society for Research in Child Development, Denver, CO.

Lorenz, K. (1943). Die angeborenen Formen moeglicher Erfahrung. (The innate conditions of the possibility of experience.) *Zeitschrift fuer Tierpsychologie, 5,* 235–409.

Lorenz, K. (1965). *Evolution and modification of behavior.* Chicago: University of Chicago Press.

Lucariello, J., & Nelson, K. (1986). Context effects on lexical specificity in maternal and child discourse. *Journal of Child Language, 13,* 507–522.

Lykken, D. (1968). Statistical significance in psychological research. *Psychological Bulletin, 70,* 151–159.

MacWhinney, B. (1978). The acquisition of morphophonology. *Monographs of the Society for Research in Child Development, 43,* (1–2, Serial No. 174).

MacWhinney, B. (1982). Basic syntactic processes. In S. Kuczaj, (Ed.), *Language development. (Vol.1). Syntax and semantics* (pp. 73–136). Hillsdale, NJ: Erlbaum.

MacWhinney, B. (Ed.). (1987a). *Mechanisms of language acquisition.* Hillsdale, NJ: Erlbaum.

MacWhinney, B. (1987b). Preface. In B. MacWhinney (Ed.), *Mechanisms of language acquisition* (pp. ix-xii). Hillsdale, NJ: Erlbaum.

MacWhinney, B. (1987c). The competition model. In B. MacWhinney (Ed.), *Mechanisms of language acquisition* (pp. 249–308). Hillsdale, NJ: Erlbaum.

MacWhinney, B. (1989). Competition and teachability. In M. L. Rice & R. L. Schiefelbusch (Eds.), *The teachability of language* (pp. 63–104). Baltimore, MD: Paul Brookes.

Mahoney, G. (1983). A developmental analysis of communication between mothers and infants with Down's syndrome. *Topics in Early Childhood Special Education, 3,* 63–76.

Malinowski, B. (1923). The problem of meaning in primitive languages. In C. K. Ogden & I. A. Richards (Eds.), *The meaning of meaning* (pp. 296–336). New York: Harcourt, Brace & World.

Malsheen, B. (1980). Two hypotheses for phonetic clarification in the speech of mothers to children. In G. Yeni-Komshian, J. F. Kavanagh, & C. H. Ferguson (Eds.), *Child phonology* (Vol. 2, pp. 173–184). New York: Academic Press.

Maratsos, M. (1983). Some current issues in the study of the acquisition of grammar. In J. H. Flavell & E. M. Markman (Ed.), *Cognitive development. Handbook of child psychology* (Vol. 3, pp. 707–786).

Masur, E. F. (1982). Mothers' responses to infants' object-related gestures: Influences on lexical development. *Journal of Child Language, 9,* 23–30.

McCarthy, D. (1930). *The language development of the preschool child.* Institute of Child Welfare, Monograph Series No. 4, Minneapolis: University of Minnesota Press.

McCarthy, D. (1946). Language development in children. In L. Carmichael (Ed.), *A manual of child psychology* (pp.476–581). New York: John Wiley & Sons.

McCarthy, D. (1954). Language development in children. In L. Carmichael (Ed.), *Manual of child psychology* (pp. 492–630). New York: John Wiley & Sons.

McCarthy, D. A. (1961). Affective aspects of language learning. *Newsletter, APA Division of Developmental Psychology,* 1–11.

McDougall, W. (1908). *Introduction to social psychology.* New York: Putnam.

McLaughlin, B. (1981). Differences and similarities between first- and second-language learning. In H. Winitz (Ed.), *Native language and foreign language acquisition* (pp. 23–32). *Annals of the New York Academy of Sciences, 379.* New York: The New York Academy of Sciences.

McLean, M. & Vincent, L. 1984. The use of expansions as a language intervention technique in the natural environment. *Journal of the Division for Early Childhood, 9,* (1),57–66.

McLoyd, V. C. (1990). Minority children: Introduction to the special issue. *Child Development, 61,* 263–266.

McNeill, D. (1966). Developmental psycholinguistics. In F. Smith & G. A. Miller (Eds.), *The genesis of language. A psycholinguistic approach* (pp. 15–84). Cambridge, MA: MIT Press.

McNeill, D. (1971). The capacity for the ontogenesis of grammar. In D. I. Slobin (Ed.), *The ontogenesis of grammar* (pp.17–40). New York: Academic Press.

Meehl, P. E. (1978). Theoretical risks and tabular asterisks: Sir Karl, Sir Ronald, and the slow progress in soft psychology. *Journal of Consulting and Clinical Psychology, 46,* 806–834.

Mehler, J., Jusczyk, P., Lambertz, G., Halsted, N., Bertoncini, J., & Armiel-Tison, C. (1988). A precursor of language acquisition in young infants. *Cognition, 29,* 143–178.

Meichenbaum, D. (1977). *Cognitive behavior modification. An integrative approach* (pp. 346–380). New York: Plenum.

Meisel, J. M. (1995). Parameters in acquisition. In P. Fletcher & B. MacWhinney (Eds.), *The handbook of child language* (pp. 10–35). Oxford: Blackwell.

Melton, A. W. (Ed.).(1964). *Categories of human learning.* New York- Academic Press.

Menyuk, P., Liebergott, J. W., & Schultz, M. C. (1995). *Early language development in full-term and premature infants.* Hillsdale, NJ: Erlbaum.

Mervis, C. B., & Mervis, C. A. (1982). Leopards are kitty-cats: Object labeling by mothers for their 13-month-olds. *Child Development, 53*, 267–273.

Mervis, C. B., & Rosch, E. (1981). Categorization of natural objects. In M. R. Rosenzweig & L. W. Porter (Eds.), *Annual Review of psychology* (Vol. 32, pp. 89–115). Palo Alto, CA: Annual Review, Inc.

Meumann, F. (1902). *Die Sprache des Kindes*. Leipzig: Engelmann.

Miller, G. E. (1970). Four philosophical problems of psycholinguistics. *Philosophy of Science, 37* (2), 183–191.

Miller, P. J. (1982). *Amy, Wendy and Beth: Language learning in south Baltimore*. Austin: University of Texas Press.

Milner, E. (1951). A study of the relationship between reading readiness in grade on school children and patterns of parent–child interaction. *Child Development, 22*, 95–112.

Moerk, E. L. (1972). Principles of dyadic interaction in language learning. *Merrill-Palmer Quarterly, 18*, 229–257.

Moerk, E. L. (1974a). Changes in verbal child–mother interactions with increasing language skills of the child. *Journal of Psycholinguistic Research, 3*, 101–116.

Moerk, E. L. (1974b). A design for multivariate analysis of language behaviour and language development. *Language and Speech, 17*, 240–254.

Moerk, E. L. (1975a). Verbal interactions between children and their mothers during the preschool years. *Developmental Psychology, 11*, 788–794.

Moerk, E. L. (1975b). Piaget's research as applied to language development. *Merrill-Palmer Quarterly, 21*, 151–170.

Moerk, E. L. (1975c). The multiple channels of the young child's communicative behavior. *Linguistics, 160*, 21–32.

Moerk, E. L. (1976). Processes of language teaching and training in the interactions of mother–child dyads. *Child Development, 47*, 1064–1078.

Moerk, E. L. (1977). *Pragmatic and semantic aspects of early language development*. Baltimore, MD: University Park Press.

Moerk, E. L. (1978). Determiners and consequences of verbal behaviors of young children and their mothers. *Developmental Psychology, 14*, 537–545.

Moerk, E. L. (1980). Relationships between parental input frequencies and children's language acquisition: A reanalysis of Brown's data. *Journal of Child Language. 7*, 105–118.

Moerk, E. L. (1981). To attend or not to attend to unwelcome reanalysis? A reply to Pinker. *Journal of Child Language, 8*, 627–631.

Moerk, E. L. (1983a). A behavioral analysis of controversial topics in first language acquisition: reinforcements, corrections, modeling, input frequencies, and the three-term contingency pattern. *Journal of Psycholinguistic Research, 12*, 129–155.

Moerk, E. L. (1983b). *The mother of Eve—As a first language teacher*. Norwood, NJ: Ablex.

Moerk, E. L. (1985a). Analytic, synthetic, abstracting and word-class defining aspects of verbal mother–child interactions. *Journal of Psycholinguistic Research, 14*, 263–287.

Moerk, E. L. (1985b). A differential interactive analysis of language teaching and learning. *Discourse Processes, 8*, 113–142.

Moerk, E. L. (1985c). Picture-book reading by mothers and young children and its impact upon language development. *Journal of Pragmatics, 9*, 547–566.

Moerk, E. L. (1986). Environmental factors in early language acquisition. In G. J. Whitehurst (Ed.), *Annals of child development* (Vol. 3, pp. 191–235). Greenwich, CT: JAI Press.

Moerk, E. L. (1989a). The fuzzy set called "imitations." In G. E. Speidel & K. E. Nelson (Eds.), *The many faces of imitation in language learning* (pp. 277–304). New York: Springer.

Moerk, E. L. (1989b). The LAD was a lady and the tasks were ill-defined. *Developmental Review, 9*, 21–57.

Moerk, E. L. (1990). Three-term contingency patterns in mother-child verbal interactions during first-language acquisition. *Journal of the Experimental Analysis of Behavior, 54*, 293–305.

Moerk, E. L. (1991). Positive evidence for negative evidence. *First Language, 11*, 219–251.

Moerk E. L. (1992). *A first language taught and learned.* Baltimore, MD: Paul Brookes.

Moerk, E. L. (1994). Corrections in first language acquisition: Theoretical controversies and factual evidence. *International Journal of Psycholinguistics, 10*, 33–58.

Moerk, E. L. (1996). Input and learning processes in first language acquisition. In H. W. Reese (Ed.), *Advances in child development and behavior*, (Vol. 26, pp. 11–228).

Moerk, E. L. (1998). El desatendido tema de los deficits en el input linguistico. *Revista de Logopedia, Foniatria, y Audiologia, 18*, (1), 9–18.

Moerk, E. L., & Moerk, C. (1979). Quotations, imitations, and generalizatons: Factual and methodological analyses. *International Journal of Behavioral Development, 2*, 43–72.

Moerk, E. L., & Vilaseca, R. (1987). Time-binding in mother–child interactions. The morphemes for past and future. *Papers and Reports on Child Language Development, 26*, 80–87.

Moerk, E. L., & Wong, N. (1976). Meaningful and structured behavioral antecedents of semantics and syntax in language. *Linguistics, 172*, 23–39.

Morgan, J. L., Bonamo, K. M., & Travis, L. L. (1995). Negative evidence on negative evidence. *Developmental Psychology, 31*, 180–197.

Morgan, J. L., & Travis, L. L. (1989). Limits on negative information in language input. *Journal of Child Language, 16*, 531–552.

Mowrer, O. H. (1960). *Learning theory and the symbolic processes.* New York: John Wiley.

Mundy-Castle, A. C. (1974). Social and technological intelligence in Western and non-Western cultures. *Universitas, 4*, 46–52.

Murphy, C. M. (1978). Pointing in the context of shared activity. *Child Development, 49*, 371–380.

Murphy, C. M., & Messer, D. J. (1977). Mothers, infants, and pointing: a study of gesture. In H. R. Schaffer (Ed.), *Studies in mother–infant interaction* (pp. 325–354). New York: Academic Press.

Murray, A. D., Johnson, J., & Peters, J. (1990). Fine-tuning utterance length to preverbal infants: Effects on later language development. *Journal of Child Language, 17*, 511–525.

Nelson, K. (1973). Structure and strategy in learning to talk. *Monographs of the Society for Research in Child Development 38*, (Nos. 1, 2, Serial no. 149).

Nelson, K. (1981). Individual differences in language development: implications for development and language. *Developmental Psychology, 17*, 170–187.

Nelson, K. (Ed.) (1989). *Narratives from the crib.* Cambridge: Harvard University Press.

Nelson, K. E. (1977). Facilitating children's syntax acquisition. *Developmental Psychology*, *13*, 101–107.

Nelson, K. E. (1987). Some observations from the perspective of the rare event cognitive comparison theory of language acquisition. In K. E. Nelson & A. van Kleeck (Eds.), *Children's language*. (Vol. 6, pp. 289–331). Hillsdale, NJ: Erlbaum.

Nelson, K. E., Carskaddon, G., & Bonvillian, J. D. (1973). Syntax acquisition: Impact of experimental variation in adult verbal interaction with the child. *Child Development, 44*, 497–504.

Nelson, K. E., Denninger, M. S., Bonvillian, J. D., Kaplan, B. J., & Baker, N. D. (1984). Maternal input adjustments and non-adjustments as related to children's linguistic advances and to language acquisition theories. In A. D. Pellegrini & T.D. Yawkey (Eds.), *The development of written and oral language in social contexts* (pp. 31–56). Norwood, NJ: Ablex.

Nelson, K. E., Welsh, J., Camarata, S. M., Butkovsky, L., & Camarata, M. (1995). Available input for language-impaired children and younger children of matched language levels. *First Language, 15*, 1–17.

Neustadt, R. E., & May, E. R. (1986). *Thinking in time. The uses of history for decision makers*. New York: The Free Press.

Newell, K. M. (1981). Skill learning. In D. Holding (Ed.), *Human skills* (pp. 203–226). New York: Wiley & Sons.

Newell, K. M. (1991). Motor skill acquisition. In M. R. Rosenzweig & L. W. Porter (Eds.), *Annual review of psychology* (Vol. 42, pp. 213–237). Palo Alto, CA: Annual Reviews, Inc.

Newport, E., Gleitman, H., & Gleitman, L. (1977). Mother, I'd rather do it myself: Some effects and non-effects of maternal speech style. In C. E. Snow & C. A. Ferguson (Eds.), *Talking to children: Language input and acquisition* (pp.109–149). Cambridge: Cambridge University Press.

Nienhuys, T. G., Cross, T. G., & Horsborough, K. M. (1984). Child variables influencing maternal speech style: Deaf and hearing children. *Journal of Communicative Disorders, 17*, 189–207.

Ninio, A. (1980a). Ostensive definition in vocabulary acquisition. *Journal of Child Language, 7*, 565–573.

Ninio, A. (1980b). Picture-book reading in mother–infant dyads belonging to two subgroups in Israel. *Child Development, 51*, 587–590.

Ninio, A. (1992). The relation of children's single word utterances to single word utterances in the input. *Journal of Child Language, 19*, 87–110.

Ninio, A., & Bruner, J. (1978). The achievements and antecedents of labelling. *Journal of Child Language, 5*, 1–15.

Nippold, M. A.. (1988). *Later language development: ages 9 through 19*. Boston: Little, Brown.

Nisbet, J. (1961). Family environment and intelligence. In A. H. Halsey, J. Floud, & C. A. Anderson (Eds.), *Education, economy and society* (pp. 273–287). Glencoe, IL: Free Press.

Ochs, E. (1982). Talking to children in Western Samoa. *Language and Society, 11*, 77–104.

Ochs, E. (1987). Input: A socio-cultural perspective. In M. Hickjmann (Ed.), *Social and functional approaches to language and thought* (pp. 305–319). Orlando, FL: Academic Press.

Ochs, E., & Schieffelin, B. B. (1983). *Acquiring conversational competence*. London: Routledge & Kegan Paul.

Ochs, E., & Schieffelin, B. B. (1984). Language acquisition and socialization: three developmental stories and their implications. In R. A. Shweder & R. A. LeVine (Eds.), *Culture theory. Essays on mind, self, and emotion* (pp. 276–320). Cambridge: Cambridge University Press.

Ong, W. J. (1982). *Orality and literacy: The technologizing of the word*. New York: Methuen.

Opie, I., & Opie, P. (1959). *The lore and language of school children*. London: Oxford University Press.

Ornstein, A. C. (Ed.). (1970). *Educating the disadvantaged*. New York: AMS Press.

Osgood, C. E. (1949). The similarity paradox in human learning. A resolution. *Psychological Review, 56*, 132–143.

Palloni, A., & Sorensen, A. B., (1990). Methods for the analysis of event history data: A didactic overview In P. B. Baltes, I. L. Featherman, & R. M. Lerner (Eds.), *Life-span development and behavior* (pp. 291–323). Hillsdale, NJ- Erlbaum.

Papousek, H., & Papousek, M. (1983). The psychobiology of the first didactic programs and toys in human infants. In A. Oliviero & M. Zapella (Eds.), *The behavior of infants* (pp. 219–239). New York: Plenum.

Papousek, M., Papousek, H., & Bornstein, M. H. (1985). The naturalistic vocal environment of young infants. In T. M. Field & N. Fox (Eds.), *Social perception in infants* (pp. 269–297). Norwood, NJ: Ablex.

Paris, S. G., & Lindauer, B. K. (1982). The development of cognitive skills during childhood. In B. B. Wolman (Ed.), *Handbook of developmental psychology* (pp. 333–349). Englewood Cliffs, NJ: Prentice-Hall.

Park, T.-Z. (1985). Plurals in child speech. *Journal of Child Language, 5*, 237–250.

Parry, M. (1971). *The making of Homeric verse*. Oxford: Clarendon Press.

Pasamanick, B. (1946). A comparative study of behavioral development of Negro children. *Journal of Genetic Psychology, 69*, 3–44.

Patterson, G. R., Littman, R. A., & Bricker, W. (1967). Assertive behavior in children: A step toward a theory of aggression. *Monographs of the Society for Research in Child Development, 32*, 1–43.

Pavenstedt, E. A. (1965). A comparison of the child-rearing environment of upper-lower and very low lower-class families. *American Journal of Orthopsychiatry, 35*, 89–98.

Pawlby, S. J. (1977). Imitative interaction. In H. R. Schaffer (Ed.), *Studies in mother–infant interaction* (pp. 203–224). New York: Academic Press.

Pearson, B. Z., Fernandez, S. C., Ledeweg, V., & Oller, D. K. (1996). The relation of input factors to lexical learning by bilingual infants. *Applied Psycholinguistics, 18*, 41–58.

Pearson, K. (1899). *The grammar of science*. London: W. Scott.

Pellegrini, A. D., Brody, G. H., & Sigel, I. E. (1985). Parents teaching strategies with their children. *Journal of Psycholinguistic Research 14*, 509–521.

Pemberton, E. F., & Watkins, R. V. (1987). Language facilitation through stories. *First Language, 7*, 79–89.

Penner, S. G. (1987). Parental responses to grammatical and ungrammatical child utterances. *Child Development, 58*, 376–384.

Pepper, S. C. (1942). *World hypotheses*. Berkeley: University of California Press.

Perez-Pereira, M. (1994). Imitations, repetitions, routines and the child's analysis of language: Insights from the blind. *Journal of Child Language, 21*, 317–337.

Perlmutter, M. (1980). A developmental study of semantic elaboration and interpretation in recognition memory. *Journal of Experimental Child Psychology, 29*, 413–427.

Peters, A. M. (1983). *The units of language acquisition.* Cambridge: Cambridge University Press.

Peterson, C., & McCabe, A. (1994). A social interactionalist account of developing decontextualized narrative skill. *Developmental Psychology, 30*, 937–948.

Petrinovich, L., & Baptista, L. (1987). Song development in the white-crowned sparrow: Modification of learned song. *Animal Behavior, 35*, 961–974.

Phillips, J. R. (1973). Syntax and vocabulary of mothers' speech to young children: Age and sex comparison. *Child Development, 44*, 182–185.

Phillips, S. U. (1983). *The invisible culture: Communication in classroom and community on the Warm Springs Indian reservation.* New York: Longman.

Piaget, J. (1936). *The origins of intelligence in children.* New York: International University Press.

Pine, J. M. (1992). Maternal style at the early one-word stage: Re-evaluating the stereotyping of the directive mother. *First Language, 12*, 169–186.

Pine, J. M. (1994). Environmental correlates of variation in lexical style: Interactional style and the structure of the input. *Applied Psycholinguistics, 15*, 355–370.

Pinker, S. (1994). *The language instinct.* New York: W. Morrow & Co.

Planck, M. (1950). *Scientific autobiography and other papers.* London: Williams & Norgate.

Platt, C. B., & MacWhinney, B. (1983). Error assimilation as a mechanism in language learning. *Journal of Child Language, 10*, 401–414.

Popper, K. (1935/1959). *The logic of scientific discovery.* New York: Harper & Row.

Popper, K. R. (1962). *Conjectures and refutations.* New York: Basic Books.

Power, T. G. (1985). Mother and father–infant play: A developmental analysis. *Child Development, 56*, 1514–1524.

Preyer, W. (1882). *Die Seele des Kindes.* Leipzig: T. Grieben.

Pye, C. (1992). The acquisition of K'iche' Maya. In D. I. Slobin (Ed.), *The crosslinguistic study of language acquisition* (Vol. 3, pp. 221–308). Hillsdale, NJ: Erlbaum.

Rabain, J. R. (1979). *L'enfant du lignage. Du sevrage a la classe d'age chez les Wolof du Senegal.* (Child of the lineage: From weaning to age-graded peer group among the Wolof of Senegal). Paris: Payot.

Rabain-Jamin, J. R. (1994). Language and socialization of the child in African families living in France. In P. M. Greenfield & R. R. Cocking (Eds.), *Cross- cultural roots of minority child development* (pp. 147–166). Hillsdale, NJ: Erlbaum.

Raph, J. B. (1965). Language development in socially disadvantaged children. *Review of Educational Research, 35*, 389–400.

Ratner, N. B. (1984). Patterns of vowel modification in mother-child speech. *Journal of Child Language, 11*, 557–578.

Ratner, N. B. (1988). Patterns of vocabulary selection in speech to very young children. *Journal of Child Language, 15*, 481–492.

Reber, A. S., & Allen, R. (1978). Analogy and abstraction strategies in synthetic grammar learning: A functionalist interpretation. *Cognition, 6*, 189–221.

Reger, Z. (1990). Mothers' speech in different social groups in Hungary. In G.Conti-Ramsden & C. E. Snow (Eds.), *Children's language* (Vol. 7, pp. 197–222). Hillsdale, NJ: Erlbaum.

Reger, Z., & Gleason, J. B. (1991). Romani child–directed speech and children's language among Gypsies in Hungary. *Language in Society, 20*, 601–617.

Reimann, B. (1989). Formen und Funktionen elterlicher Korrekturen in der fruehen Kind-Eltern-Kommunikation. *Linguistische Studien, Reihe A, 199*, 133–142.

Reimann, B. (1991). Syntagmatisch orientierte Reaktionen in Frühphasen des Spracherwerbs. *Zeitschrift für Psychologie, 199*, 45–54.

Reimann, B., & Budwig, N. (1992). Verweise mit Pronomen: formale und funktionale Aspekte in fruehen Phasen des Spracherwerbs. *Zeitschrift fuer Psychologie, 200*, 61–77.

Rheingold, H. L., Gewirtz, J. L., & Ross, H. W. (1959). Social conditioning of vocalization in the infant. *Journal of Comparative and Physiological Psychology, 52*, 68–73.

Rice, M. L. (1990). Preschooler's QUIL: Quick incidental learning of words. In G. Conti-Ramsden & C. E. Snow (Eds.), Children's language (Vol. VII, pp. 171–195). Hillsdale, NJ: Erlbaum.

Rice, M. L., Buhr, J. C., & Nemeth, M. (1990). Fast mapping word-learning abilities of language-delayed preschoolers. *Journal of Speech and Hearing Disorders, 55*, 33–42.

Rice, M. L., & Schiefelbusch, R. L. (Eds.).(1989). *The teachability of language*. Baltimore, MD: Paul H. Brookes.

Richards, B., & Robinson, P. (1993). Environmental correlates of child copula verb growth. *Journal of Child Language, 20*, 343–362.

Richelle, M. (1973). Analyse formelle et analyse functionelle du comportement verbal. *Bulletin de Psychologie, 26*, 252–259.

Rocissano, L., & Yatchmink, Y. (1983). Language skill and interactive patterns in prematurely born toddlers. *Child Development, 54*, 1229–1241.

Rogoff, B. (1990). *Apprenticeship in thinking: Cognitive development in social context*. New York: Oxford University Press.

Rogoff, B., & Gardner, W. (1984). Adult guidance of cognitive development. In B. Rogoff & J. Lave (Eds.) *Everyday cognition. Its development in social context* (pp. 95–116). Cambridge, MA: Harvard University Press.

Rome-Flanders, T., Cronk, C., & Gourde, C. (1995). Maternal scaffolding in mother–infant games and its relationship to language development: A longitudinal study. *First Language, 15*, 339–355.

Rondal, J. A. (1978). Maternal speech to normal and Down's Syndrome children matched for mean length of utterance. In C. E. Meyers (Ed.), *Quality of life in severely and profoundly mentally retarded people: Research foundations for improvement* (pp. 193–265). Washington, DC: American Association on Mental Deficiency.

Rondal, J. A. (1979). "Maman est au courant": une etude des connaissances maternelles quant aux aspects formels du langage de jeune enfant. *Enfance, 2*, 185–195.

Rondal, J. A. (1981). On the nature of linguistic input to language-learning children. *International Journal of Psycholinguistics, 8*, 75–107.

Rondal, J. A. 1985. *Adult–child interaction and the process of language acquisition*. New York: Praeger.

Rondal, J. A. (1995). *Exceptional language development in Down syndrome*. New York: Cambridge University Press.

Rondal, J., & Cession, A. (1990). Input evidence regarding the semantic bootstrapping hypothesis. *Journal of Child Language, 17*, 711–717.

Root, M. D. (1973). Language, rules, and complex behavior. In K. Gunderson (Ed.), *Language, mind, and knowledge: Minnesota studies in the philosophy of science* (Vol. 7, pp. 321–343). Minneapolis: University of Minnesota Press.

Rorty, R. (1979). *Philosophy and the mirror of nature*. Princeton, NJ: Princeton University Press.

Ruke-Dravina, D. V. (1977). Modifications of speech addressed to young children in Latvian. In C. E. Snow & C. A. Ferguson (Eds.), *Talking to children: Language input and acquisition* (pp. 237–253). Cambridge: Cambridge University Press.

Rumelhart, D., McClelland, J., & the PDP Research Group (1986). *Parallel distributed processing: Explorations in the microstructure of cognition*. Cambridge, MA: Bradford Books.

Sachs, J. (1979). Topic selection in parent–child discourse. *Discourse Processes, 2*, 145–153.

Sachs, J. (1983). Talking about the there and then: The emergence of displaced reference in parent-child discourse. In K. E. Nelson (Ed.), *Children's language* (Vol. 4, pp. 1–28). Hillsdale, NJ: Erlbaum.

Sackett, G. P. (1979). The lag sequential analysis of contingency and cyclicity in behavioral interaction research. In J. D. Osofsky (Ed.), *Handbook of infant development*. New York: Wiley.

Sackett, G. P. (1980). Lag sequential analysis as a data reduction technique in social interaction research. In D. B. Swain, R. C. Hawkins, L. O. Walker, & J. H. Penticuffs (Eds.), *Exceptional infant* (Vol. 4). New York: Brunner/Mazel.

Sampson, G. (1997). *Educating Eve. The 'language instinct' debate*. London: Cassell.

Savic, S. (1975). Aspects of adult-child communication: The problem of question acquisition. *Journal of Child Language, 2*, 251–260.

Savic, S. (1977). Quelques fonctions des questions posees par les adultes aux jeunes enfants. In J. P. Bronckart, P. Malrieu, M. Siguan-Soler, H. Sinclair, T. Slama-Cazacu, & A. Tabouret-Keller (Eds.), *La genese de la parole*. Paris: Presses Universitaires de France.

Saxton, M. (1992). Negative evidence versus negative feedback: A critical review. *Child Language Seminar*, University of Glasgow.

Saxton, M. (1993). Does negative input work? *First Language, 13*, 409–411.

Schachter, J. (1984). A universal input condition. In W. E. Rutherford (Ed.), *Language universals and second language acquisition*. Philadelphia: John Benjamin.

Scherer, N. J., & Olswang, L. B. (1984). Role of mother's expansions in stimulating children's language production. *Journal of Speech and Hearing Research, 27*, 387–396.

Schieffelin, B. B. (1979a). *How Kaluli children learn what to say, what to do, and how to feel: An ethnographic study of the development of communicative competence*. Doctoral Dissertation: Columbia University. (University Microfilms, No. 1416).

Schieffelin, B. B. (1979b). Getting it together: An ethnographic approach to the study of the development of competence. In E. Ochs & B. B. Schieffelin (Eds.), *Developmental pragmatics* (pp. 73–103). New York: Academic Press.

Schieffelin, B. B. (1990). *The give and take of everyday life: language and socialization of Kaluli children.* Cambridge, MA: Cambridge University Press.

Schlesinger, I. M. (1971). Learning grammar: From pivot to realization rule. In R. Huxley & E. Ingram (Eds.), *Language acquisition: Models and methods* (pp. 79–89). New York: Academic Press.

Schlesinger, I. M. (1974). Relational concepts underlying language. In R. L. Schiefelbusch & L. L. Lloyd (Eds.), *Language perspectives—acquisition, retardation and intervention.* Baltimore, MD: University Park Press.

Schmidt, R. A. (1975). A schema theory of discrete motor learning. *Psychological Review, 82,* 225–260.

Schneider, W., & Detweiler, M. (1987). A connectionist/control architecture for working memory. In G. H. Bower (Ed.), *The psychology of learning and motivation* (Vol. 21, pp. 53–119). San Diego: Academic Press.

Schneiderman, M. H. (1983). 'Do what I mean, not what I say!' Changes of mothers' action-directives to young children. *Journal of Child Language, 10,* 357–367.

Schumacher, J. B. (1976). *Mothers' expansions: Their characteristics and effects on the child.* Unpublished doctoral dissertation. University of Kansas, Lawrence.

Schumacher, J. B., & Sherman, J. A. (1978). Parent as intervention agent. In R. L. Schiefelbusch (Ed.), *Language intervention strategies* (pp. 237–315). Baltimore, MD: University Park Press.

Scribner, S., & Cole, M. (1981). *The psychology of literacy.* Cambridge: Harvard University Press.

Searle, J. R. (1969). *Speech acts.* New York: Cambridge University Press.

Seitz, S., & Stewart, C. (1975). Imitations and expansions: Some developmental aspects of mother–child communications. *Developmental Psychology, 11,* 763–768.

Seliger, H. W. (1977). Does practice make perfect? A study of interaction patterns and L2 competence. *Language Learning, 27,* 263–278.

Shatz, M. (1982). On mechanisms of language acquisition: Can features of the communicative environment account for development? In E. Wanner & L. R. Gleitman (Eds.), Language acquisition: The state of the art. (pp. 102–127). Cambridge: Cambridge Univ. Press.

Shatz, M. (1991). Using cross-cultural research to inform us about the role of language in development: Comparisons of Japanese, Korean, English, and of German, American English, and British English. In M. Bornstein (Ed.), *Cultural approaches to parenting* (pp. 139–153). Hillsdale, NJ: Erlbaum.

Shatz, M., & Gelman, R. (1973). The development of communication skills: Modifications in the speech of young chilren as a function of listener. *Monographs of the Society for Research in Child Development, 38* (No. 5, Serial No. 152).

Shatz, M., Hoff-Ginsberg, E., & Maciver, D. (1989). Induction and the acquisition of English auxiliaries: The effects of differentially enriched input. *Journal of Child Language, 16,* 121–140.

Sherrod, K. B., Friedman, S., Crawley, S., Drake, D., & Devieux, J. (1977). Maternal language to prelinguistic infants: Syntactic aspects. *Child Development, 48*, 1662–1665.

Shirai, Y., & Andersen, R. W. (1995). The acquisition of tense-aspect morphology: A prototype account. *Language, 71*, 743–762.

Shore, C. M. (1995). *Individual differences in language development*. Thousand Oaks, CA: Sage.

Shweder, R. A. (1984). Anthropology's romantic rebellion against the Enlightenment, or there's more to thinking than reasons and evidence. In R. A. Shweder & R. A. LeVine (Eds.), *Culture theory. Essays on mind, self, and emotion* (pp. 27–66). New York: Cambridge University Press.

Sigel, I. E. (1986). Early social experience and the development of representational competence. In W. Fowler (Ed.), *Early experience and the development of competence* (pp. 49–65). San Francisco: Jossey-Bass.

Sigel, I. E., & McGillicuddy-Delisi, A. V. (1984). Parents as teachers of their children: A distancing behavior model. In A. Pellegrini & T. Yawkey (Eds.), *The development of oral and written language in social contexts* (pp. 71–92). Norwood, NJ: Ablex.

Silverman, I. W., & Geiringer, E. (1973). Dyadic interaction and conservation induction: A test of Piaget's equilibration model. *Child Development, 44*, 815–820.

Simon, H. (1969). *The sciences of the artificial*. Cambridge, MA: MIT Press.

Simon, H. A. (1978). Information processing theory of human problem solving. In W. K. Estes (Ed.), *Handbook of learning and cognitive processes. Vol. 5: Human information processing* (pp. 271–295). Hillsdale, NJ: Erlbaum.

Simon, H. A. (1985). Human nature in politics: The dialogue of psychology with political science. *The American Political Science Review, 79*, 293–304.

Simon, H. A. (1990). Invariants of human behavior. In M. R. Rosenzweig & L. W. Porter (Eds.), *Annual review of psychology,* (Vol. 41, pp. 1–19). Palo Alto, CA: Annual Review Press.

Sinclair, A., Jarvella, R. J., & Levelt, W. J. M. (Eds.). (1978). *The child's conception of language*. New York: Springer.

Sinclair, H. (1971). Sensorimotor action patterns as a condition for the acquisition of syntax. In R. Huxley & E. Ingram (Eds.), *Language acquisition: Models and methods* (pp. 121–130). New York: Academic Press.

Skinner, B. F. (1953). *Science and human behavior*. New York: Macmillan.

Skinner, B. F. (1957). *Verbal behavior*. New York: Appleton-Century-Crofts.

Slama-Cazacu,T. (1983). Theoretical prerequisites for a contemporary applied linguistics. In B. Bain (Ed.), *The sociogenesis of language and human conduct* (pp. 257–271). New York: Plenum.

Slamecka, N. J., & Graf, P. (1978). The generation effect: Delineation of phenomenon. *Journal of Experimental Psychology: Human Learning and Memory, 4*, 592–604.

Slobin, D. I. (1968). Imitation and grammatical development in children. In N. S. Endler, L. R. Boulter & H. Osser (Eds.), *Contemporary issue in developmental psychology* (pp. 437–444). New York: Holt, Rinehart & Winston.

Slobin, D. I. (1975). On the nature of talk to children. In E. H. Lenneberg & E. Lenneberg (Eds.), *Foundations of language development. A multidisciplinary approach* (pp. 283–297). New York: Academic Press.

Slobin, D. I. (Ed.). (1985). *The crosslinguistic study of language acquisition.* (Vols. 1–2). Hillsdale, NJ: Erlbaum.

Slobin, D. I. (Ed.). (1992). *The crosslinguistic study of language acquisition.* (Vol. 3). Hillsdale, NJ: Erlbaum.

Slobin, D. I. (Ed.). (1997). *The crosslinguistic study of language acquisition* (Vol. 4). Hillsdale, NJ: Erlbaum.

Slotkin, J. S. (1965). *Readings in early anthropology.* Chicago, IL: Aldine.

Smith, C. B., Adamson, L. B., & Bakeman, R. (1988). Interactional predictors of early language. *First Language, 8,* 143–156.

Smolak, L., & Weintraub, M. (1983). Maternal speech: Strategy or response? *Journal of Child Language, 10,* 369–380.

Snow, C. E. (1972). Mothers' speech to children learning language. *Child Development 43,* 549–565.

Snow, C. E. (1977a). Mothers' speech research: From input to interaction. In C. E. Snow & C. A. Ferguson (Eds.), *Talking to children. Language input and acquisition* (pp. 31–51). Cambridge, MA: Cambridge University Press.

Snow, C. E. (1977b). The development of conversation between mothers and babies. *Journal of Child Language, 4,* 1–22.

Snow, C. E. (1978). The conversational context of language acquisition. In R. N. Campbell & P. T. Smith (Eds.), *Recent advances in the psychology of language* (pp. 253–269). New York: Plenum Press.

Snow, C. E. (1979). The role of social interaction in language acquisition. In W. A. Collins (Ed.), *Children's language and communication. The Minnesota Symposia on child psychology* (Vol.12, pp. 157–182). Hillsdale, NJ: Erlbaum.

Snow, C. E. (1983). Literacy and language: Relationships during the preschool years. *Harvard Educational Review, 53,* 165–189.

Snow, C. E. (1986). Conversations with children. In P. Fletcher & M. Garman (Eds.), *Language acquisition* (pp. 69–89). New York: Cambridge University Press.

Snow, C. E. (1989). Understanding social interaction and language acquisition; sentences are not enough. In M. Bornstein & S. E. Bruner (Eds.), *Intraction in human development* (pp. 83–103). Hillsdale, NJ: Erlbaum.

Snow, C. E. (1995). Issues in the study of input: Fine tuning, universality, individual and developmental differences, and necessary causes. In P. Fletcher & B. MacWhinney (Eds.), *The handbook of child language* (pp. 180–193). Oxford: Blackwell.

Snow, C. E., Arlman-Rupp, A., Hassing, Y., Jobse, J., Joosten, J., & Vorster, J. (1976). Mothers' speech in three social classes. *Journal of Psycholinguistic Research, 5,* 2–20.

Snow, C. E., Dubber, C., & de Blauw, A. (1987). Routines in mother-child interaction. In L. Fegans & D. C. Farran (Eds.), *The language of children reared in poverty.* (pp. 53–72). New York: Academic Press.

Snow, C. E., & Goldfield, B. A. (1983). Turn the page please: Situation-specific language acquisition. *Journal of Child Language, 10,* 551–569.

Snow, C. E., Nathan, D., & Perlmann, R. (1985). Assessing children's knowledge about book reading. In L. Galda & A. D. Pellegrini (Eds.), *Play, language, and stories: The development of children's literate behavior* (pp. 167–181). Norwood, NJ: Ablex.

Snow, C. E., Perlmann, R., & Nathan, D. (1987). Why routines are different: Toward a multiple-factors mode of relation between input and language acquisition. In K. E. Nelson & A. van Kleeck (Eds.), *Children's language* (Vol. 6, pp. 65–97). Hillsdale, NJ: Erlbaum.

Soderbergh, R. (1974). *Barnets Sprackutveckling och dess konsekvenser foer pedagogiken.* Institutionen foer Nordiska Spraok, University of Stockholm.

Sokolov, J. L. (1993a). A local contingency analysis of the fine-tuning hypothesis. *Developmental Psychology, 29,* 1008–1023.

Sokolov, J. L. (1993b). *Learning from error.* Poster presented at the meeting of the Society for Research in Child Development, New Orleans, March, 1993.

Sokolov, J. L., & Snow, C. E. (Eds.).(1994). *Handbook of research in language development using CHILDES.* Hillsdale, NJ: Lawrence Erlbaum.

Sonnenschein, S., & Whitehurst, G. J. (1984). Developing refential communication: A hierarchy of skills. *Child Development, 55,* 1936–1945.

Speidel, G. E. (1987). Conversation and language learning in the classroom. In K. E. Nelson & A. van Kleeck (Eds.), *Children's language.* (Vol. 6, pp. 99–135). Hillsdale, NJ: Erlbaum.

Speidel, G. E. (1993). The comprehension reading lesson as a setting for language apprenticeship. In E. N. Roberts (Ed.), *Advances in applied developmental psychology.* (Vol. 7, pp. 274–274). Norwood, NJ: Ablex.

Speidel, G. E., & Nelson, K. E. (Eds.). (1989). *The many faces of imitation in language learning.* New York: Springer.

Spitz, R. A., & Wolff, K. M. (1946). Anaclitic depression: An inquiry into the genesis of psychiatric conditions in early childhood. In A. Freud et al. (Eds.), *The psychoanalytic study of the child* (Vol. II, pp. 313–342). New York: International Universities Press.

Stafford, L. (1987). Maternal input to twin and singleton children: Implications for language acquisition. *Human Communication Research, 13,* 429–462.

Stern, C., & Stern W. (1928/1987). *Die Kindersprache.* Darmstadt: Wissenschaftliche Buchgesellschaft.

Stern, D. N., Spieker, S., Barnett, R. K., & MacKain, K. (1983). The prosody of maternal speech: Infant age and context related changes. *Journal of Child Language, 10,* 1–15.

Stern, H. H. (1978). French immersion in Canada: Achievements and directions. *Canadian Modern Language Review, 34,* 836–854.

Stern, H. H. (1983). *Fundamental concepts of language teaching.* Oxford: Oxford University Press.

Stoel-Gammon, C., & Cabral, L. S. (1977). Learning how to tell it like it is: The development of the reportative function in children's speech. *Papers and Reports of Child Language Development, 17,* 64–71.

Swain, M. (1985). Communicative competence: Some roles of comprehensible input and comprehensible output in its development. In S. M. Gass & C. G. Madden (Eds.), *Input in second language acquisition* (pp. 235–253). Cambridge, MA: Newbury Press.

Swain, M., & Lapkin, S. (1982). *Evaluating bilingual education: A Canadian example.* Clevedon, Avon: Multilingual Matters.

Taine, H. (1870). *De l'acquisition du langage chez des enfants et dans l'especie humaine.* Paris: Librairie Baillière.

Tannen, D. (1982). The oral/literate continuum in discourse. In D. Tannen (Ed.), *Spoken and written language: Exploring orality and literacy* (pp. 1–16). Norwood, NJ: Ablex.

Tannen, D. (1989). *Talking voices: Repetition, dialogue, and imagery in conversational discourse*. Cambridge: Cambridge University Press.

Tannen, D. (1990). *You just don't understand*. New York: Ballantine.

Tartter, V. C. (1986). *Language processes*. New York: Holt, Rinehart & Winston.

Teale, W. H. (1986). Home background and young children's literacy development. In W. T. Teale & E. Sulzby (Eds.). *Emergent literacy: Writing and reading* (pp.173–206). Norwood, NJ: Ablex.

Templin, M. C. (1957). *Certain language skills in children: Their development and interrelationships*. Institute of Child Welfare Monograph Series, No. 26, Minneapolis: University of Minnesota Press.

Tenenbaum, H., & Leaper, C. (1998). Gender effects on Mexican-descent parents' questions and scaffolding during toy play: A sequential analysis. *First Language, 18*, 129–147.

Tharp, R. G. (1994). Intergroup differences among Native Americans in socialization and child cognition: An ethnogenetic analysis. In P. M. Greenfield & R. R. Cocking (Eds.), *Cross-cultural roots of minority child development* (pp. 87–105). Hillsdale, NJ: Erlbaum.

Thompson, D. (1983). *Children of the wilderness*. Victoria: Australia: Currey O'Neil Ross.

Thorndike, E. L. (1903). *Educational psychology*. New York: Teachers College. Columbia University.

Tiedemann, D. (1787). *Beobachtungen uber die Entwicklung der Seelenfahigkeit bei Kindern*. Altenburg, Germany: Bonde

Tiegerman, E., & Siperstein, M. (1984). Individual patterns of interaction in the mother–child dyad: Implications for parent intervention. *Topics in Language Disorders, 4* (4), 50–61.

Tizard, B., & Hughes, M. (1984). *Young children learning*. Cambridge, MA: Harvard University Press.

Tolman, E. C. (1949). There is more than one kind of learning. *Psychological Review, 56*, 144–155.

Tomasello, M., Conti-Ramsden, G., & Ewert, B. (1990). Young children's conversations with their mothers and fathers: Differences in breakdown and repair. *Journal of Child Language, 17*, 115–130.

Tomasello, M., & Farrar, J. (1986). Object permanence and relational words: A lexical training study. *Journal of Child Language, 13*, 495–505.

Tomasello, M., & Heron, C. (1988). Down the garden path: Inducing and correcting overgeneralization errors in the foreign language classroom. *Applied Psycholinguistics, 9*, 237–246.

Tomasello, M., Mannle, S., & Kruger, A. C. (1986). Linguistic environment of 1- to 2-year-old twins. *Developmental Psychology, 22*, 169–176.

Tough, J. (1977). Children and programmes: How shall we educate the young child. In A. Davies (Ed.), *Language and learning in early childhood* (pp. 60–88). London: Heinemann.

Tough, J. (1982). Children's use of language and learning to read. In R. P. Parker & F.A. Davis (Eds.), *Developing literacy* (pp. 55–67). Newark, DE: International Reading Association.

Tulving, E., & Thomson, D. M. (1973). Encoding specificity and retrieval processes in episodic memory. *Psychological Review, 80*, 352–373.

Tuma, N. B., & Hannan, M. T. (1979). Dynamic analysis of event histories. *American Journal of Sociology, 84*, 820–854.

Uribe, F. M. T., LeVine, R. A., & LeVine, S. E. (1994). Maternal behavior in a Mexican community: The changing environments of children. In P. M. Greenfield & R. R. Cocking (Eds.), *Cross-cultural roots of minority child development* (pp. 41–54). Hillsdale, NJ: Erlbaum.

Uzgiris, I. (1984). Imitation in infancy: Its interpersonal aspects. In M. Perlmutter (Ed.), *Minnesota symposium on child psychology* (Vol. 17, pp. 1–32). Hillsdale, NJ: Erlbaum.

Valentine, E. S. (1986). *Great and desperate cures*. New York: Basic Books.

Valian, V., & Coulson, S. (1988). Anchor points in language learning: The role of marker frequency. *Journal of Memory and Language, 27*, 71–86.

van der Geest, T. (1977). Some interactional aspects of language acquisition. In C. E. Snow & C. A. Ferguson (Eds.), *Talking to children: Language input and acquisition* (pp. 89–107). Cambridge: Cambridge University Press.

Vygotsky, L. (1962). *Thought and language*. Cambridge, MA: MIT Press. (Original work published 1934)

Wagner, K. R. (1985). How much do children say in a day? *Journal of Child Language, 12*, 475–487.

Walters, J., Connor, R., & Zunich, M. (1964). Interaction of mothers and children from lower-class families. *Child Development, 35*, 433–440.

Wanska, S. K., & Bedrosian, J. L. (1986). Topic and communicative intent in mother-child discourse. *Journal of Child Language, 13*, 523–535.

Ward, M. C. (1971). *Them children. A study of language learning*. Prospect heights, IL: Waveland Press.

Warren, S. F., & Kaiser, A. P. (1986). Incidental language teaching: A critical review. *Journal of Speech and Hearing Disorders, 51*, 251–299.

Warren, S. F., & Rogers-Warren, A. K. (1985). *Teaching functional language*. Baltimore, MD: University Park Press.

Watkins, C. W. (1988). Effects of cognitive level and selected stimulus variables on augmentative communication learning. *Dissertation Abstracts International*, Vol. 49(3-B), Sep. 1988, 711.

Watson-Gegeo, K. A., & Gegeo, D. (1986). Calling-out and repeating routines in Kwara'ae children's language socialization. In B. B. Schieffelin & E. Ochs (Eds.), *Language socialization across cultures* (pp. 17–50). Cambridge: Cambridge University Press.

Weeks, D. L., & Hoogestraat, J. (Eds.).(1998). *Time, memory, and the verbal arts*. London: Associated University Presses.

Weikart, D. P., Bond, J. T., & McNeil, J. T. (1978). *The Ypsilanty Perry preschool project: Preschool years and longitudinal results through fourth grade*. Ypsilanti, MI: Educational Research Foundation.

Weir, R. H. (1962). *Language in the crib*. The Hague: Mouton.

Wellman, H. M., & Lempers, J. D. (1977). The naturalistic communicative abilities of two-year-olds. *Child Development, 48*, 1052–1057.

Wells, C. G. (1978). Talking with children, the complementary roles of parents and teachers. *English in Education, 12* (2), 15–38.

Wells, C. G. (1979). Variation in child language. In P. Fletcher & M. Garman (Eds.), *Language acquisition* (pp. 377–395). New York: Cambridge University Press.

Wells, C. G. (1985). *Language development in the preschool years.* Cambridge: Cambridge University Press.

Wells, C. G. (1986). *The meaning makers: Children learning language and using language to learn.* London: Heinemann.

Wells, C. G., Barnes, S., Gutfreund, M., & Satterly, D. (1983). Characteristics of adult speech which predict children's language development. *Journal of Child Language, 10,* 65–84.

Werker, J. F., & Macleod, P. J. (1989). Infant preferences for both male- and female infant-directed talk: A developmental study of attentional and affective responsiveness. *Canadian Journal of Psychology, 43,* 230–246.

Werner, H. (1940). *Comparative psychology of mental development.* New York: International Universities Press.

Wertsch, J. (1979). From social interaction to higher psychological processes. *Human Development, 22,* 1–22.

Wesche, M. B. (1994). Input and interaction in second language acquisition. In C. Gallaway & B. J. Richards (Eds.), *Input and interaction in language acquisition* (pp. 219–249). Cambridge: Cambridge University Press.

Wexler, K., & Culicover, P. (1980). *Formal principles of language acquisition.* Cambridge, MA: MIT Press.

Wheeler, M. A. (1983). Mothers' speech in context: Age changes and language lessons. *Journal of Child Language, 10,* 259–263.

Whitehurst, G. J., & de Baryshe, B. D. (1989). Observational learning and language acquisition: Principles of learning, systems, and tasks. In G. E. Speidel & K. E. Nelson (Eds.), *The many forms of imitation in language learning* (pp. 251–276). New York: Springer.

Whitehurst, G. J., Falco, F. L., Lonigan, C. J., Fischel, J. E., DeBaryshe, B. D., Valdez-Mechaca, M. C., & Caulfield, M. (1988). Accelerating language development through picture book rading. *Developmental Psychology, 24,* 552–559.

Whitehurst, G. J., & Sonnenschein, S. (1985). The development of communication: A functional analysis. In G. J. Whitehurst (Ed.), *Annals of child developmentg* (Vol. 2, pp. 1–48). Greenwich, CT: JAI Press.

Whitehurst, G. J., & Valdez-Mechacha, M. (1988). What is the role of reinforcement in early language acquisition? *Child Development, 59,* 430–440.

Wiener, N. (1950). *The human use of human beings.* New York: Houghton Mifflin.

Wijnen, F., Krikhaar, E., & Den Os, E. (1994). The (non)realization of unstressed elements in children's utterances: Evidence for a rhythmic constraint. *Journal of Child Language, 21,* 59–83.

Williams, F., & Naremore, C. (1969). On the functional analysis of social class differences in modes of speech. *Speech Monographs, 36,* 77–102.

Wilson, F. O. (1975). *Sociobiology: The new synthesis.* Cambridge: Harvard University Press.

Wode, H. (1978). Free vs. bound morphemes in three types of language acquisition. *Interlanguage Studies Bulletin, 3*, 6–22.

Wong-Fillmore, L. (1976). *The second time around: Cognitive and social strategies in second language acquisition.* Doctoral dissertation, Stanford University, Stanford, CA.

Wood, D. J. (1980). Teaching the young child some relationships between social interaction, language, and thought. In D. R. Olson (Ed.), *The social foundation of language and thought* (pp. 280–296). New York: Norton.

Yoder, P. J., & Warren, S. F. (1998). Maternal responsivity predicts the prelinguistic communication intervention that facilitates generalized intentional communication. *Journal of Speech and hearing Research, 41*, 1207–1219.

Young, V. H. (1970). Family and childhood in a southern Negro community. *American Anthropology, 72*, 269–288.

Youssef, V. (1994). 'To be or not to be': Formulaic and frame-based acquisition of the copula in Trinidad. *First Language, 14*, 263–282.

Zajonc, R. B. (1983). Validating the confluence model. *Psychological Bulletin, 93*, 457–480.

Zajonc, R. B., & Bargh, J. (1980). Birth order and intellectual development. *Psychological Review, 82*, 74–88.

Zilzel, E. (1942). The genesis of the concept of physical law. *Philosophical Review, 51*, 245–279.

Author Index

Subject Index